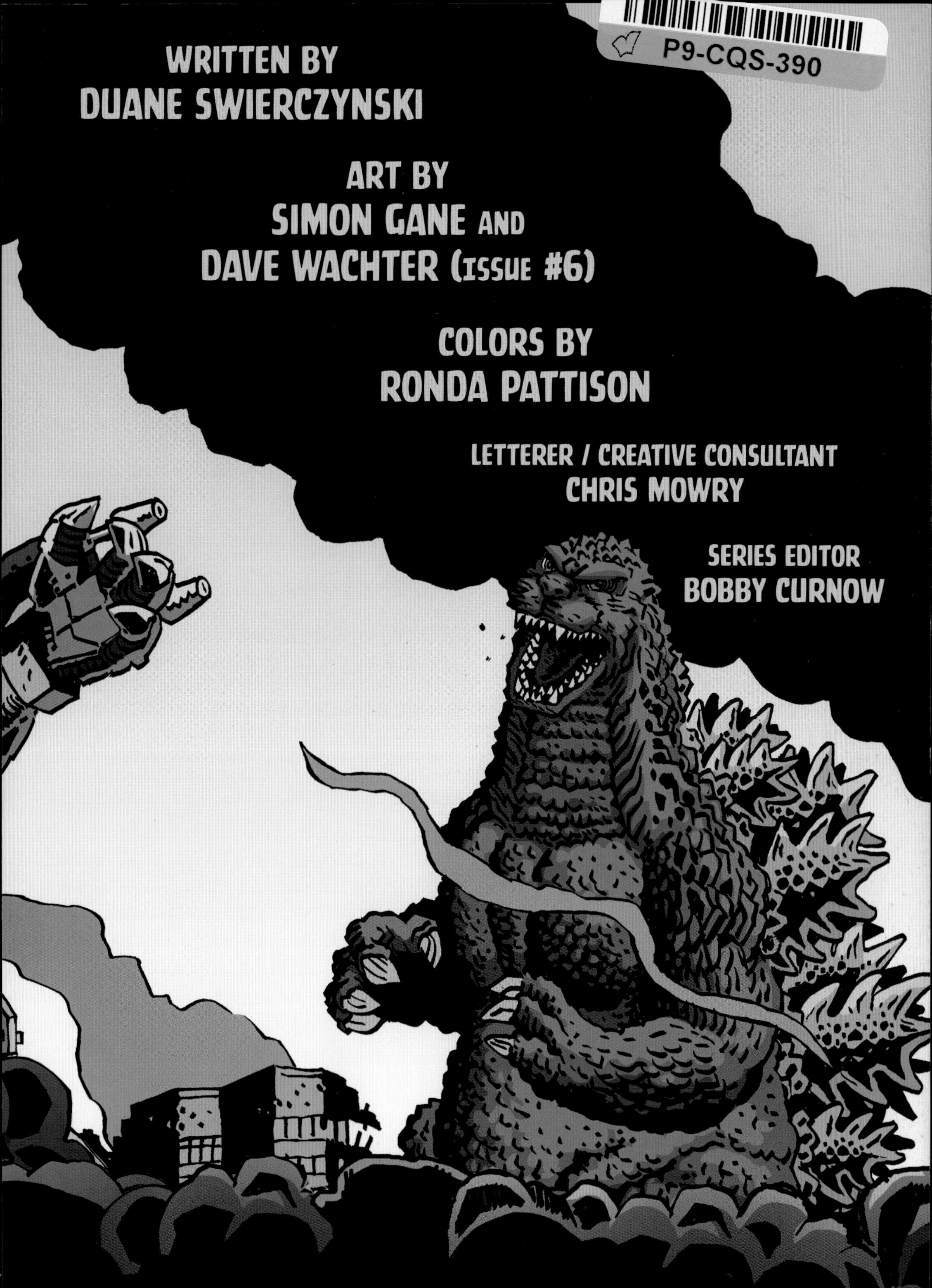

WRITTEN BY
DUANE SWIERCZYNSKI

ART BY
SIMON GANE AND
DAVE WACHTER (ISSUE #6)

COLORS BY
RONDA PATTISON

LETTERER / CREATIVE CONSULTANT
CHRIS MOWRY

SERIES EDITOR
BOBBY CURNOW

COVER BY ZACH HOWARD, COLORS BY NELSON DANIEL
COLLECTION EDITS BY JUSTIN EISINGER AND ALONZO SIMON
COLLECTION DESIGN BY CHRIS MOWRY

ART BY ZACH HOWARD
COLORS BY NELSON DANIEL

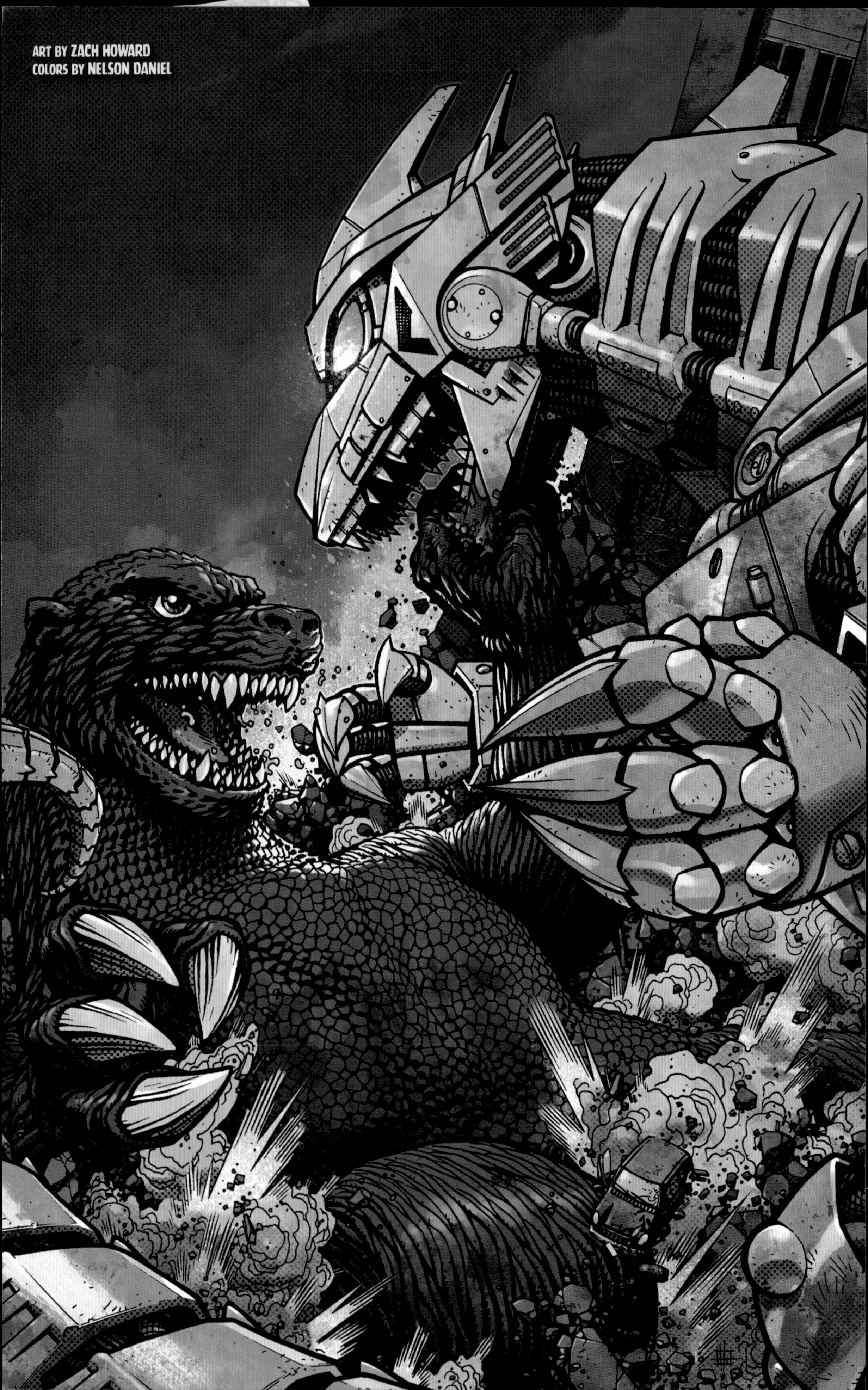

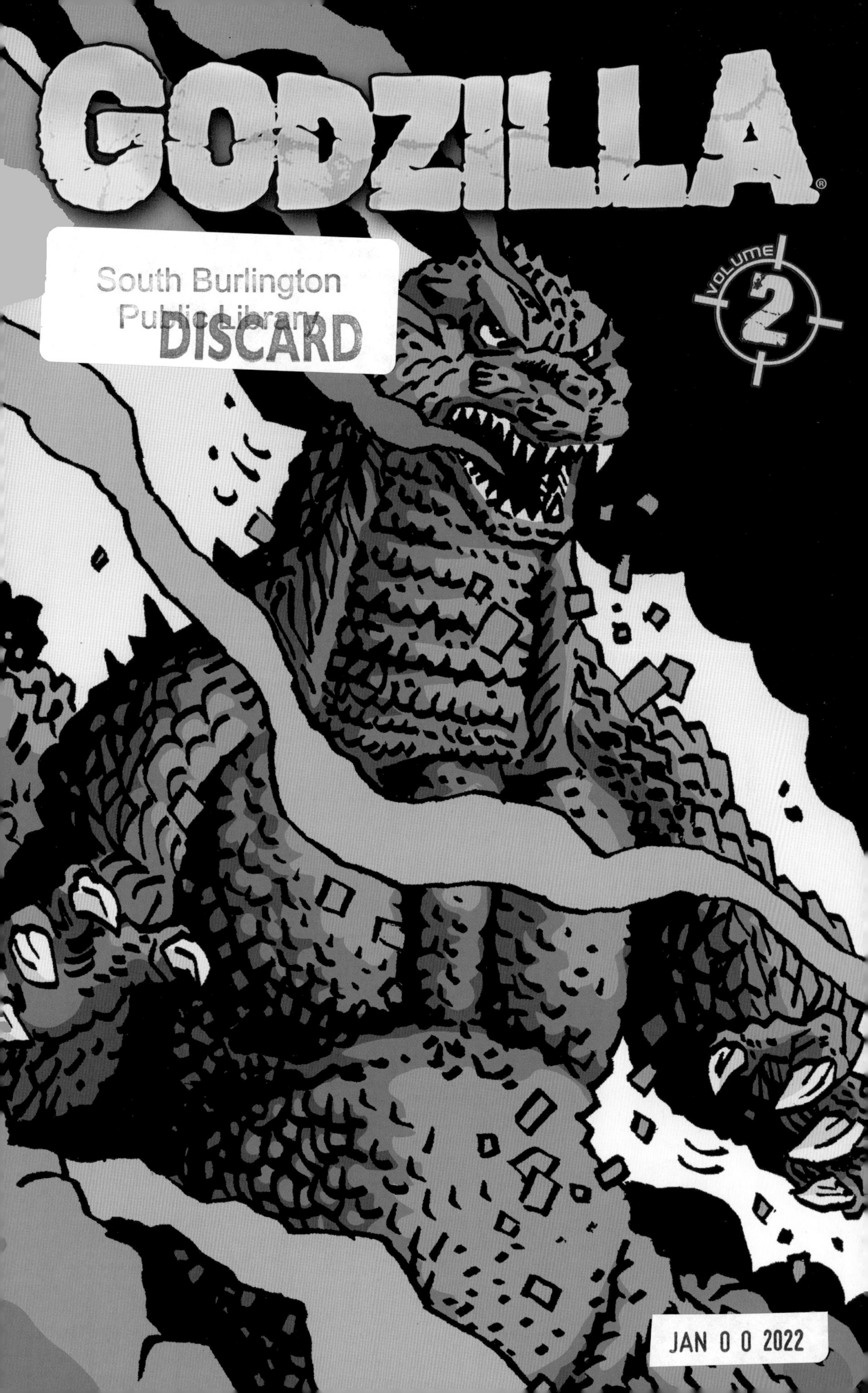
GODZILLA®
VOLUME 2

MFS-3

ISBN: 978-1-61377-584-4

17 16 15 14   2 3 4 5

IDW founded by Ted Adams, Alex Garner, Kris Oprisko, and Robbie Robbins

Special thanks to Yoshiko Fukuda and everyone at Toho for their invaluable assistance.

www.IDWPUBLISHING.com

Ted Adams, CEO & Publisher
Greg Goldstein, President & COO
Robbie Robbins, EVP/Sr. Graphic Artist
Chris Ryall, Chief Creative Officer/Editor-in-Chief
Matthew Ruzicka, CPA, Chief Financial Officer
Alan Payne, VP of Sales
Dirk Wood, VP of Marketing
Lorelei Bunjes, VP of Digital Services

Originally published as GODZILLA Issues #5–8.

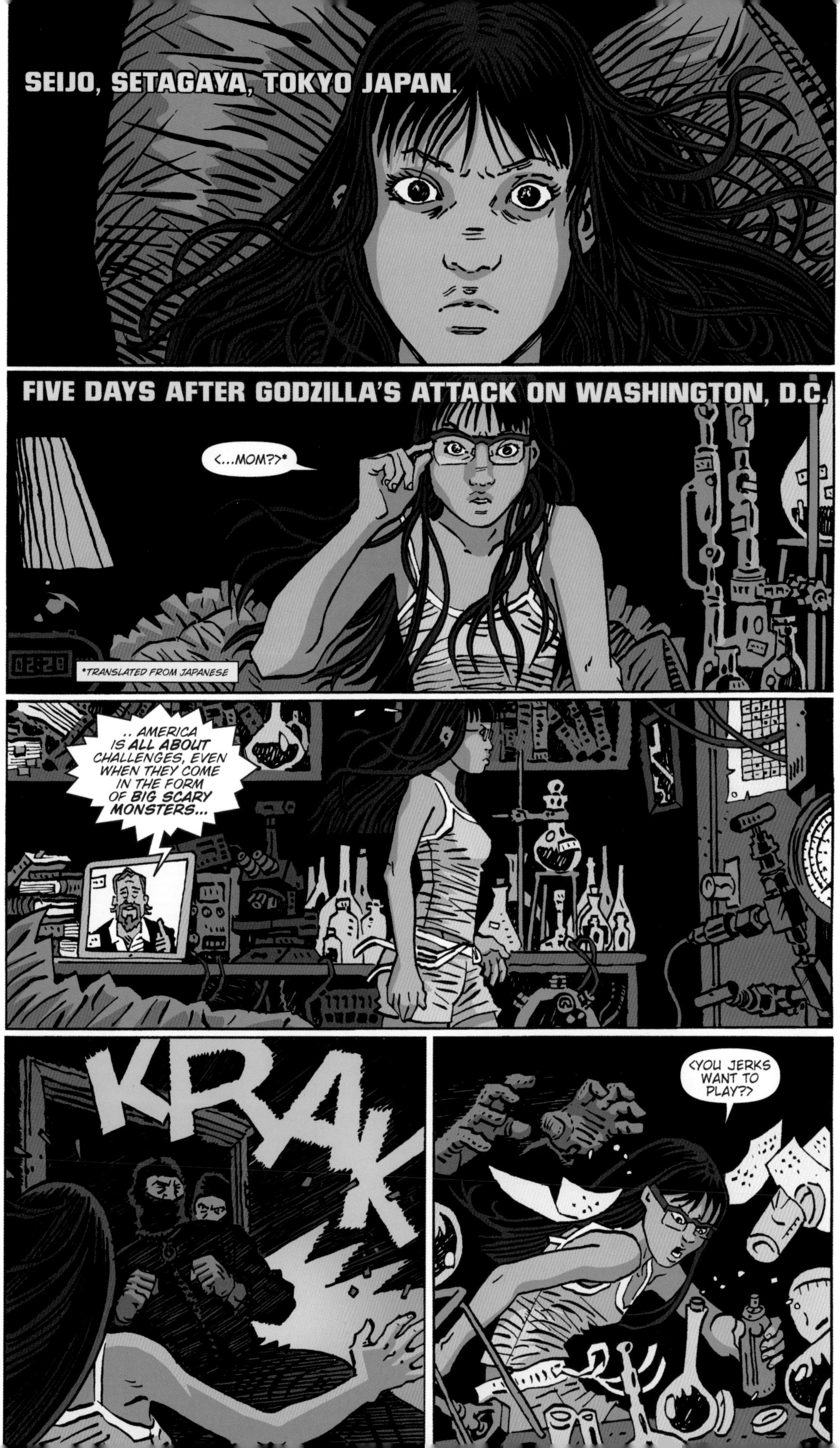
SEIJO, SETAGAYA, TOKYO JAPAN.
FIVE DAYS AFTER GODZILLA'S ATTACK ON WASHINGTON, D.C.
<...MOM?>*
02:28
*TRANSLATED FROM JAPANESE
.. AMERICA IS ALL ABOUT CHALLENGES, EVEN WHEN THEY COME IN THE FORM OF BIG SCARY MONSTERS...
KRAK
<YOU JERKS WANT TO PLAY?>

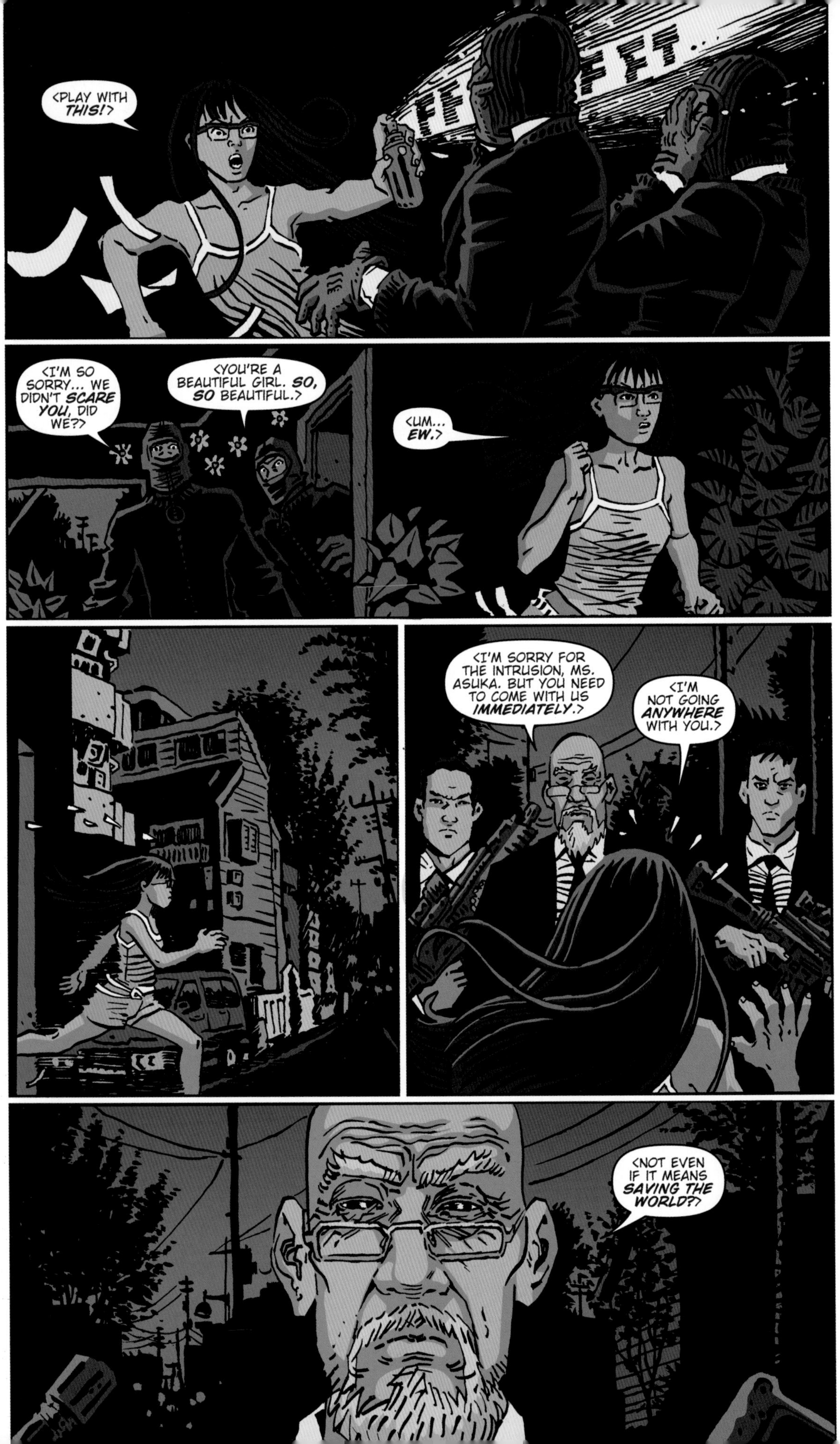
<PLAY WITH THIS!>
FFFFT...
<I'M SO SORRY... WE DIDN'T SCARE YOU, DID WE?>
<YOU'RE A BEAUTIFUL GIRL. SO, SO BEAUTIFUL.>
<UM... EW.>
<I'M SORRY FOR THE INTRUSION, MS. ASUKA. BUT YOU NEED TO COME WITH US IMMEDIATELY.>
<I'M NOT GOING ANYWHERE WITH YOU.>
<NOT EVEN IF IT MEANS SAVING THE WORLD?>

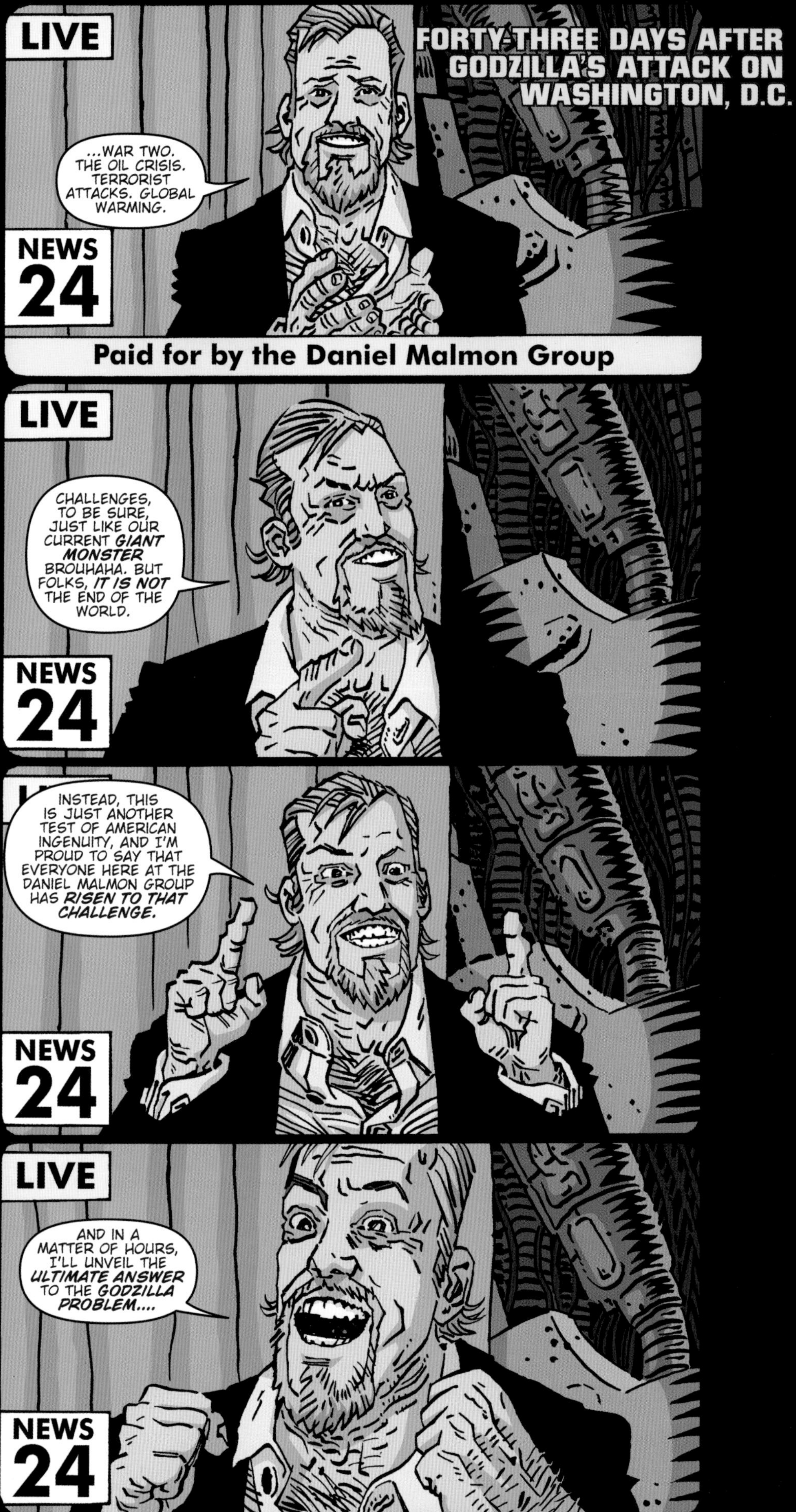

LIVE
FORTY-THREE DAYS AFTER GODZILLA'S ATTACK ON WASHINGTON, D.C.
...WAR TWO. THE OIL CRISIS. TERRORIST ATTACKS. GLOBAL WARMING.
NEWS 24
Paid for by the Daniel Malmon Group
LIVE
CHALLENGES, TO BE SURE, JUST LIKE OUR CURRENT *GIANT MONSTER* BROUHAHA. BUT FOLKS, *IT IS NOT* THE END OF THE WORLD.
NEWS 24
INSTEAD, THIS IS JUST ANOTHER TEST OF AMERICAN INGENUITY, AND I'M PROUD TO SAY THAT EVERYONE HERE AT THE DANIEL MALMON GROUP HAS *RISEN TO THAT CHALLENGE.*
NEWS 24
LIVE
AND IN A MATTER OF HOURS, I'LL UNVEIL THE *ULTIMATE ANSWER* TO THE *GODZILLA PROBLEM....*
NEWS 24

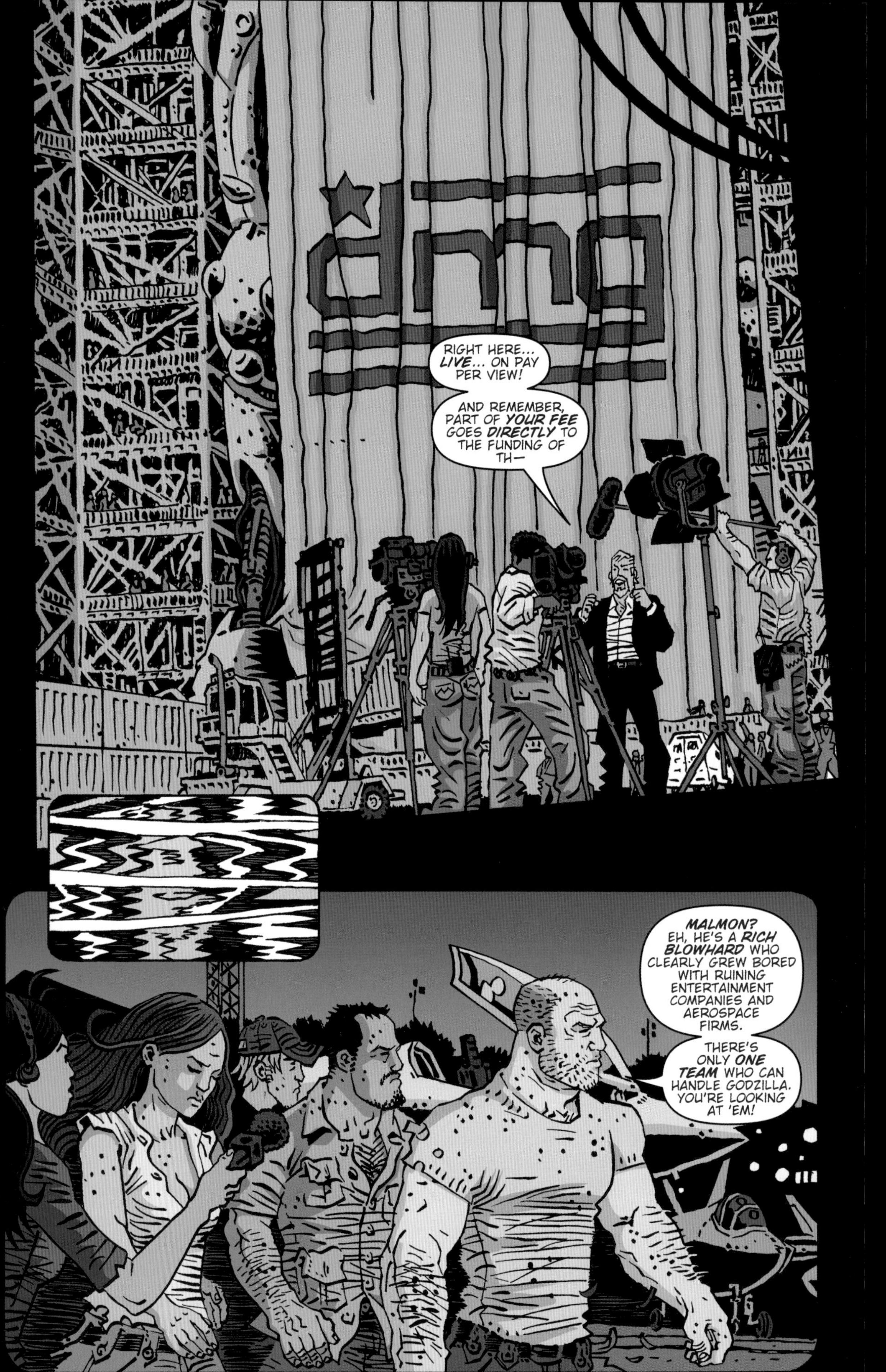

RIGHT HERE... *LIVE*... ON PAY PER VIEW!
AND REMEMBER, PART OF ***YOUR FEE*** GOES ***DIRECTLY*** TO THE FUNDING OF TH—
MALMON? EH, HE'S A ***RICH BLOWHARD*** WHO CLEARLY GREW BORED WITH RUINING ENTERTAINMENT COMPANIES AND AEROSPACE FIRMS.
THERE'S ONLY ***ONE TEAM*** WHO CAN HANDLE GODZILLA. YOU'RE LOOKING AT 'EM!

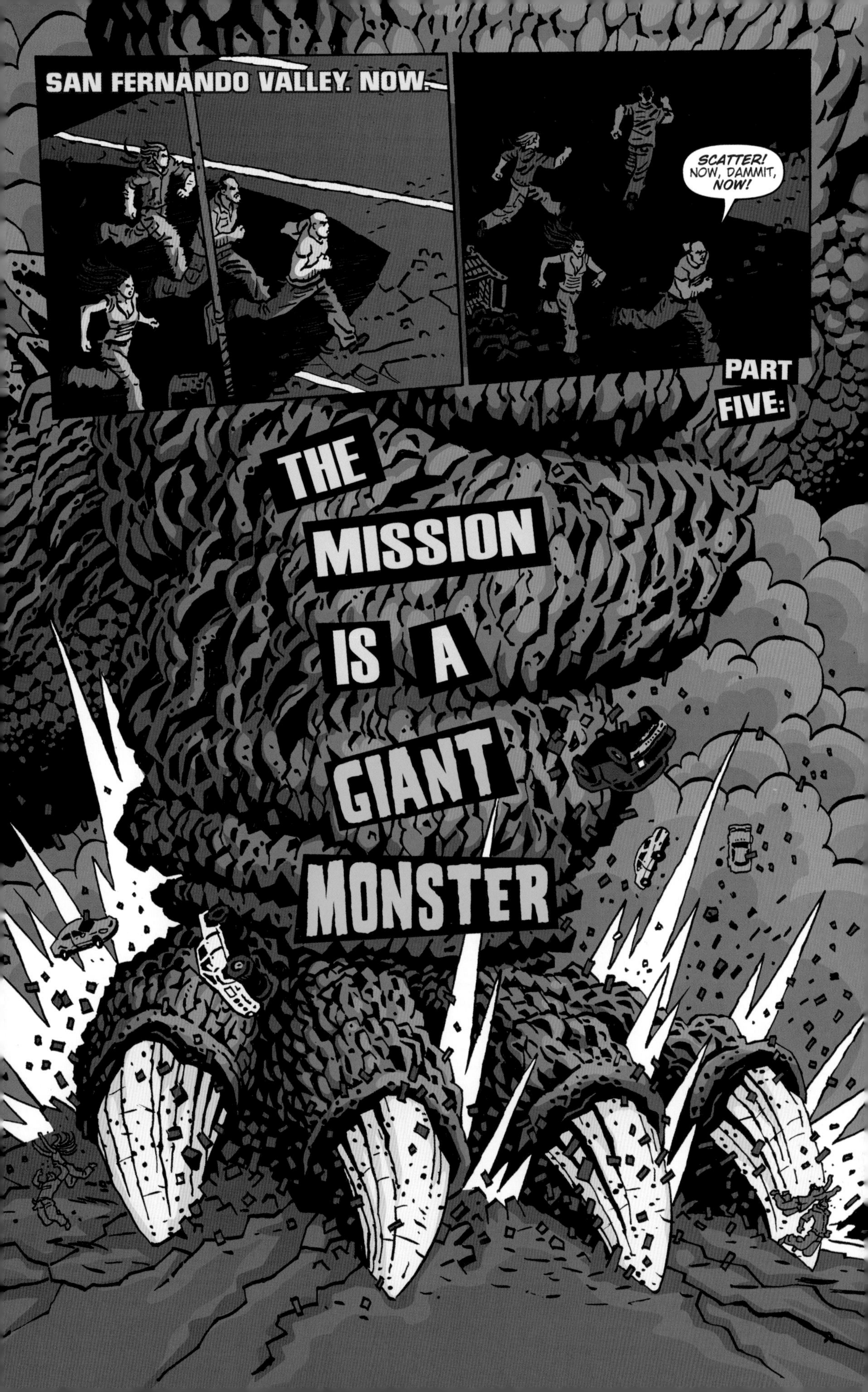
SAN FERNANDO VALLEY. NOW.
SCATTER! NOW, DAMMIT, NOW!
PART FIVE:
THE MISSION IS A GIANT MONSTER

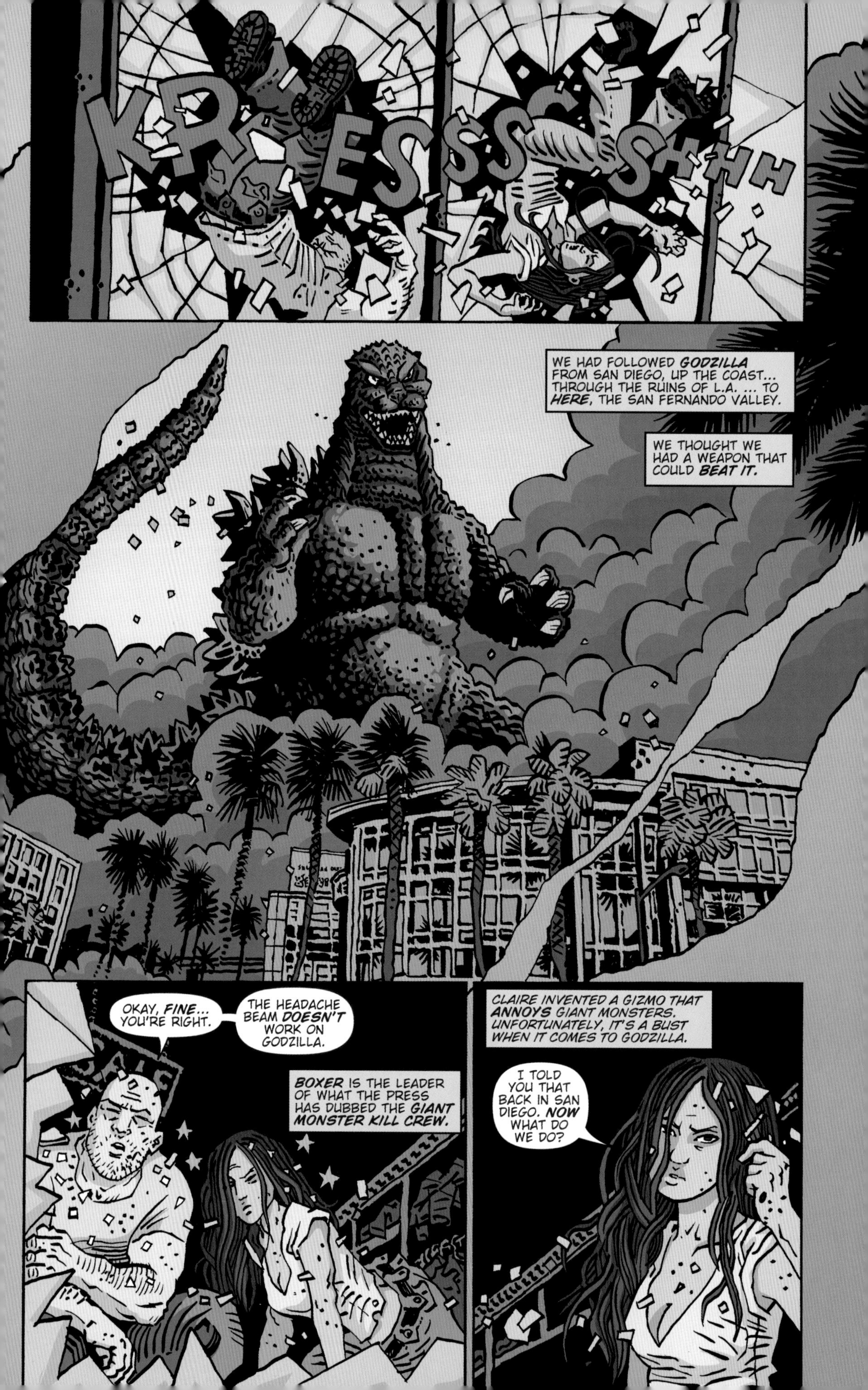
KRRESSSSHHH
WE HAD FOLLOWED GODZILLA FROM SAN DIEGO, UP THE COAST... THROUGH THE RUINS OF L.A. ... TO HERE, THE SAN FERNANDO VALLEY.
WE THOUGHT WE HAD A WEAPON THAT COULD BEAT IT.
OKAY, FINE... YOU'RE RIGHT.
THE HEADACHE BEAM DOESN'T WORK ON GODZILLA.
BOXER IS THE LEADER OF WHAT THE PRESS HAS DUBBED THE GIANT MONSTER KILL CREW.
CLAIRE INVENTED A GIZMO THAT ANNOYS GIANT MONSTERS. UNFORTUNATELY, IT'S A BUST WHEN IT COMES TO GODZILLA.
I TOLD YOU THAT BACK IN SAN DIEGO. NOW WHAT DO WE DO?

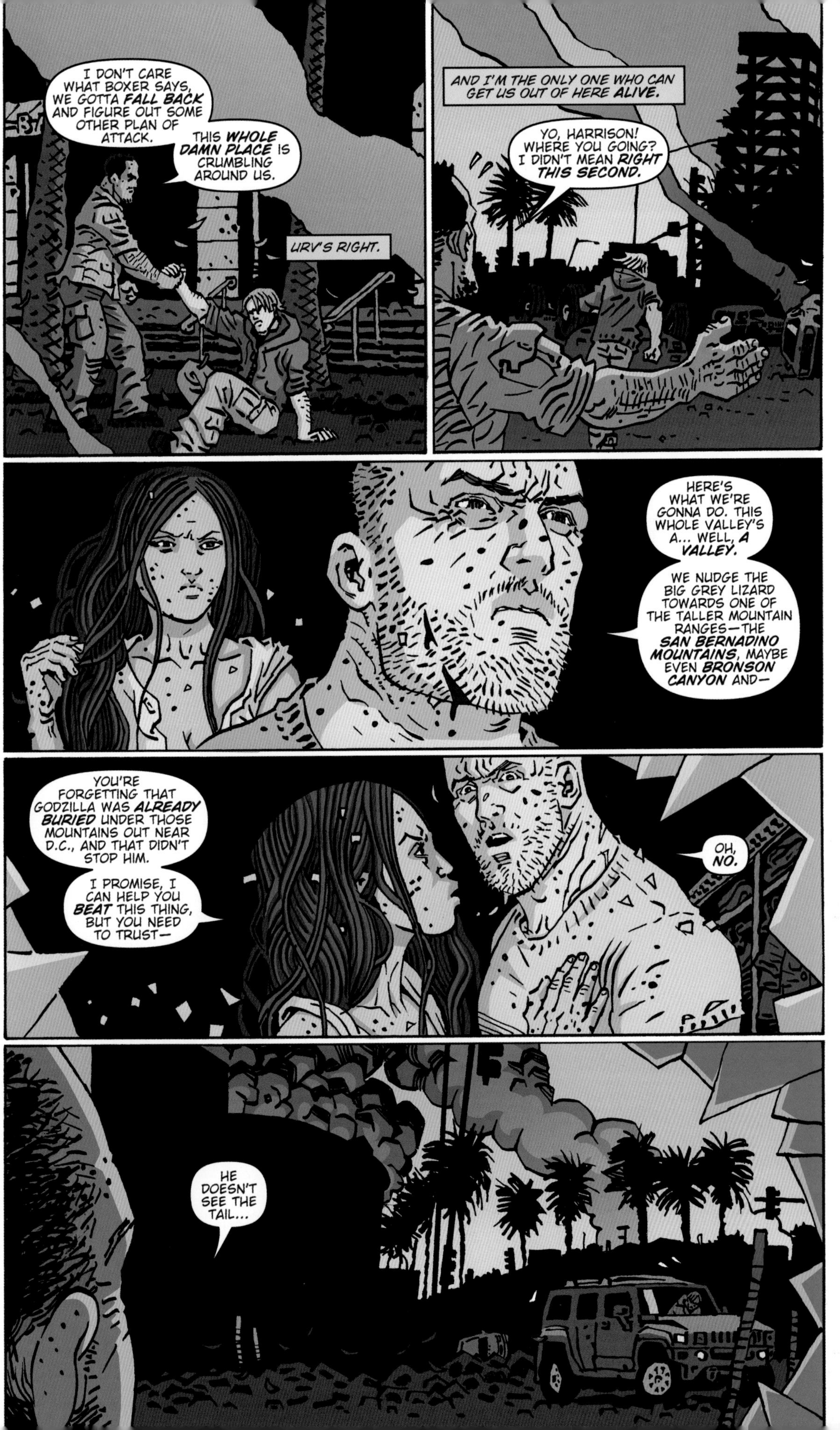
I DON'T CARE WHAT BOXER SAYS, WE GOTTA FALL BACK AND FIGURE OUT SOME OTHER PLAN OF ATTACK.
THIS WHOLE DAMN PLACE IS CRUMBLING AROUND US.
URV'S RIGHT.
AND I'M THE ONLY ONE WHO CAN GET US OUT OF HERE ALIVE.
YO, HARRISON! WHERE YOU GOING? I DIDN'T MEAN RIGHT THIS SECOND.
HERE'S WHAT WE'RE GONNA DO. THIS WHOLE VALLEY'S A... WELL, A VALLEY.
WE NUDGE THE BIG GREY LIZARD TOWARDS ONE OF THE TALLER MOUNTAIN RANGES—THE SAN BERNADINO MOUNTAINS, MAYBE EVEN BRONSON CANYON AND—
YOU'RE FORGETTING THAT GODZILLA WAS ALREADY BURIED UNDER THOSE MOUNTAINS OUT NEAR D.C., AND THAT DIDN'T STOP HIM.
I PROMISE, I CAN HELP YOU BEAT THIS THING, BUT YOU NEED TO TRUST—
OH, NO.
HE DOESN'T SEE THE TAIL...

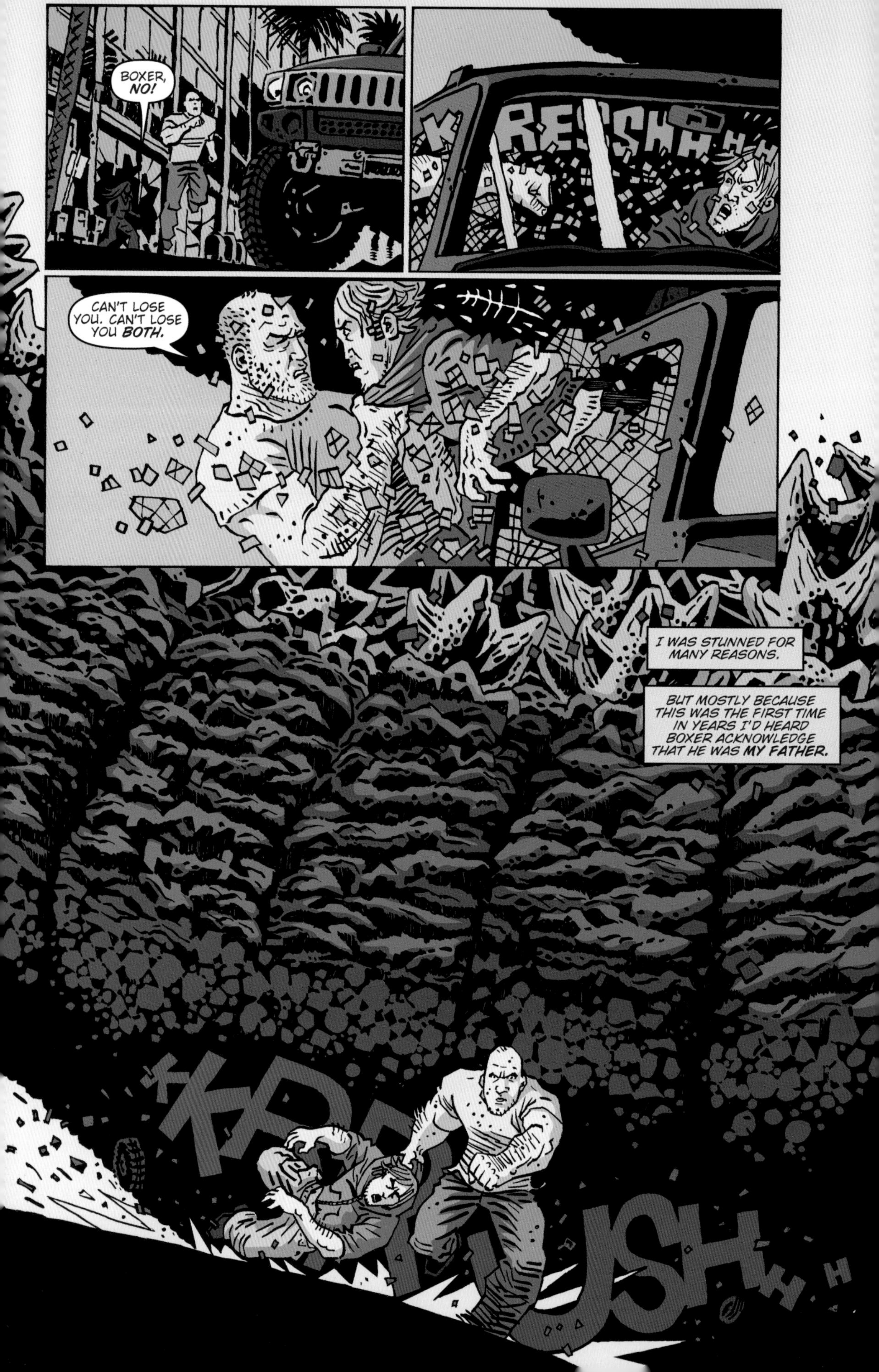

BOXER, NO!
KRESSHHHH
CAN'T LOSE YOU. CAN'T LOSE YOU BOTH.
I WAS STUNNED FOR MANY REASONS.
BUT MOSTLY BECAUSE THIS WAS THE FIRST TIME IN YEARS I'D HEARD BOXER ACKNOWLEDGE THAT HE WAS MY FATHER.

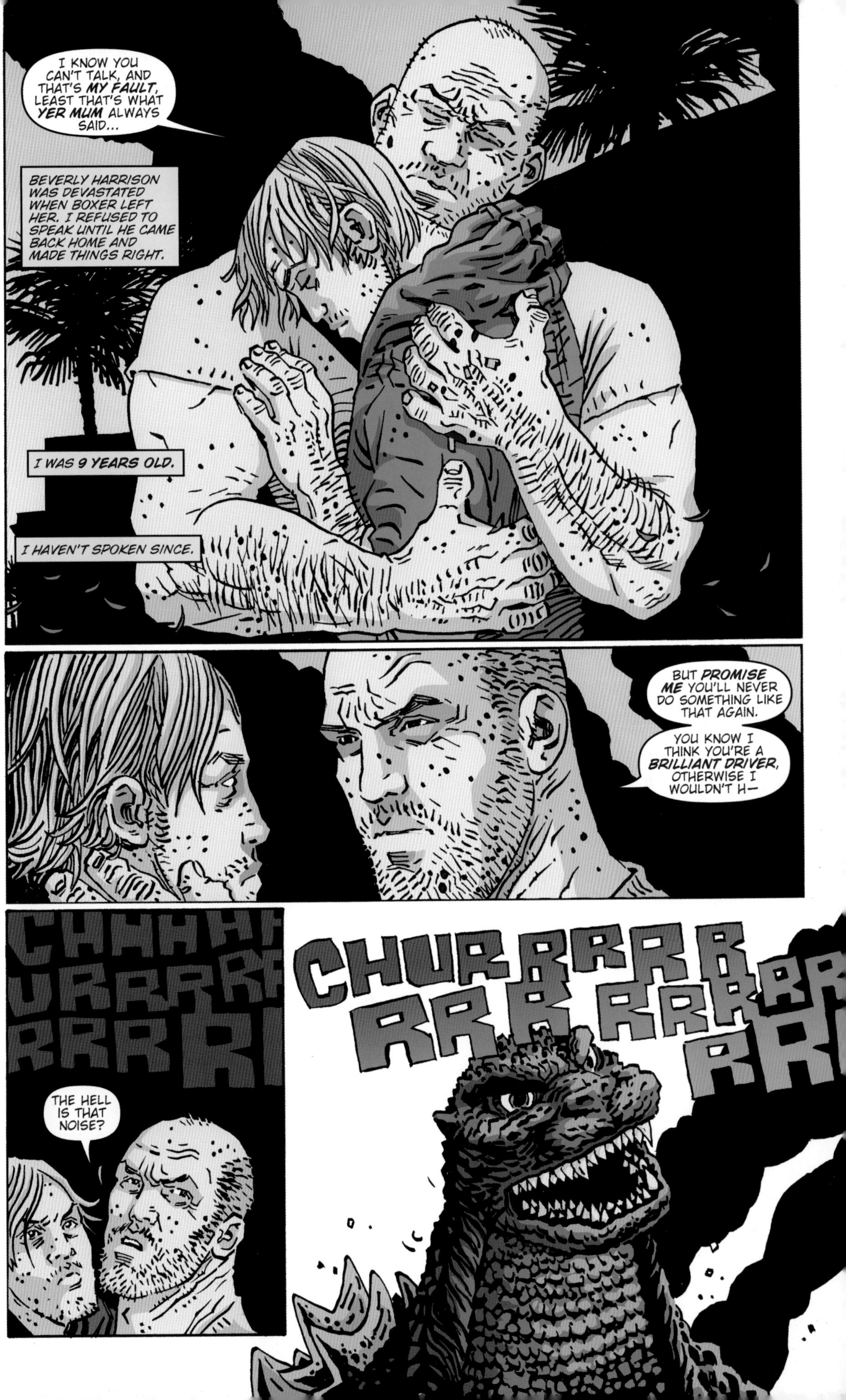
I KNOW YOU CAN'T TALK, AND THAT'S MY FAULT, LEAST THAT'S WHAT YER MUM ALWAYS SAID...
BEVERLY HARRISON WAS DEVASTATED WHEN BOXER LEFT HER. I REFUSED TO SPEAK UNTIL HE CAME BACK HOME AND MADE THINGS RIGHT.
I WAS 9 YEARS OLD.
I HAVEN'T SPOKEN SINCE.
BUT PROMISE ME YOU'LL NEVER DO SOMETHING LIKE THAT AGAIN.
YOU KNOW I THINK YOU'RE A BRILLIANT DRIVER, OTHERWISE I WOULDN'T H—
CHHHH URRRR RRRR
THE HELL IS THAT NOISE?
CHURRRR RRRRRRRR RRR

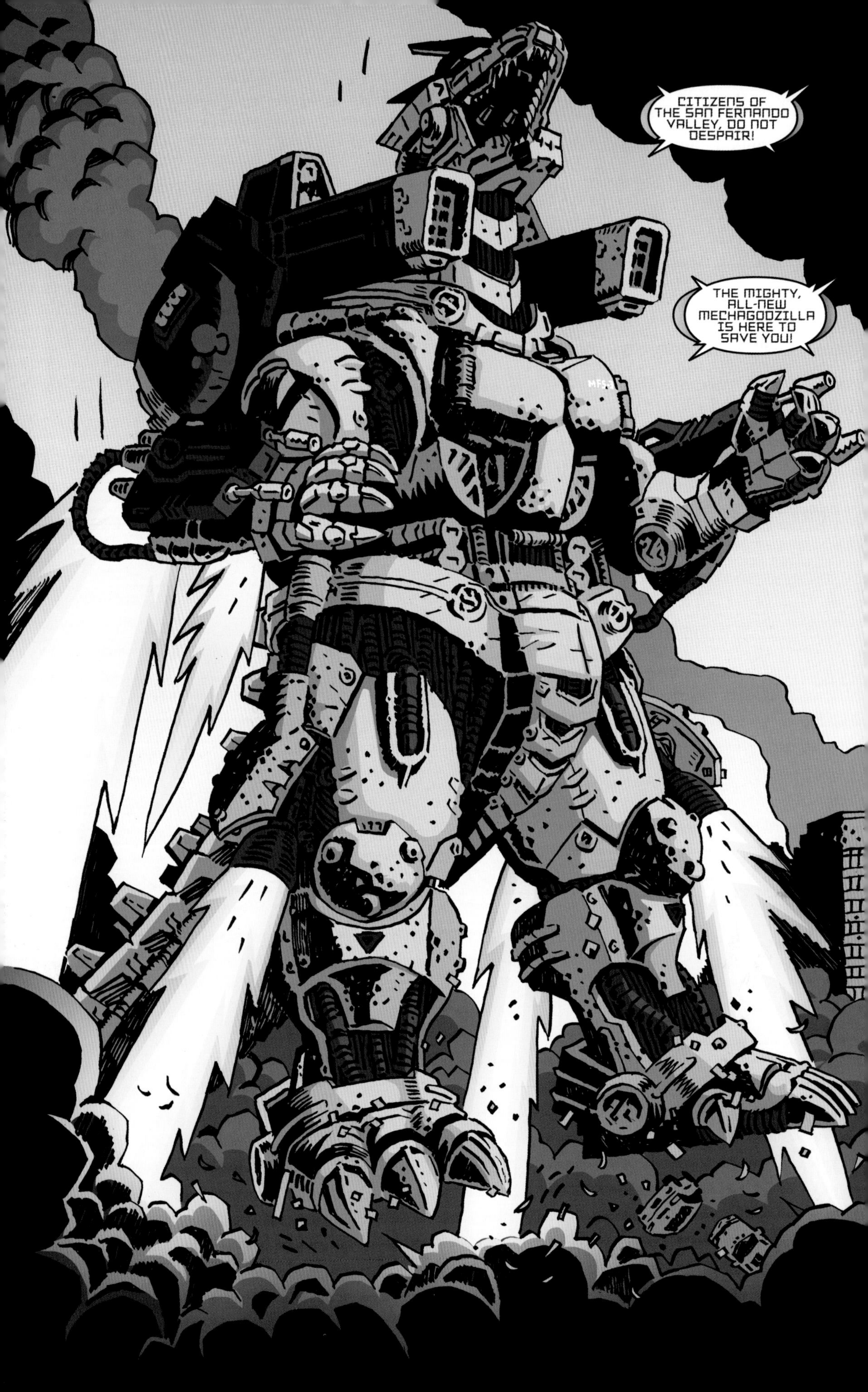
CITIZENS OF THE SAN FERNANDO VALLEY, DO NOT DESPAIR!
THE MIGHTY, ALL-NEW MECHAGODZILLA IS HERE TO SAVE YOU!

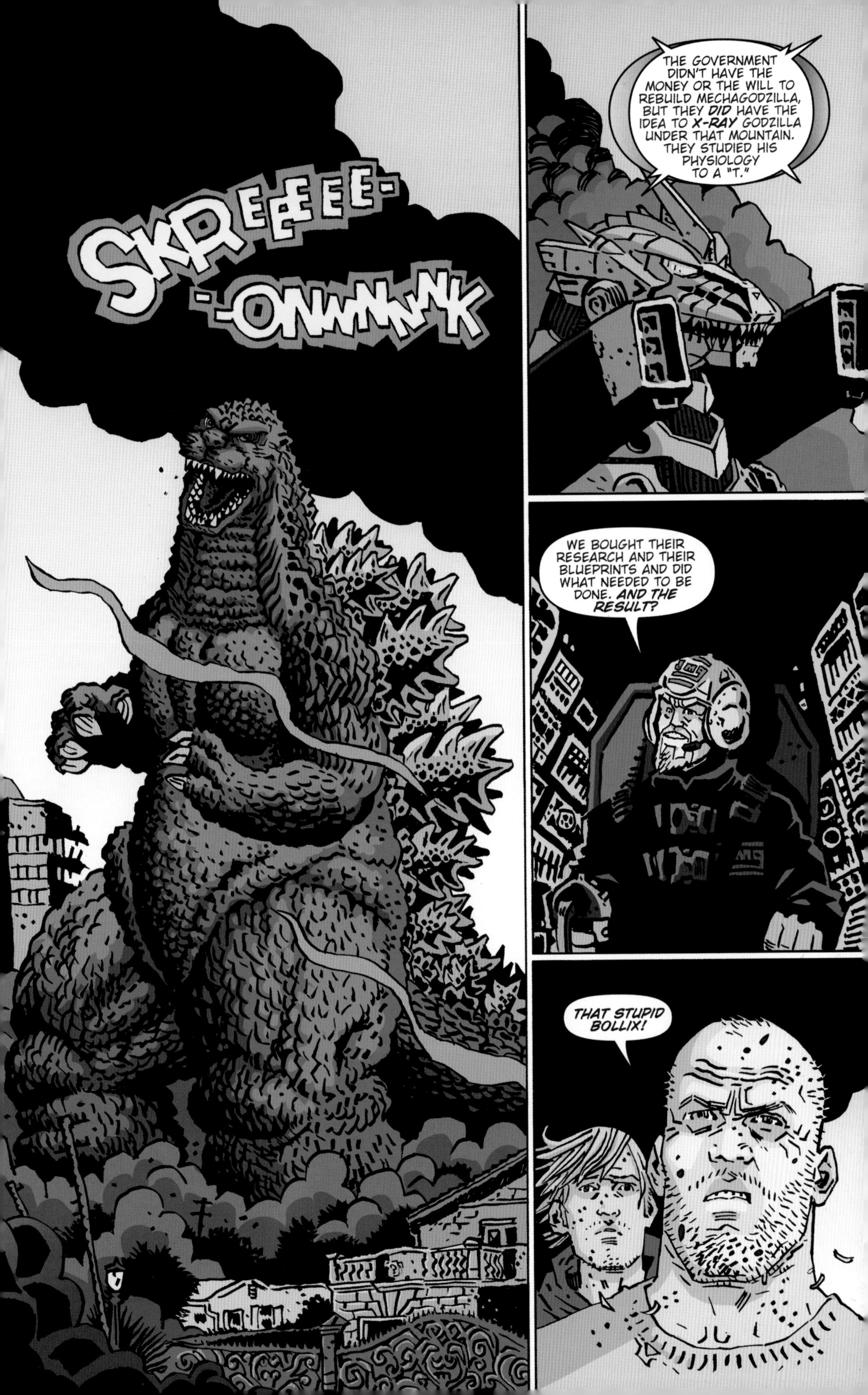
SKREEEEE-
-ONNNNK
THE GOVERNMENT DIDN'T HAVE THE MONEY OR THE WILL TO REBUILD MECHAGODZILLA, BUT THEY *DID* HAVE THE IDEA TO *X-RAY* GODZILLA UNDER THAT MOUNTAIN. THEY STUDIED HIS PHYSIOLOGY TO A "T."
WE BOUGHT THEIR RESEARCH AND THEIR BLUEPRINTS AND DID WHAT NEEDED TO BE DONE. *AND THE RESULT?*
THAT STUPID BOLLIX!

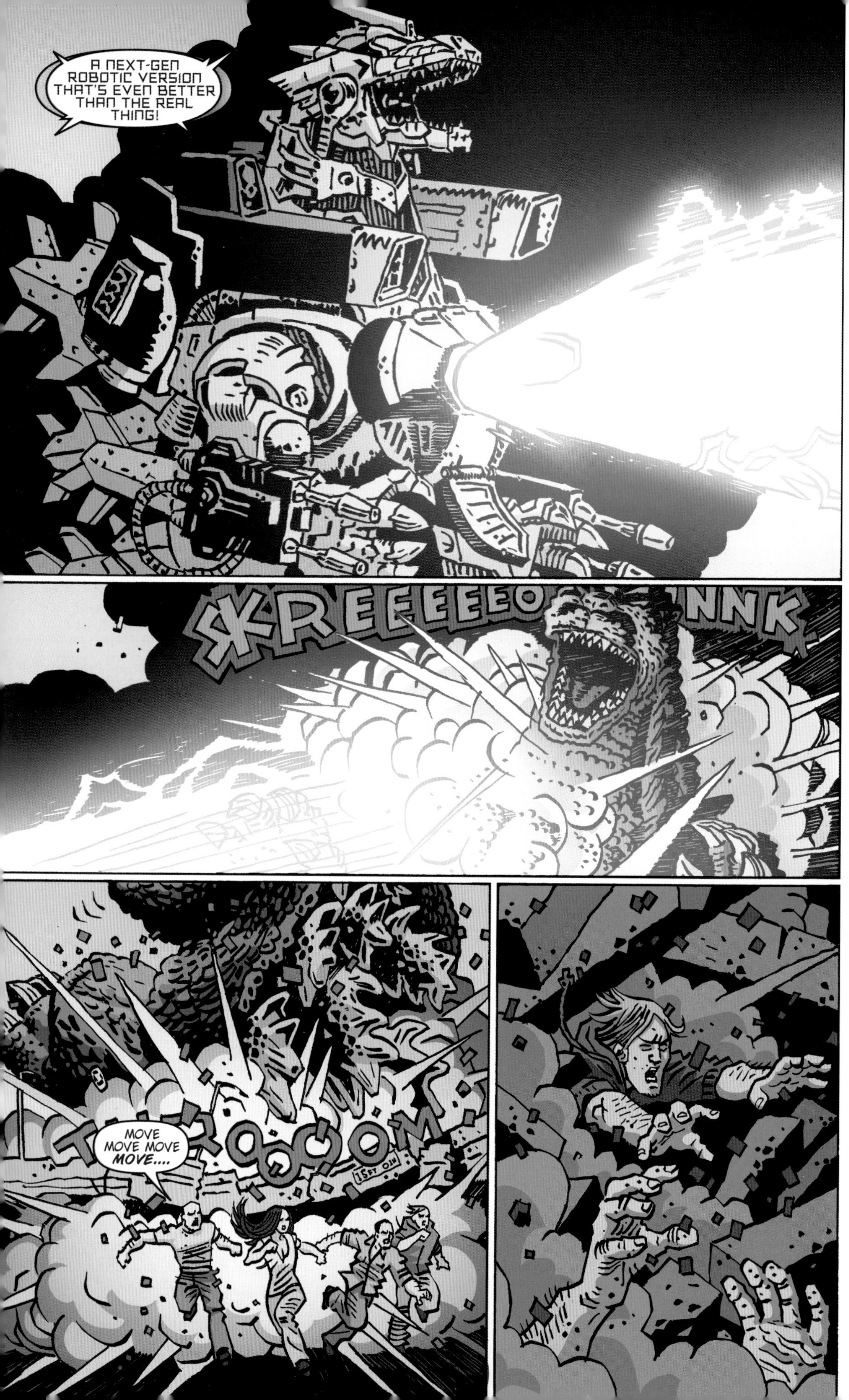
A NEXT-GEN ROBOTIC VERSION THAT'S EVEN BETTER THAN THE REAL THING!
SKREEEEEO
NNK
MOVE MOVE MOVE *MOVE*....

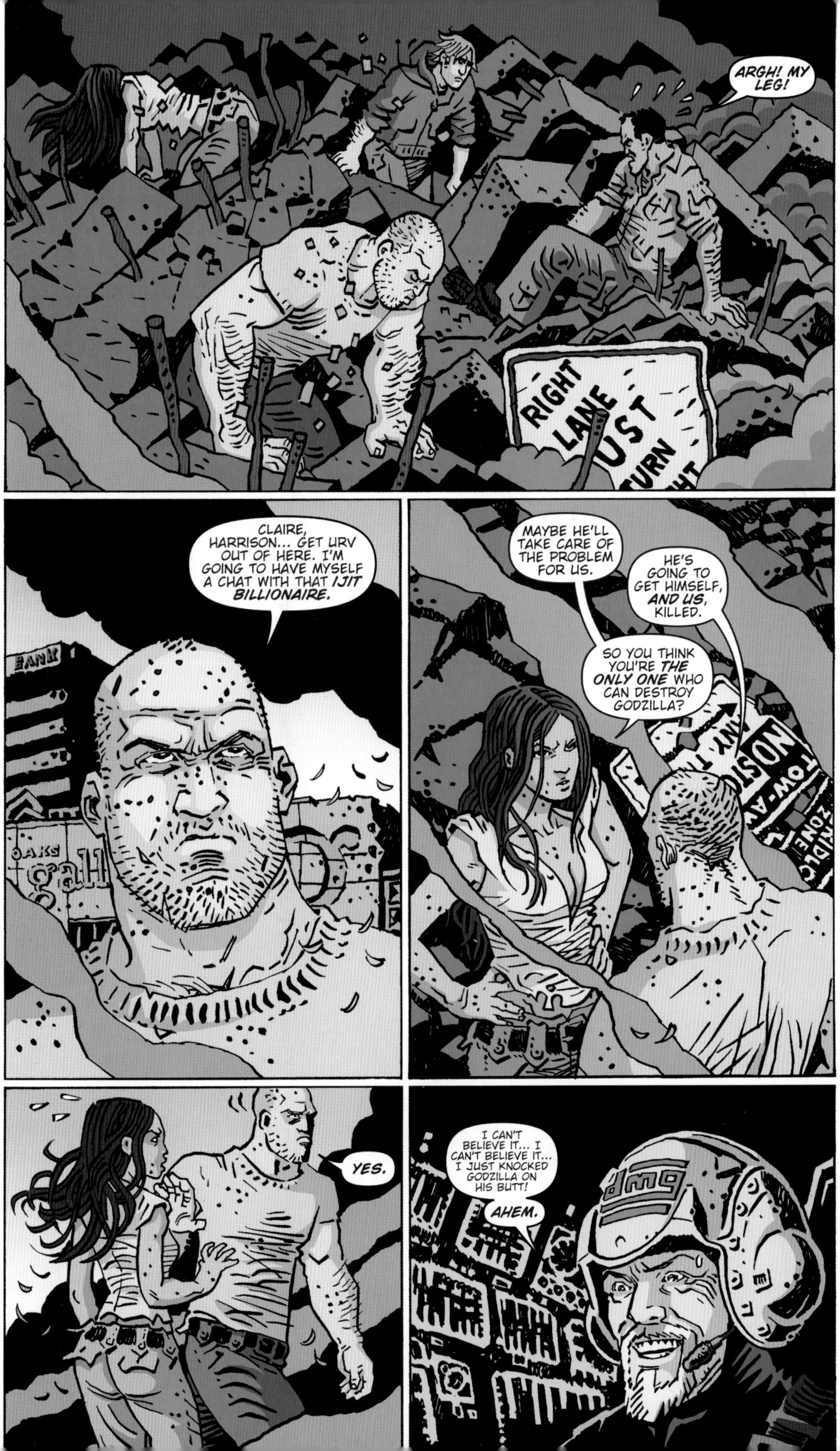
ARGH! MY LEG!
RIGHT LANE UST TURN
CLAIRE, HARRISON... GET URV OUT OF HERE. I'M GOING TO HAVE MYSELF A CHAT WITH THAT IJIT BILLIONAIRE.
BANK
MAYBE HE'LL TAKE CARE OF THE PROBLEM FOR US.
HE'S GOING TO GET HIMSELF, AND US, KILLED.
SO YOU THINK YOU'RE THE ONLY ONE WHO CAN DESTROY GODZILLA?
YES.
I CAN'T BELIEVE IT... I CAN'T BELIEVE IT... I JUST KNOCKED GODZILLA ON HIS BUTT!
AHEM.

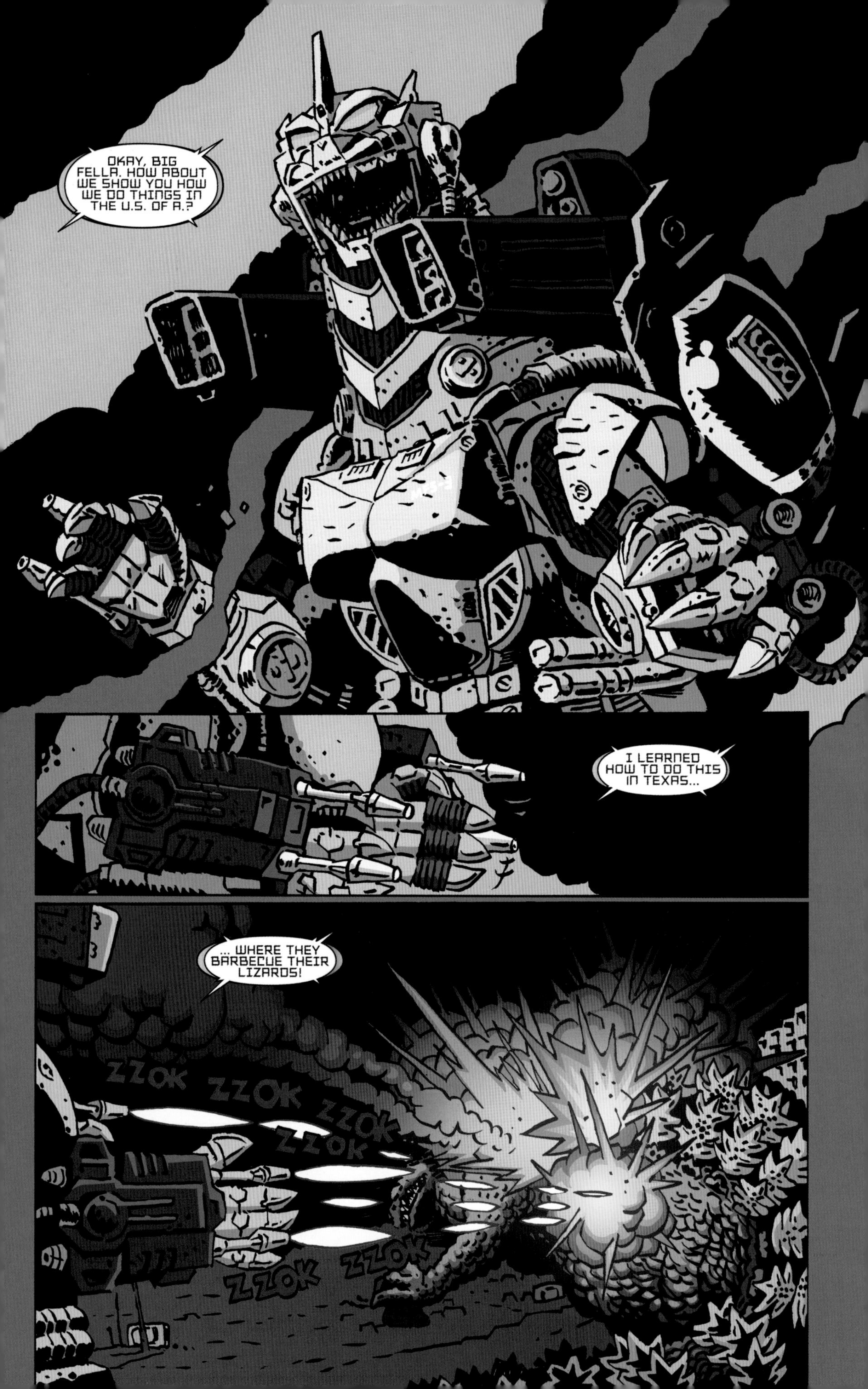
OKAY, BIG FELLA. HOW ABOUT WE SHOW YOU HOW WE DO THINGS IN THE U.S. OF A.?
I LEARNED HOW TO DO THIS IN TEXAS...
... WHERE THEY BARBECUE THEIR LIZARDS!
ZZOK
ZZOK
ZZOK
ZZOK
ZZOK
ZZOK

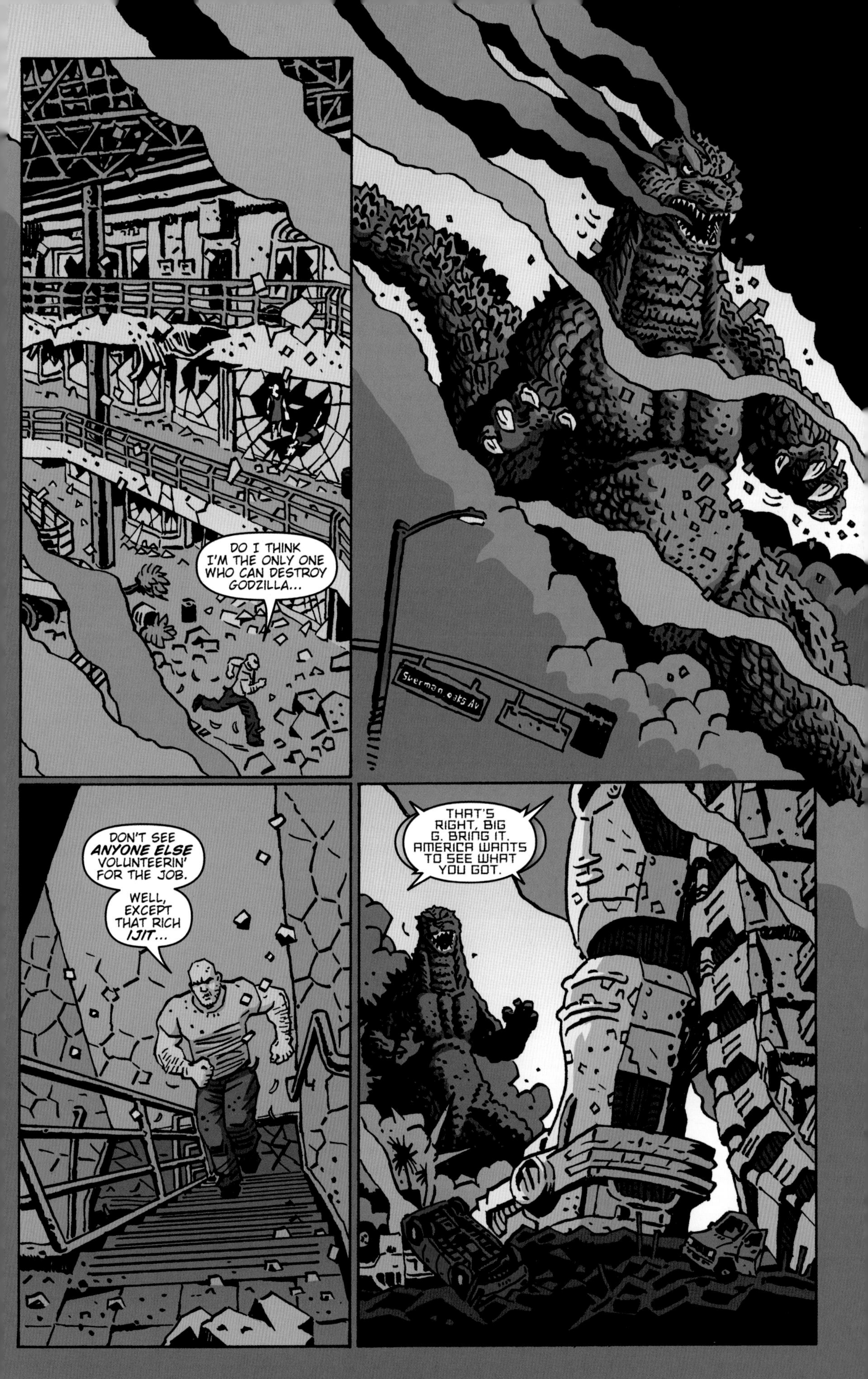
DO I THINK I'M THE ONLY ONE WHO CAN DESTROY GODZILLA...
Sherman oaks Av
DON'T SEE ANYONE ELSE VOLUNTEERIN' FOR THE JOB.
WELL, EXCEPT THAT RICH IJIT...
THAT'S RIGHT, BIG G. BRING IT. AMERICA WANTS TO SEE WHAT YOU GOT.

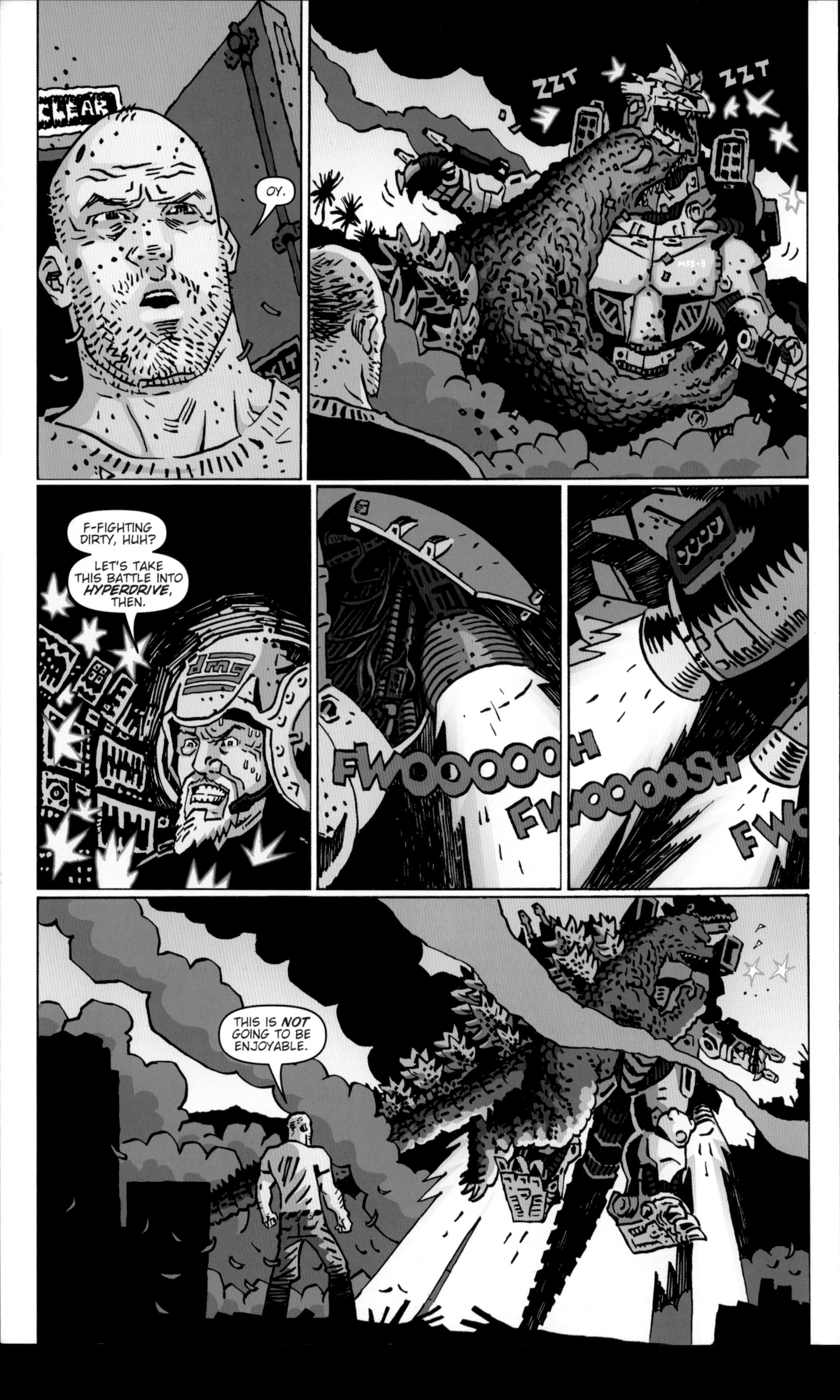
CLEAR
OY.
ZZT
ZZT
MFS-3
F-FIGHTING DIRTY, HUH?
LET'S TAKE THIS BATTLE INTO *HYPERDRIVE*, THEN.
FWOOOOOH
FWOOOOOSH
THIS IS *NOT* GOING TO BE ENJOYABLE.

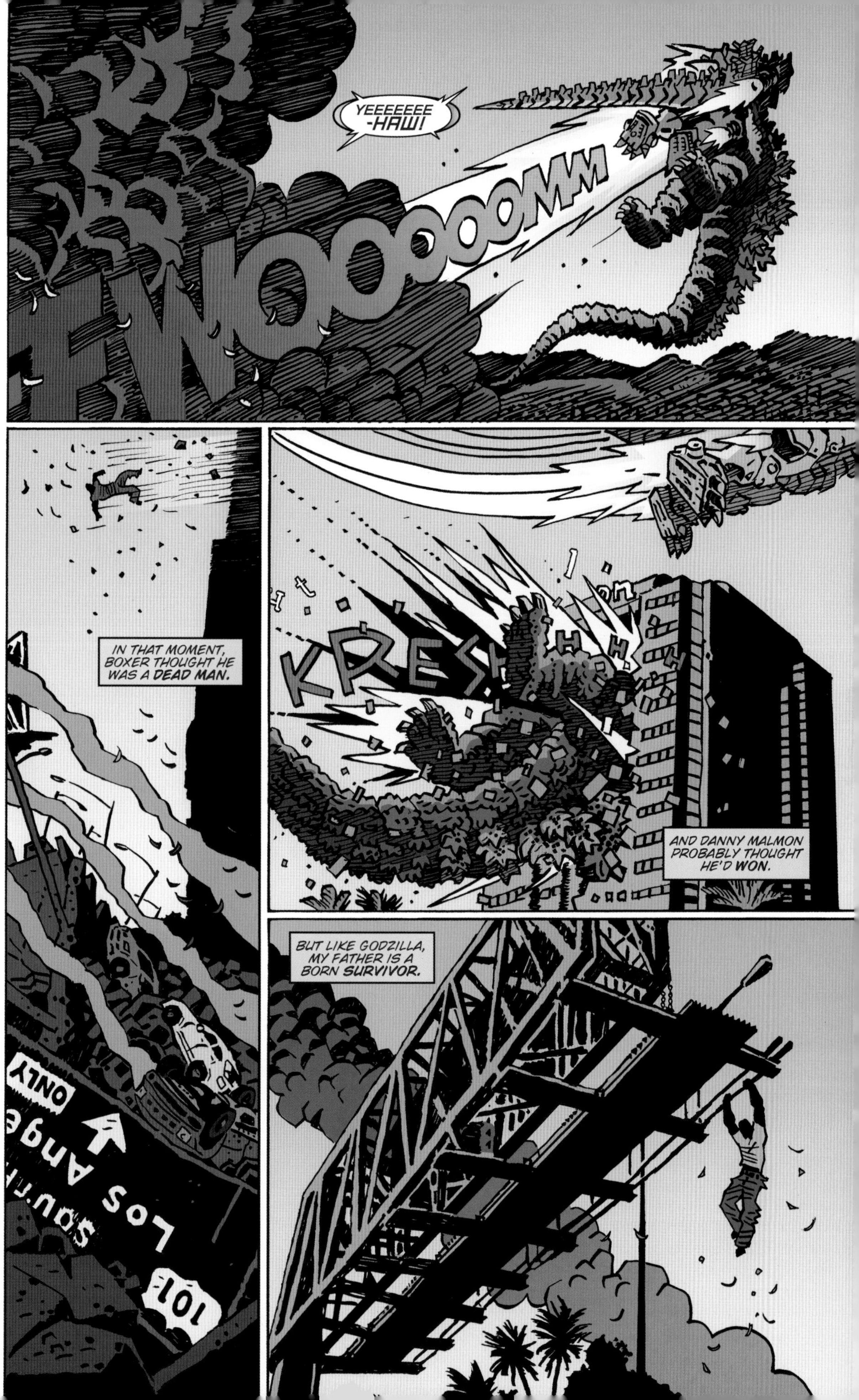
YEEEEEEE -HAW!
IN THAT MOMENT, BOXER THOUGHT HE WAS A DEAD MAN.
KRESH
AND DANNY MALMON PROBABLY THOUGHT HE'D WON.
BUT LIKE GODZILLA, MY FATHER IS A BORN SURVIVOR.
ONLY
101

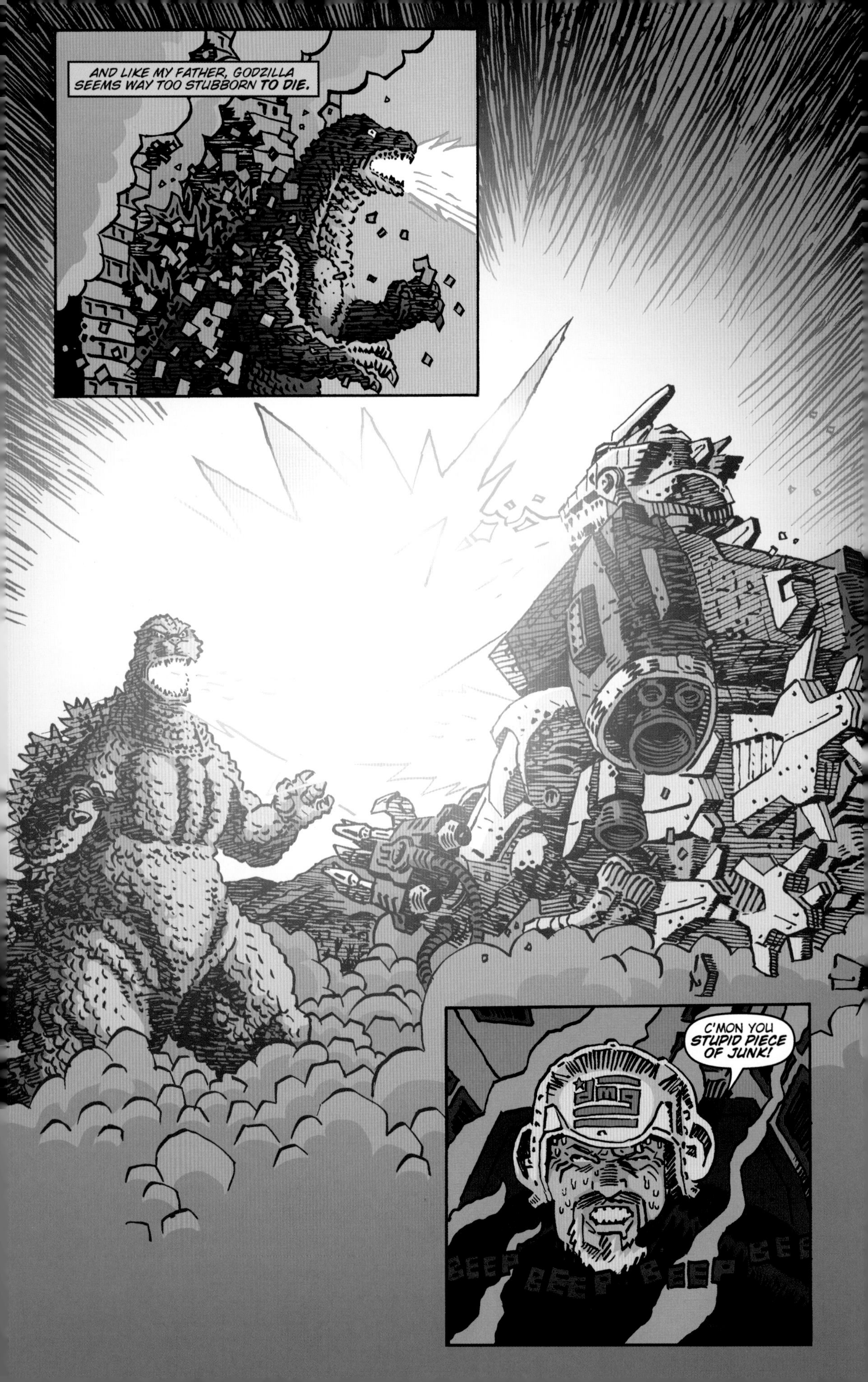
AND LIKE MY FATHER, GODZILLA SEEMS WAY TOO STUBBORN TO DIE.
C'MON YOU STUPID PIECE OF JUNK!
BEEP BEEP BEEP BEEP

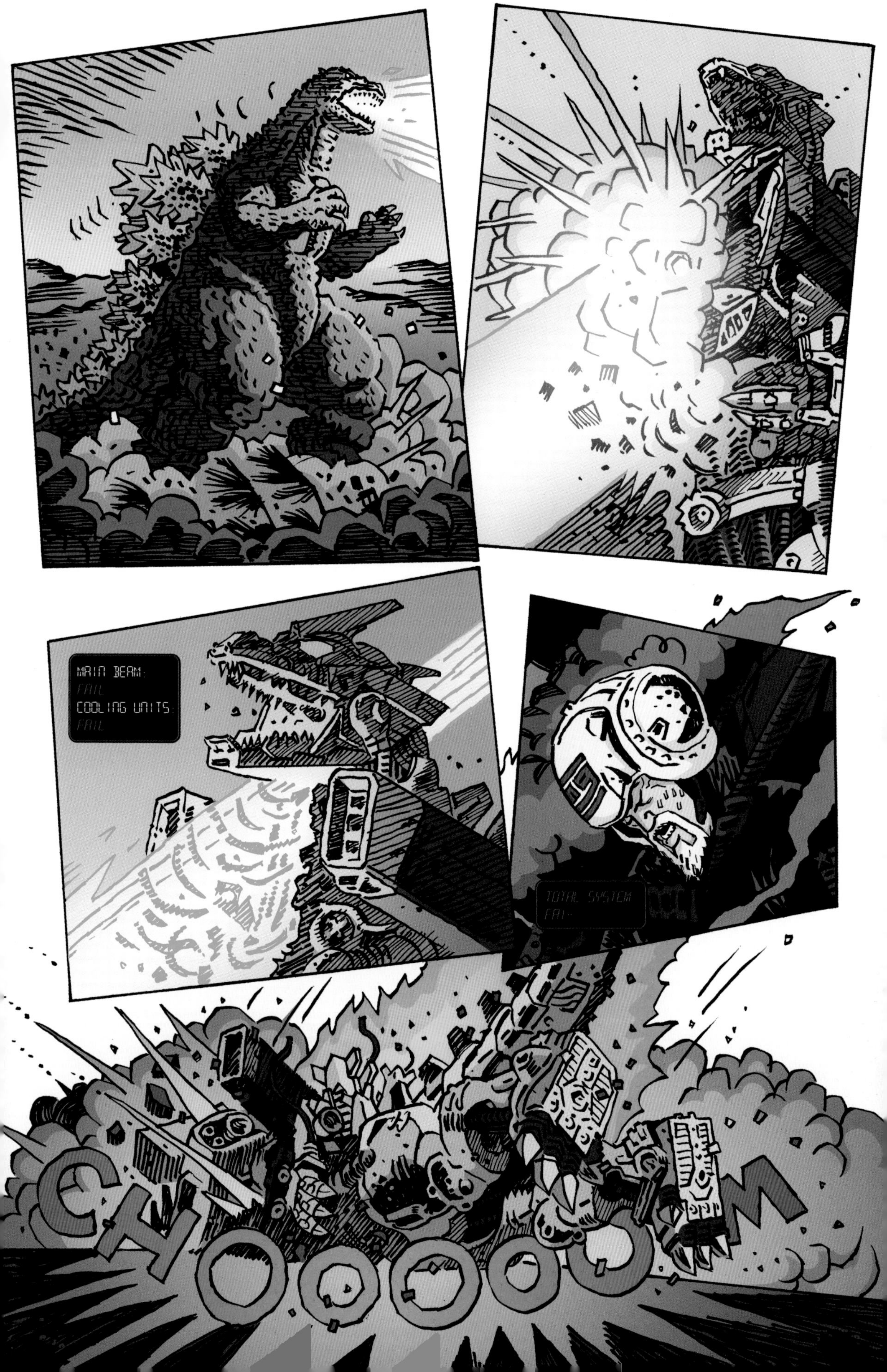
MAIN BEAM:
FAIL
COOLING UNITS:
FAIL
TOTAL SYSTEM
FAI-
CHOOOOOM

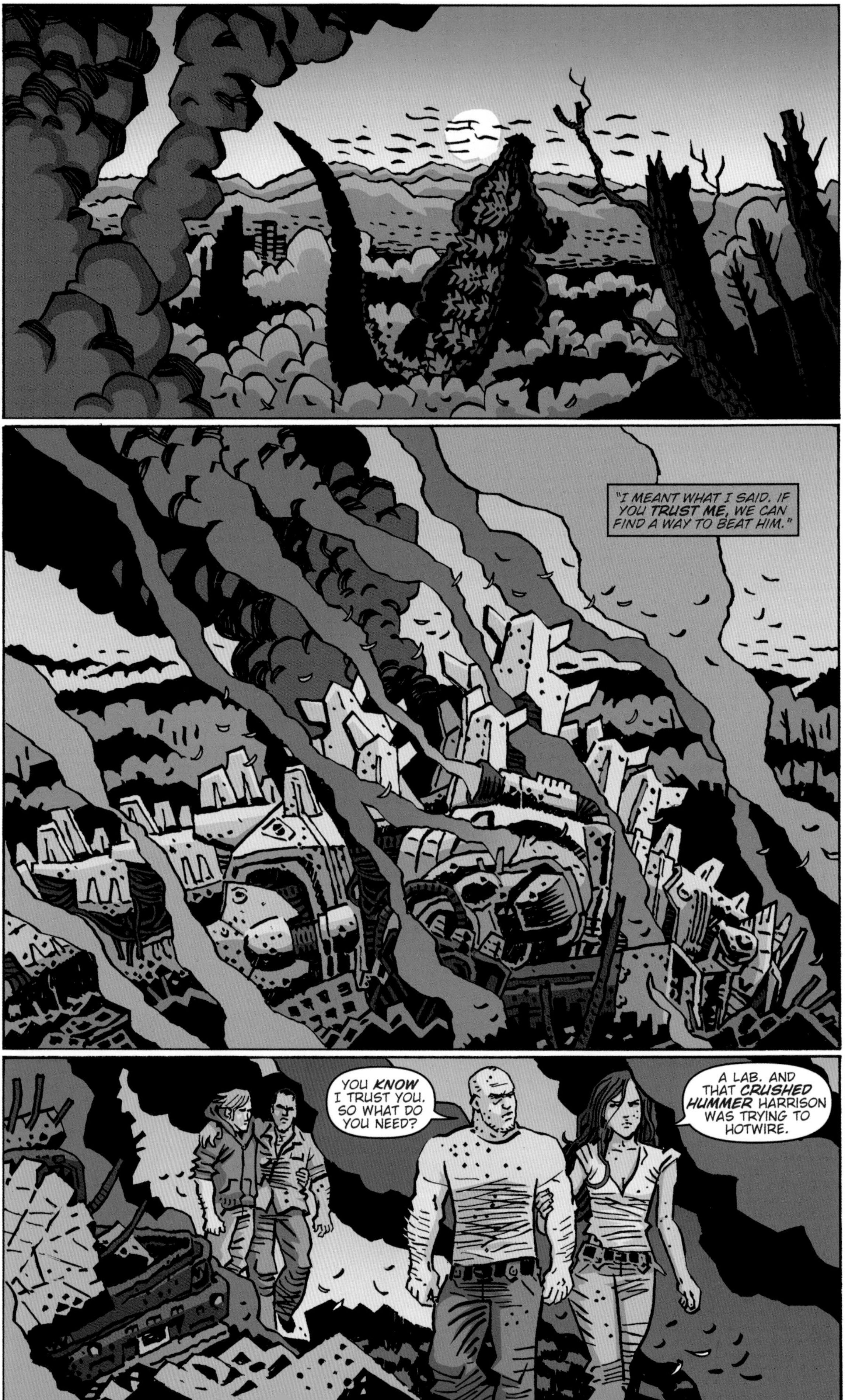
"I MEANT WHAT I SAID. IF YOU TRUST ME, WE CAN FIND A WAY TO BEAT HIM."
YOU KNOW I TRUST YOU. SO WHAT DO YOU NEED?
A LAB. AND THAT CRUSHED HUMMER HARRISON WAS TRYING TO HOTWIRE.

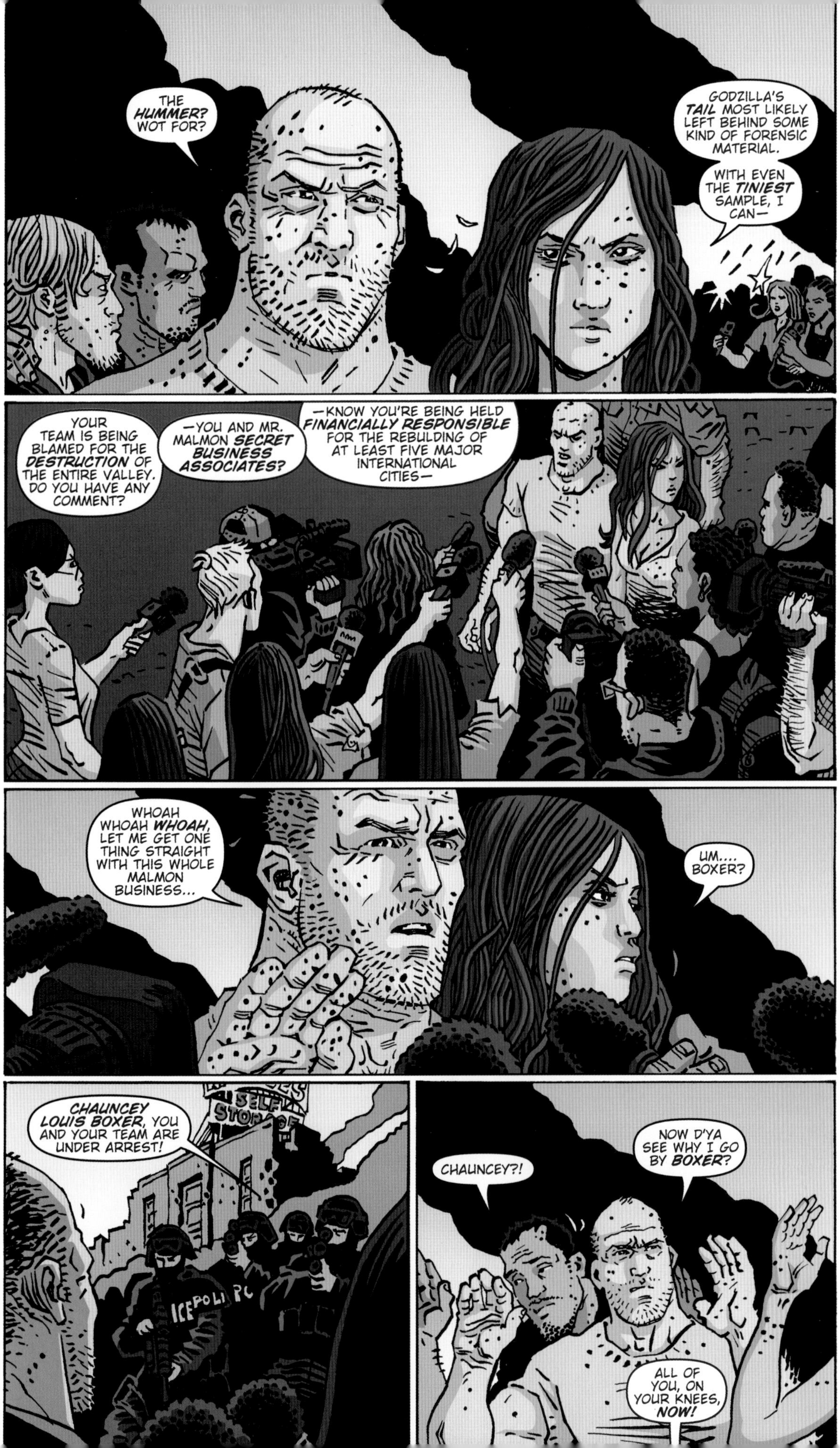
THE HUMMER? WOT FOR?
GODZILLA'S TAIL MOST LIKELY LEFT BEHIND SOME KIND OF FORENSIC MATERIAL.
WITH EVEN THE TINIEST SAMPLE, I CAN—
YOUR TEAM IS BEING BLAMED FOR THE DESTRUCTION OF THE ENTIRE VALLEY. DO YOU HAVE ANY COMMENT?
—YOU AND MR. MALMON SECRET BUSINESS ASSOCIATES?
—KNOW YOU'RE BEING HELD FINANCIALLY RESPONSIBLE FOR THE REBULDING OF AT LEAST FIVE MAJOR INTERNATIONAL CITIES—
WHOAH WHOAH WHOAH, LET ME GET ONE THING STRAIGHT WITH THIS WHOLE MALMON BUSINESS...
UM.... BOXER?
CHAUNCEY LOUIS BOXER, YOU AND YOUR TEAM ARE UNDER ARREST!
CHAUNCEY?!
NOW D'YA SEE WHY I GO BY BOXER?
ALL OF YOU, ON YOUR KNEES, NOW!

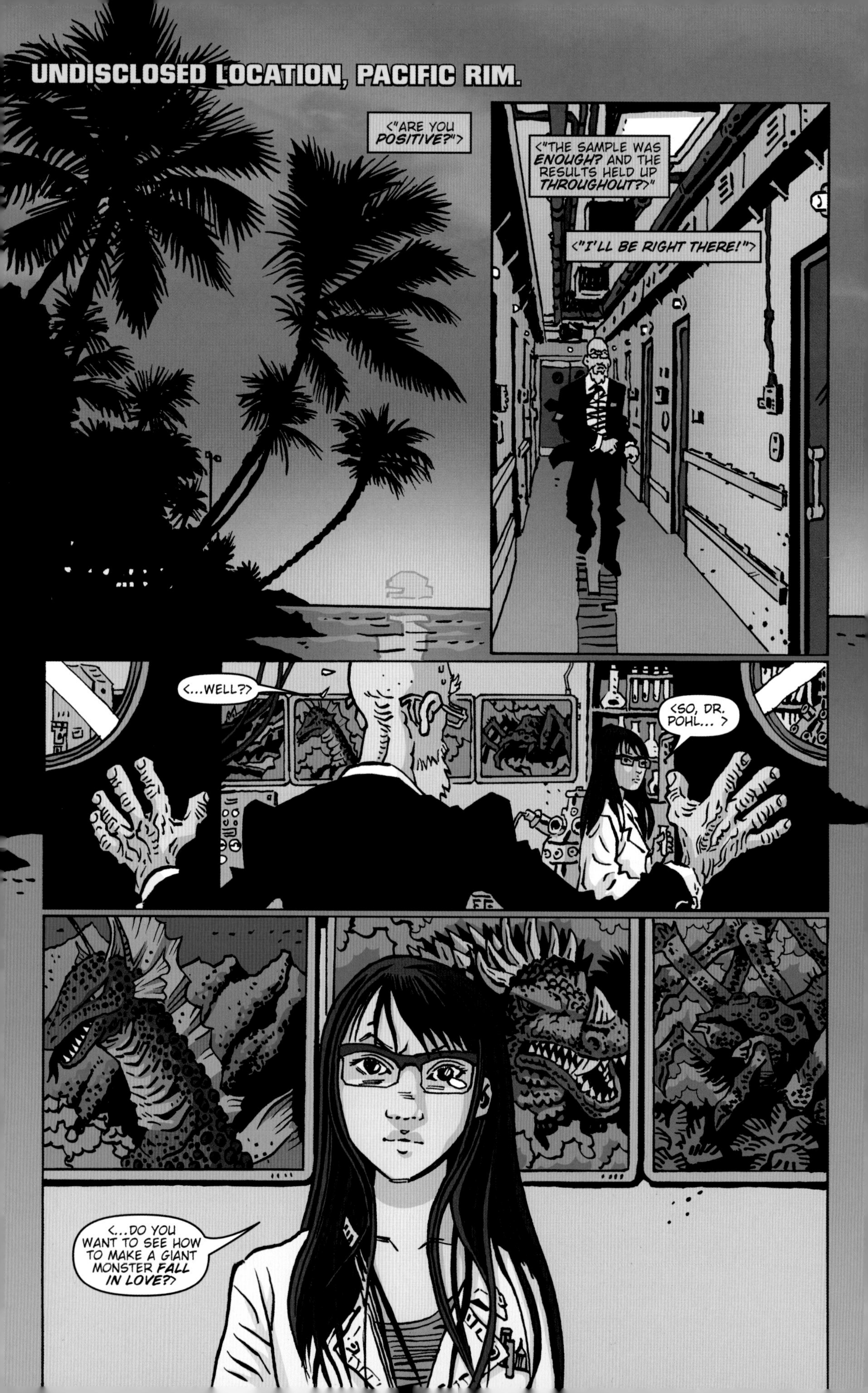
UNDISCLOSED LOCATION, PACIFIC RIM.
<"ARE YOU POSITIVE?">
<"THE SAMPLE WAS ENOUGH? AND THE RESULTS HELD UP THROUGHOUT?">
<"I'LL BE RIGHT THERE!">
<...WELL?>
<SO, DR. POHL... >
<...DO YOU WANT TO SEE HOW TO MAKE A GIANT MONSTER FALL IN LOVE?>

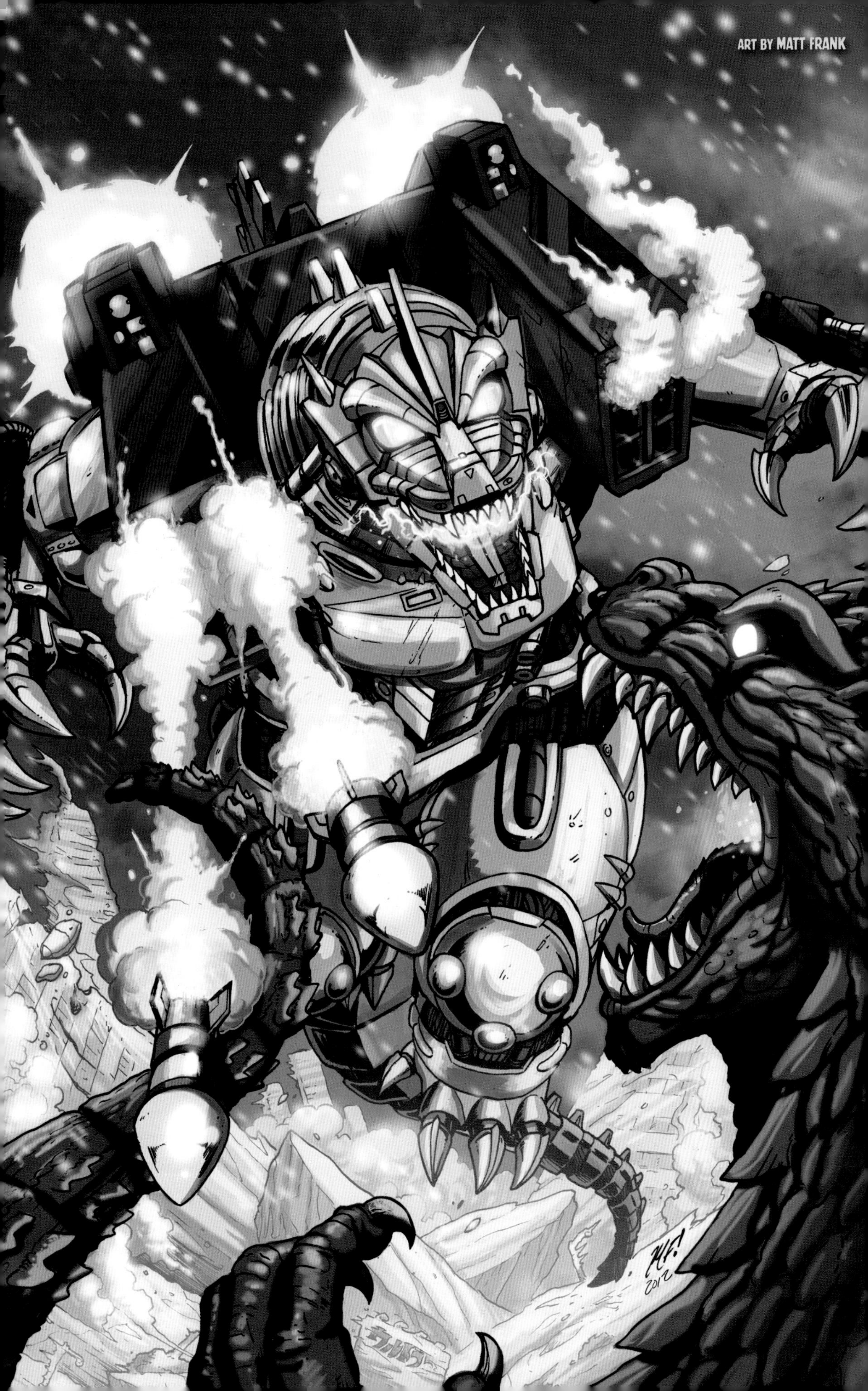
ART BY MATT FRANK

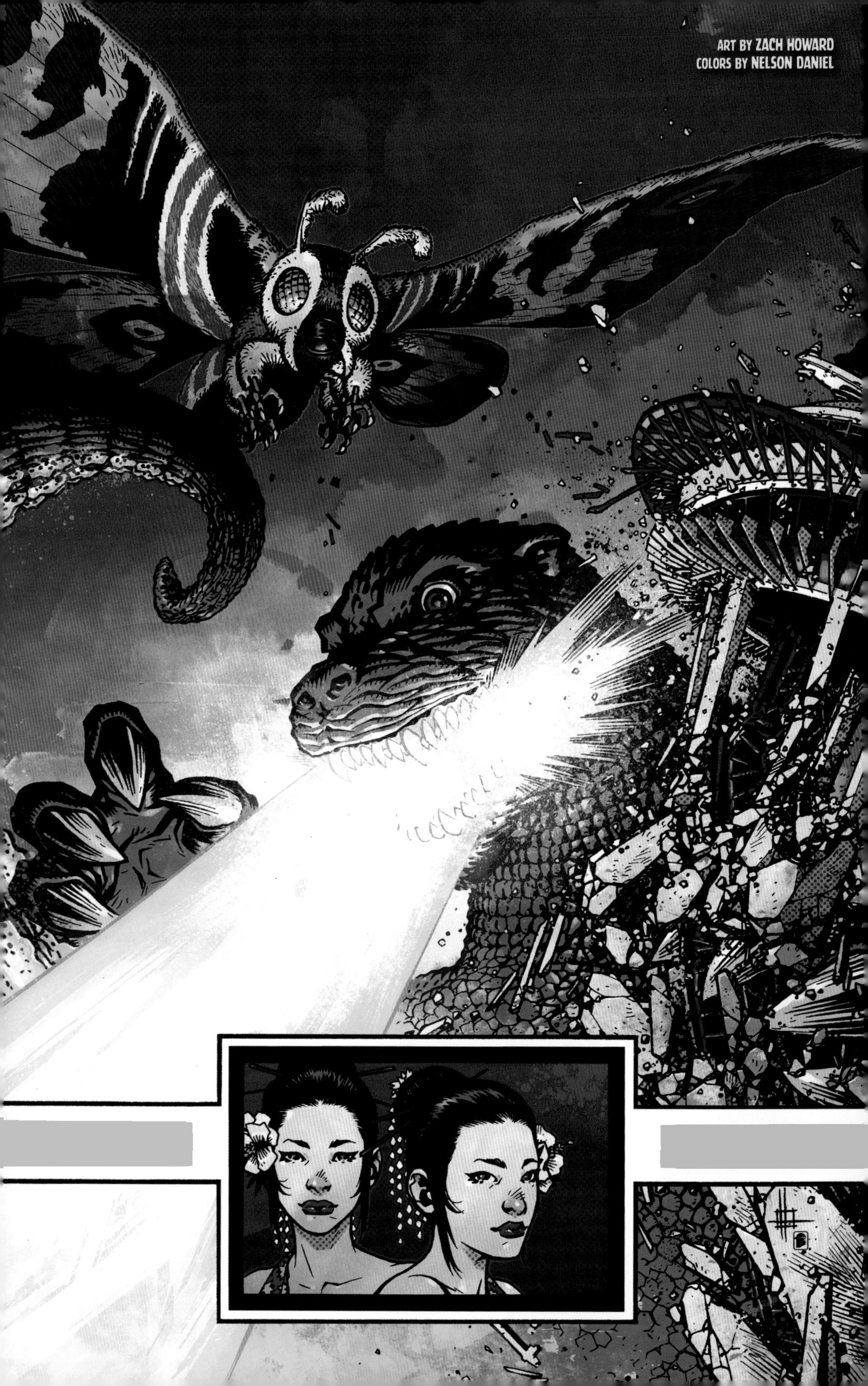
ART BY ZACH HOWARD
COLORS BY NELSON DANIEL

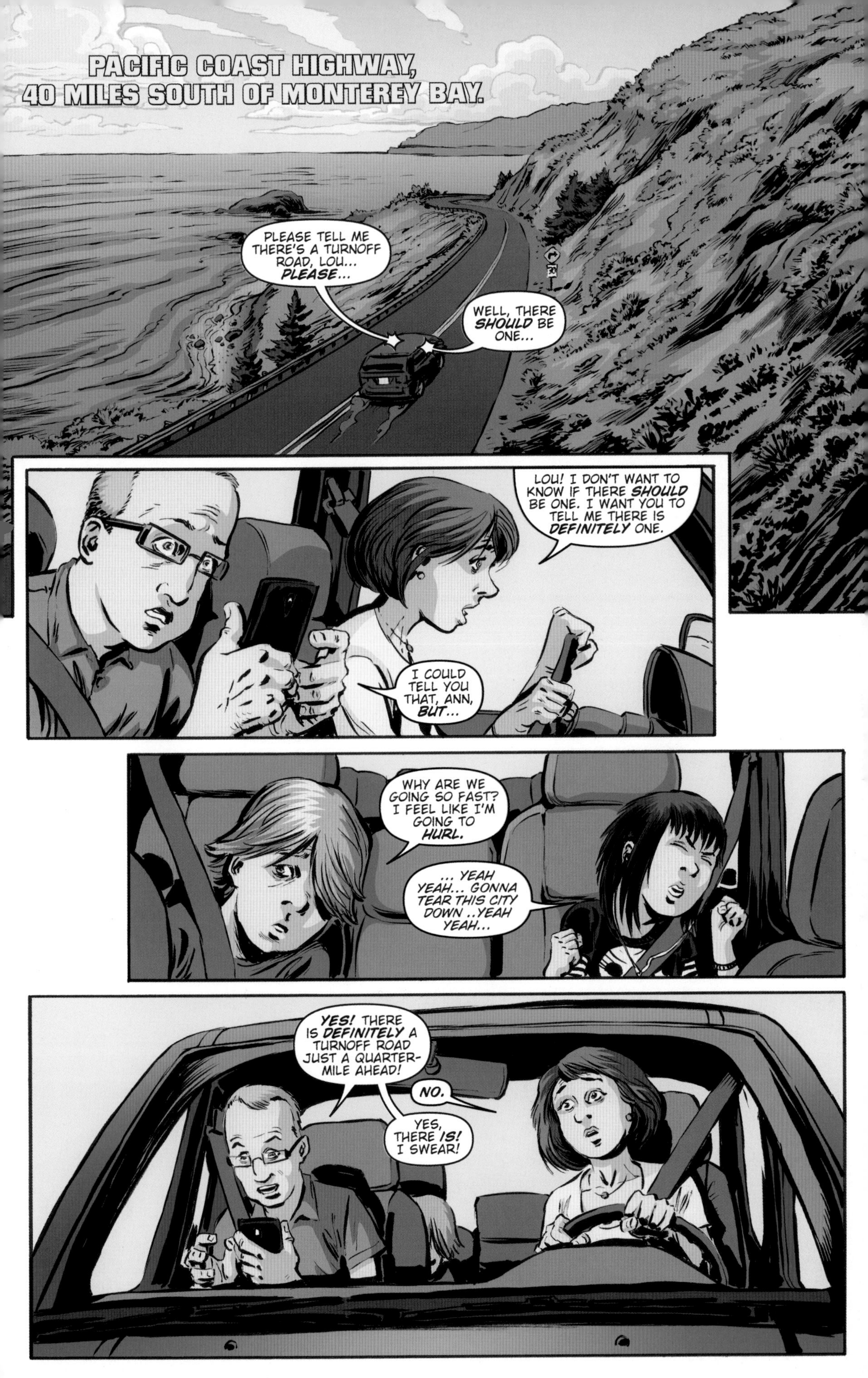
PACIFIC COAST HIGHWAY, 40 MILES SOUTH OF MONTEREY BAY.
PLEASE TELL ME THERE'S A TURNOFF ROAD, LOU... PLEASE...
WELL, THERE SHOULD BE ONE...
LOU! I DON'T WANT TO KNOW IF THERE SHOULD BE ONE. I WANT YOU TO TELL ME THERE IS DEFINITELY ONE.
I COULD TELL YOU THAT, ANN, BUT...
WHY ARE WE GOING SO FAST? I FEEL LIKE I'M GOING TO HURL.
... YEAH YEAH... GONNA TEAR THIS CITY DOWN ..YEAH YEAH...
YES! THERE IS DEFINITELY A TURNOFF ROAD JUST A QUARTER-MILE AHEAD!
NO.
YES, THERE IS! I SWEAR!

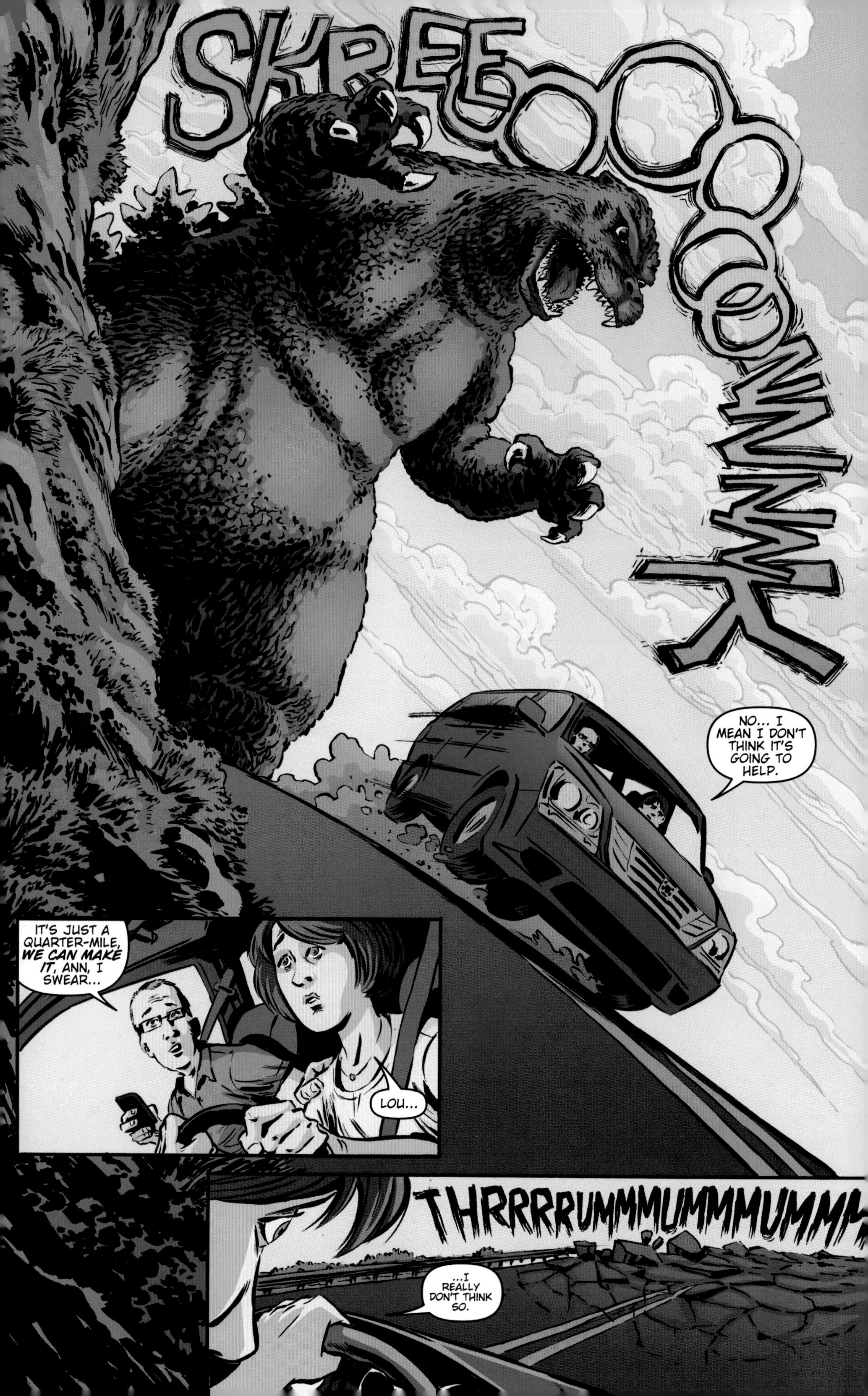
SKREEOOOOOONNNK
NO... I MEAN I DON'T THINK IT'S GOING TO HELP.
IT'S JUST A QUARTER-MILE, WE CAN MAKE IT, ANN, I SWEAR...
LOU...
THRRRRUMMMUMMMUMM
...I REALLY DON'T THINK SO.

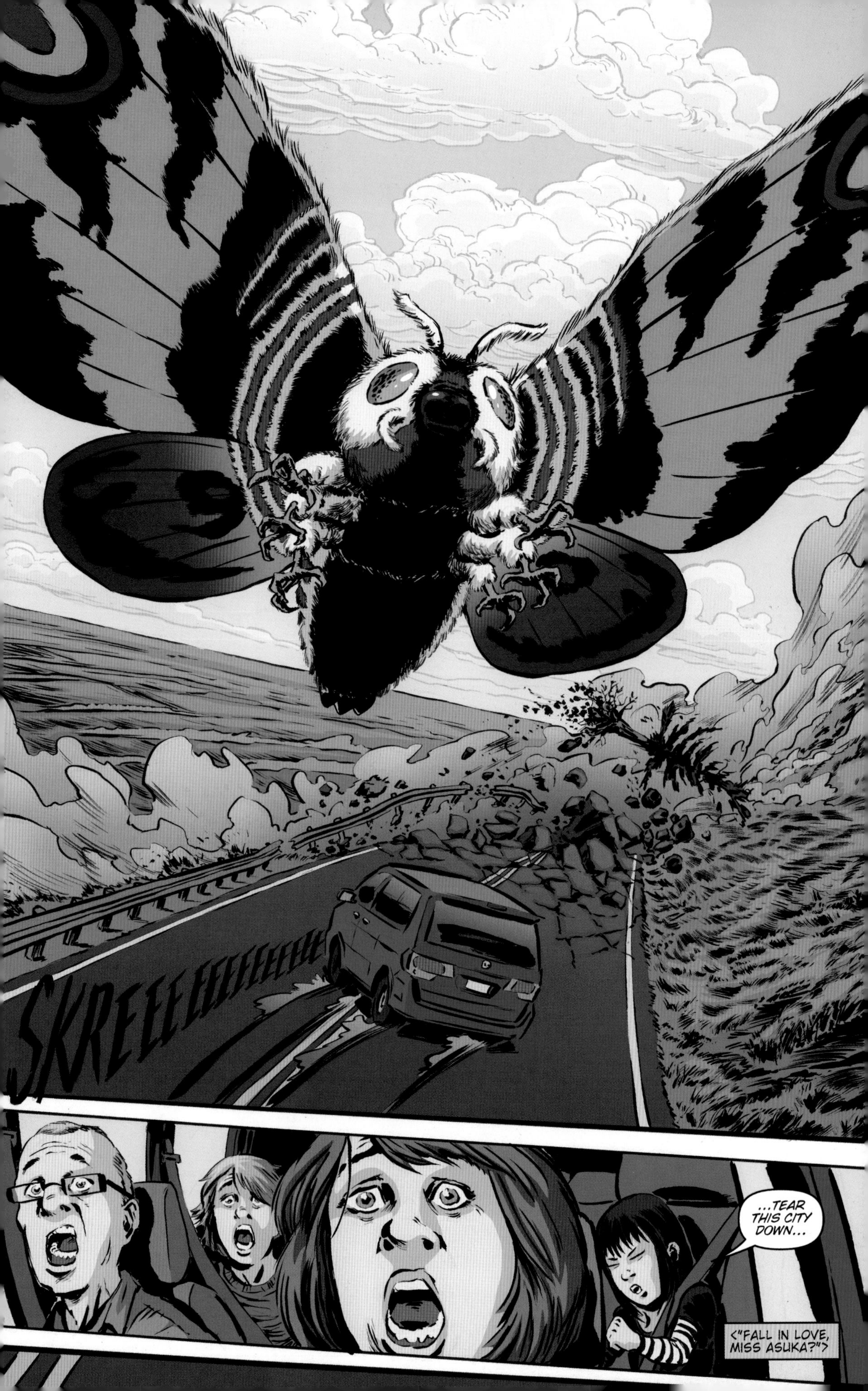
SKREEEEEEEEEEEEE
...TEAR THIS CITY DOWN...
<"FALL IN LOVE, MISS ASUKA?">

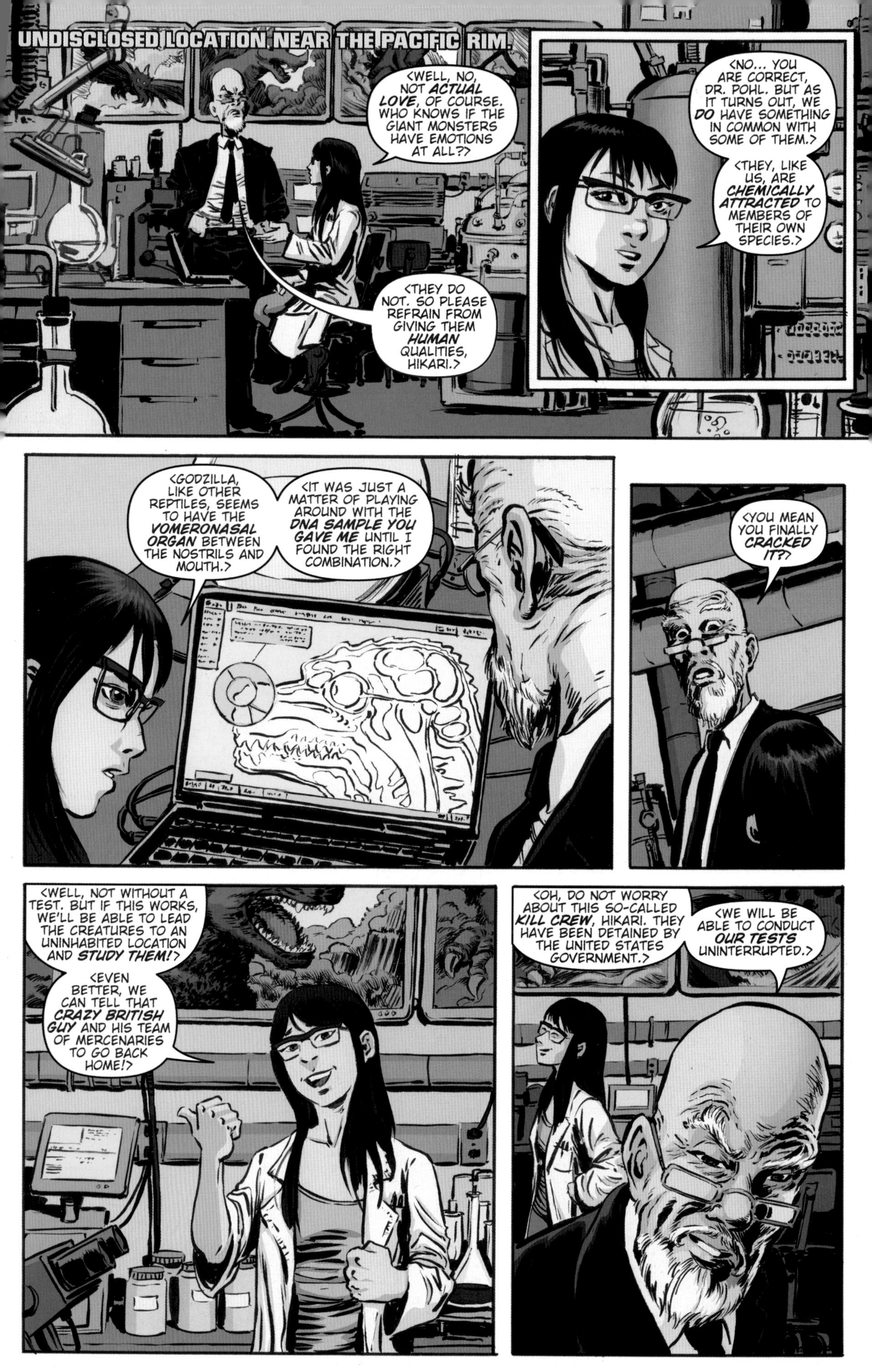

UNDISCLOSED LOCATION, NEAR THE PACIFIC RIM.
<WELL, NO, NOT ACTUAL LOVE, OF COURSE. WHO KNOWS IF THE GIANT MONSTERS HAVE EMOTIONS AT ALL?>
<THEY DO NOT. SO PLEASE REFRAIN FROM GIVING THEM HUMAN QUALITIES, HIKARI.>
<NO... YOU ARE CORRECT, DR. POHL. BUT AS IT TURNS OUT, WE DO HAVE SOMETHING IN COMMON WITH SOME OF THEM.>
<THEY, LIKE US, ARE CHEMICALLY ATTRACTED TO MEMBERS OF THEIR OWN SPECIES.>
<GODZILLA, LIKE OTHER REPTILES, SEEMS TO HAVE THE VOMERONASAL ORGAN BETWEEN THE NOSTRILS AND MOUTH.>
<IT WAS JUST A MATTER OF PLAYING AROUND WITH THE DNA SAMPLE YOU GAVE ME UNTIL I FOUND THE RIGHT COMBINATION.>
<YOU MEAN YOU FINALLY CRACKED IT?>
<WELL, NOT WITHOUT A TEST. BUT IF THIS WORKS, WE'LL BE ABLE TO LEAD THE CREATURES TO AN UNINHABITED LOCATION AND STUDY THEM!>
<EVEN BETTER, WE CAN TELL THAT CRAZY BRITISH GUY AND HIS TEAM OF MERCENARIES TO GO BACK HOME!>
<OH, DO NOT WORRY ABOUT THIS SO-CALLED KILL CREW, HIKARI. THEY HAVE BEEN DETAINED BY THE UNITED STATES GOVERNMENT.>
<WE WILL BE ABLE TO CONDUCT OUR TESTS UNINTERRUPTED.>

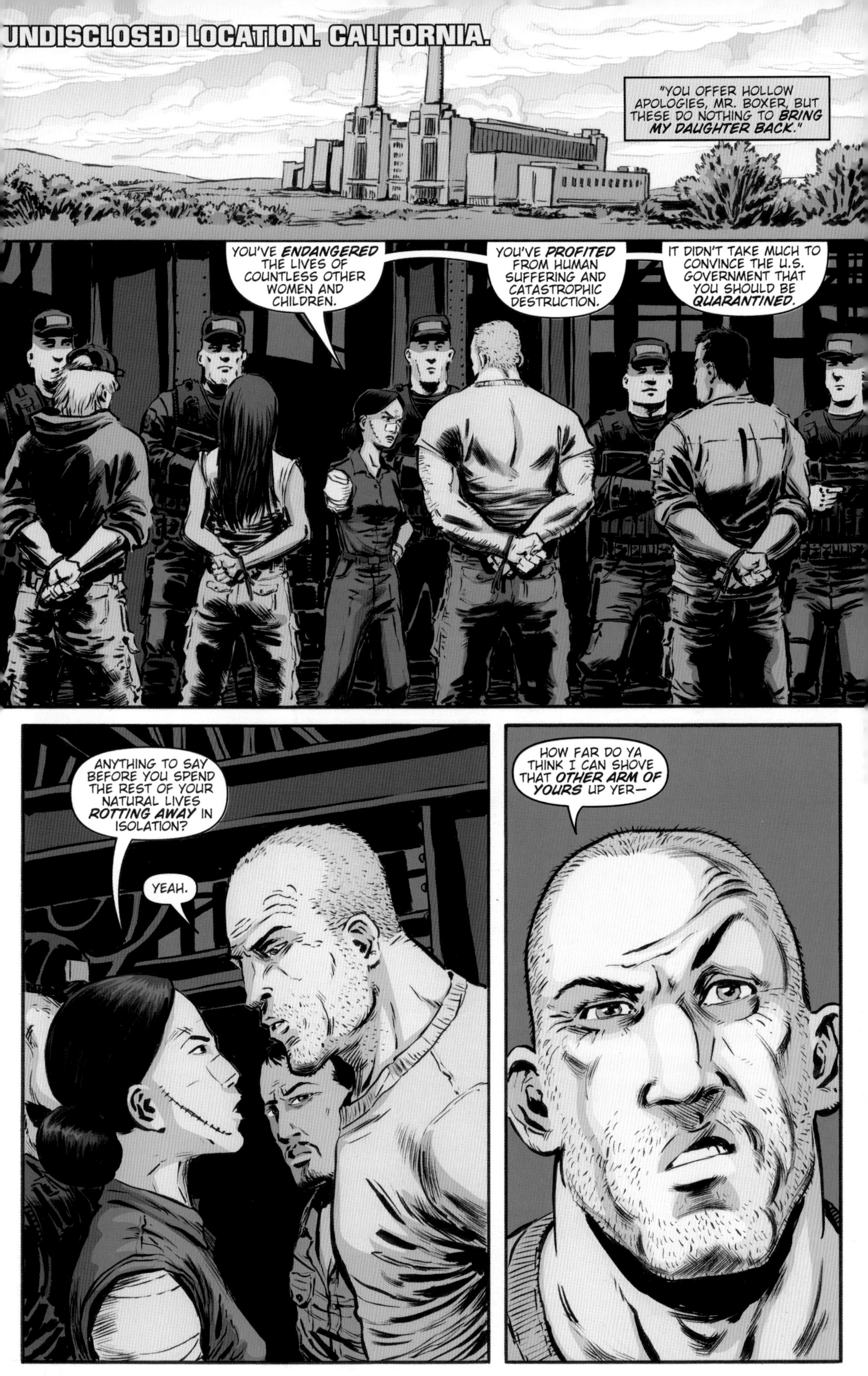
UNDISCLOSED LOCATION. CALIFORNIA.
"YOU OFFER HOLLOW APOLOGIES, MR. BOXER, BUT THESE DO NOTHING TO BRING MY DAUGHTER BACK."
YOU'VE ENDANGERED THE LIVES OF COUNTLESS OTHER WOMEN AND CHILDREN.
YOU'VE PROFITED FROM HUMAN SUFFERING AND CATASTROPHIC DESTRUCTION.
IT DIDN'T TAKE MUCH TO CONVINCE THE U.S. GOVERNMENT THAT YOU SHOULD BE QUARANTINED.
ANYTHING TO SAY BEFORE YOU SPEND THE REST OF YOUR NATURAL LIVES ROTTING AWAY IN ISOLATION?
YEAH.
HOW FAR DO YA THINK I CAN SHOVE THAT OTHER ARM OF YOURS UP YER—

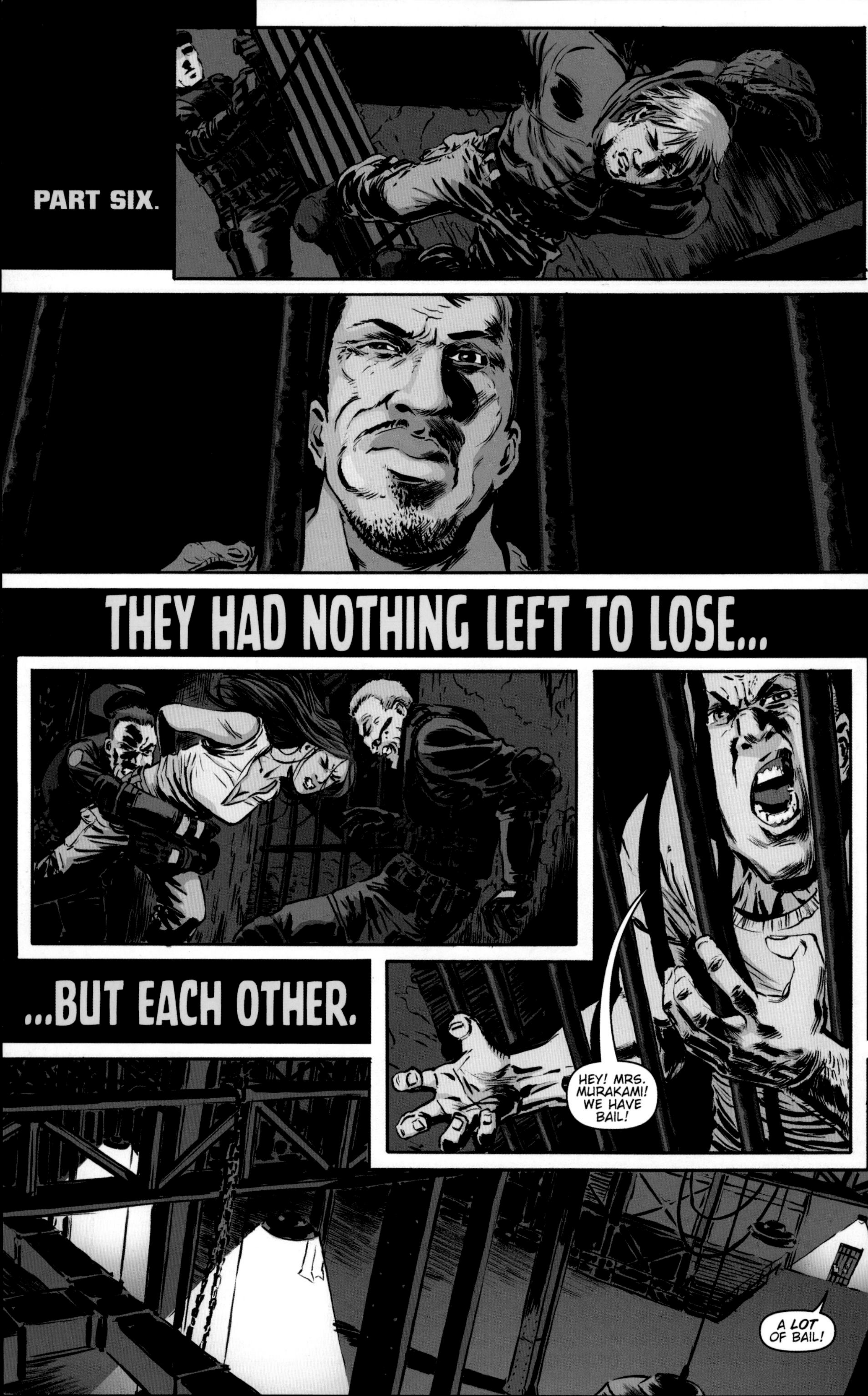
PART SIX.
THEY HAD NOTHING LEFT TO LOSE...
...BUT EACH OTHER.
HEY! MRS. MURAKAMI! WE HAVE BAIL!
A LOT OF BAIL!

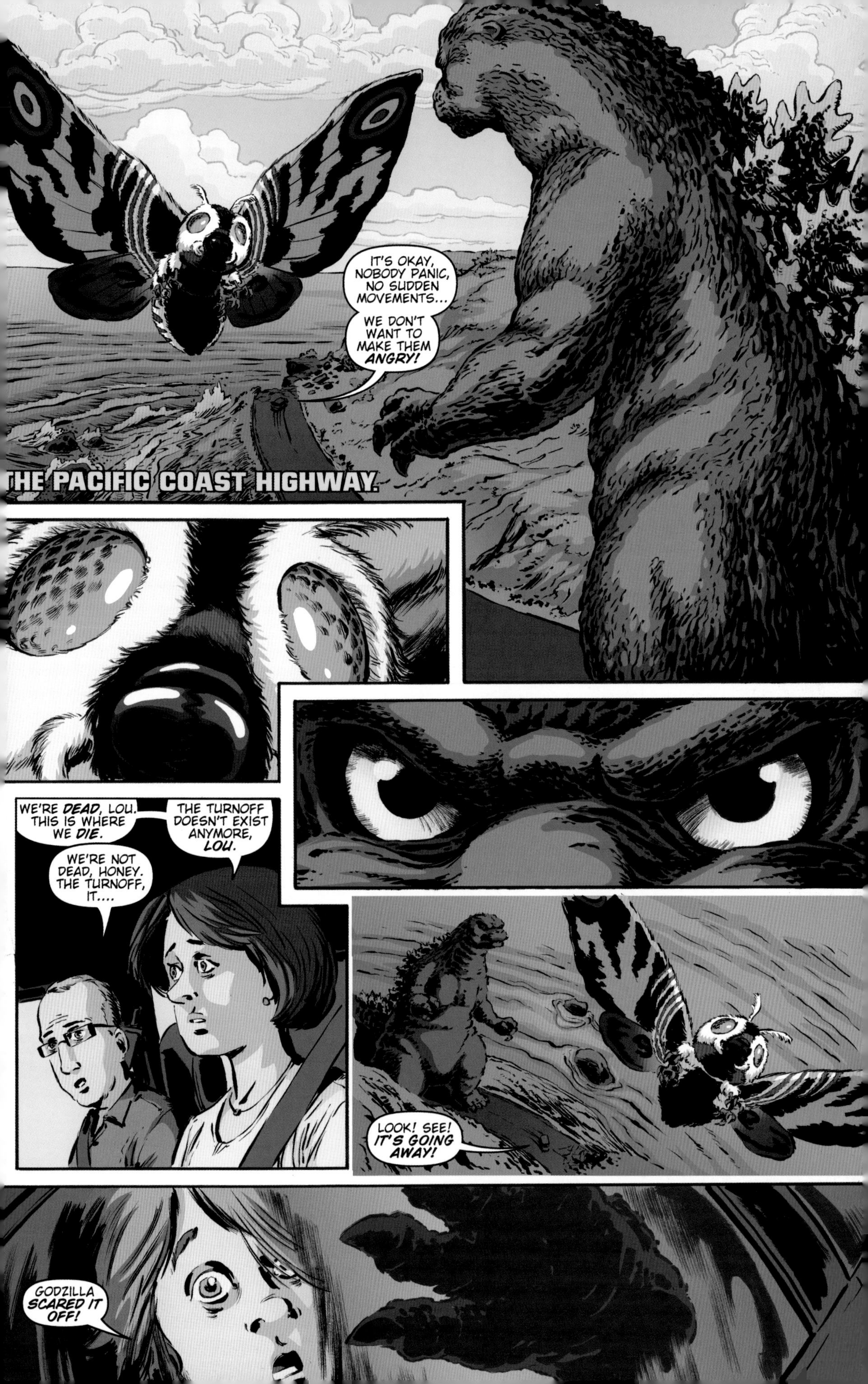

IT'S OKAY, NOBODY PANIC, NO SUDDEN MOVEMENTS...
WE DON'T WANT TO MAKE THEM ANGRY!
THE PACIFIC COAST HIGHWAY.
WE'RE DEAD, LOU. THIS IS WHERE WE DIE.
THE TURNOFF DOESN'T EXIST ANYMORE, LOU.
WE'RE NOT DEAD, HONEY. THE TURNOFF, IT....
LOOK! SEE! IT'S GOING AWAY!
GODZILLA SCARED IT OFF!

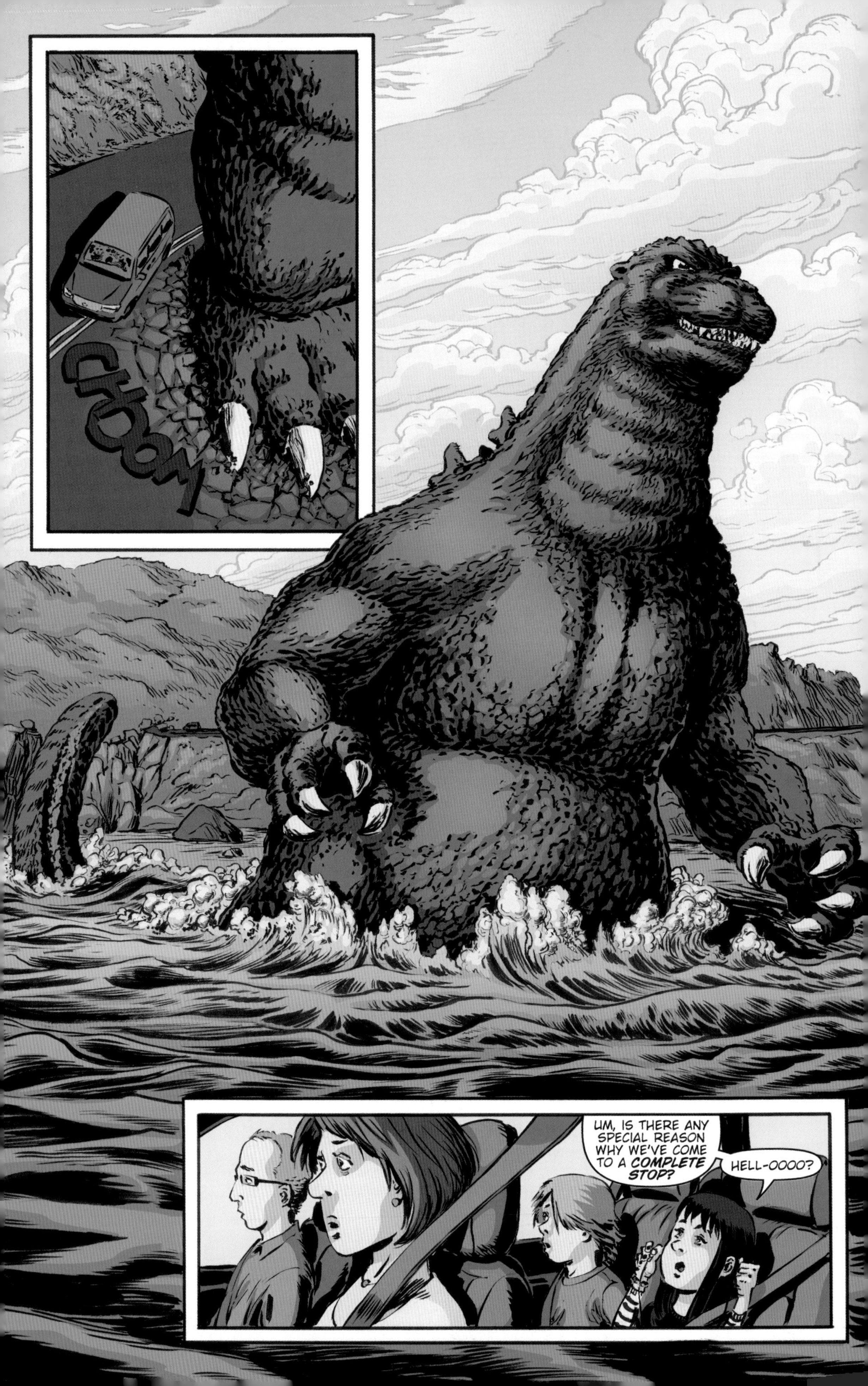
CHOOM
UM, IS THERE ANY SPECIAL REASON WHY WE'VE COME TO A COMPLETE STOP?
HELL-OOOO?

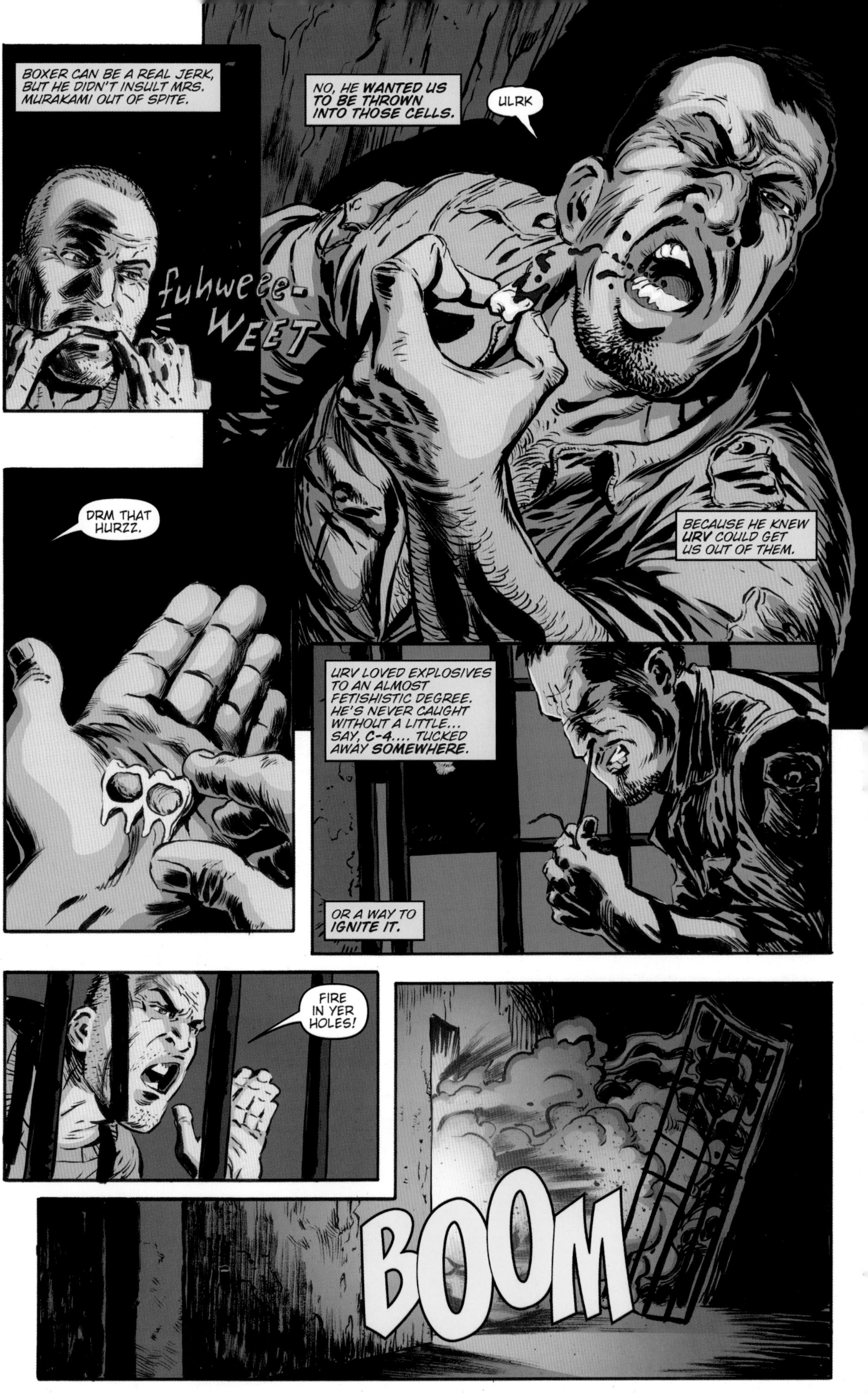

BOXER CAN BE A REAL JERK, BUT HE DIDN'T INSULT MRS. MURAKAMI OUT OF SPITE.
fuhweee-WEET
NO, HE WANTED US TO BE THROWN INTO THOSE CELLS.
ULRK
BECAUSE HE KNEW URV COULD GET US OUT OF THEM.
DRM THAT HURZZ.
URV LOVED EXPLOSIVES TO AN ALMOST FETISHISTIC DEGREE. HE'S NEVER CAUGHT WITHOUT A LITTLE... SAY, C-4.... TUCKED AWAY SOMEWHERE.
OR A WAY TO IGNITE IT.
FIRE IN YER HOLES!
BOOM

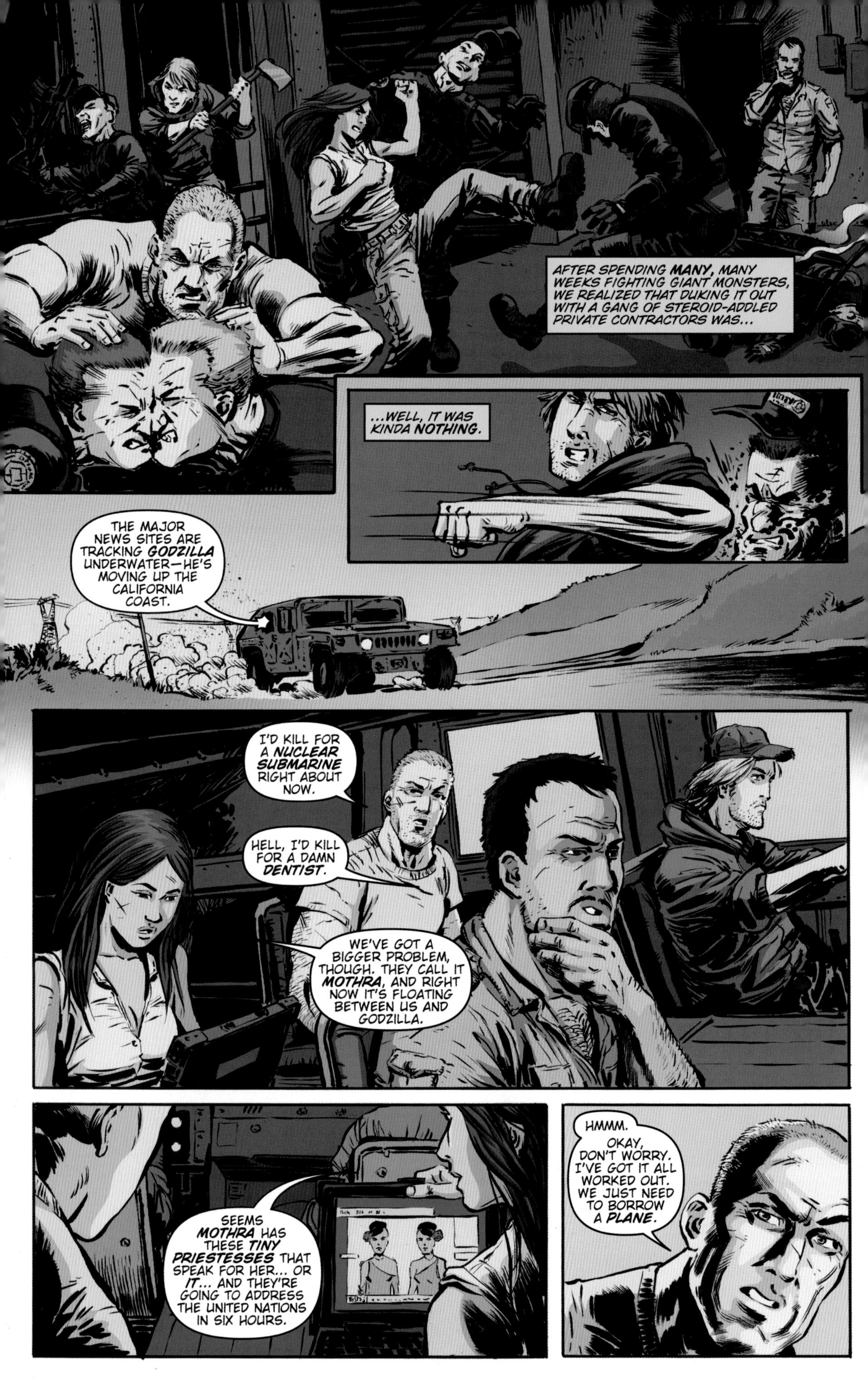
AFTER SPENDING MANY, MANY WEEKS FIGHTING GIANT MONSTERS, WE REALIZED THAT DUKING IT OUT WITH A GANG OF STEROID-ADDLED PRIVATE CONTRACTORS WAS...
...WELL, IT WAS KINDA NOTHING.
THE MAJOR NEWS SITES ARE TRACKING GODZILLA UNDERWATER—HE'S MOVING UP THE CALIFORNIA COAST.
I'D KILL FOR A NUCLEAR SUBMARINE RIGHT ABOUT NOW.
HELL, I'D KILL FOR A DAMN DENTIST.
WE'VE GOT A BIGGER PROBLEM, THOUGH. THEY CALL IT MOTHRA, AND RIGHT NOW IT'S FLOATING BETWEEN US AND GODZILLA.
SEEMS MOTHRA HAS THESE TINY PRIESTESSES THAT SPEAK FOR HER... OR IT... AND THEY'RE GOING TO ADDRESS THE UNITED NATIONS IN SIX HOURS.
HMMM.
OKAY, DON'T WORRY. I'VE GOT IT ALL WORKED OUT. WE JUST NEED TO BORROW A PLANE.

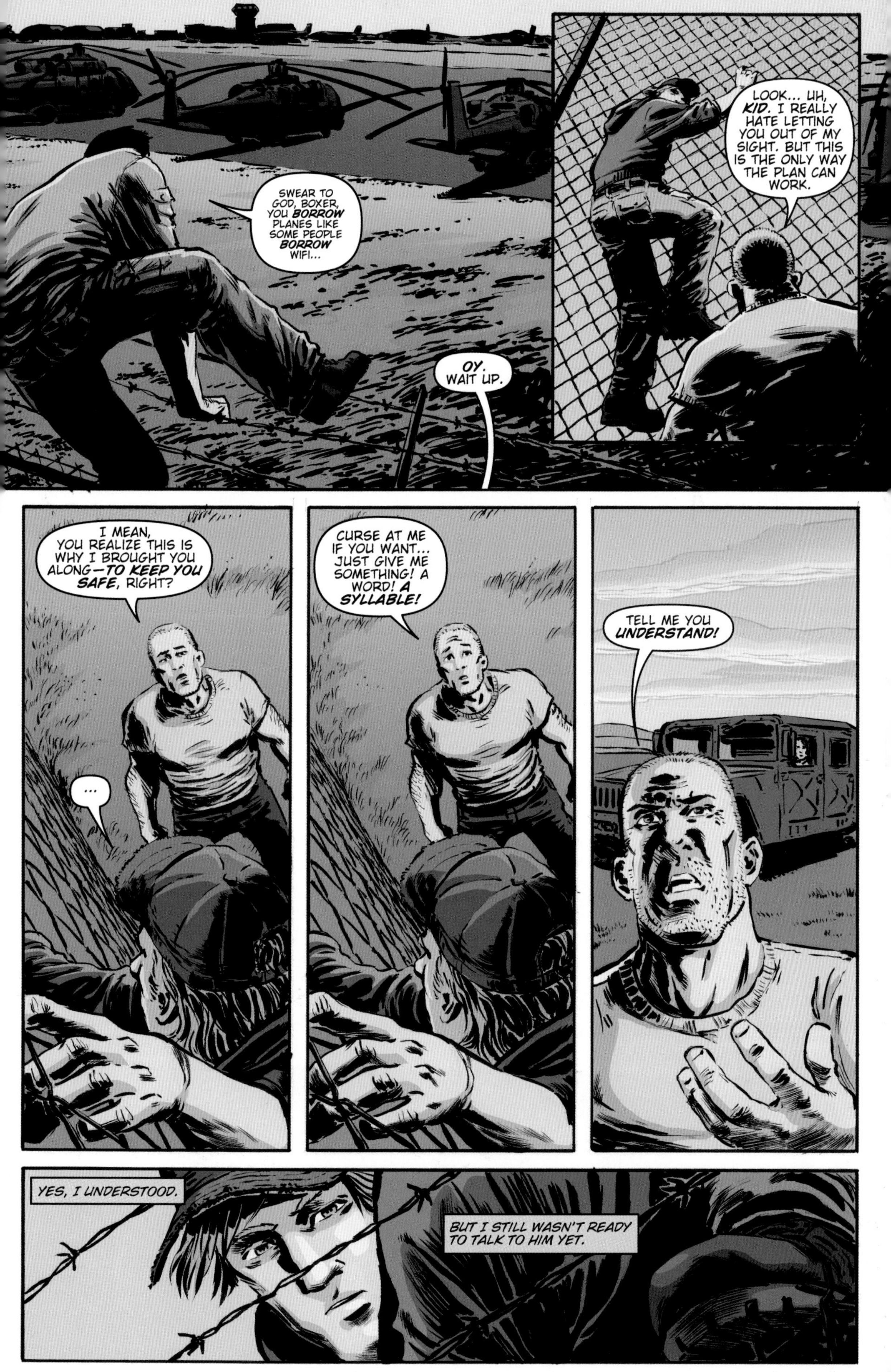
SWEAR TO GOD, BOXER, YOU **BORROW** PLANES LIKE SOME PEOPLE **BORROW** WIFI...
LOOK... UH, **KID.** I REALLY HATE LETTING YOU OUT OF MY SIGHT. BUT THIS IS THE ONLY WAY THE PLAN CAN WORK.
OY. WAIT UP.
I MEAN, YOU REALIZE THIS IS WHY I BROUGHT YOU ALONG—***TO KEEP YOU SAFE***, RIGHT?
...
CURSE AT ME IF YOU WANT... JUST GIVE ME SOMETHING! A WORD! ***A SYLLABLE!***
TELL ME YOU ***UNDERSTAND!***
YES, I UNDERSTOOD.
BUT I STILL WASN'T READY TO TALK TO HIM YET.

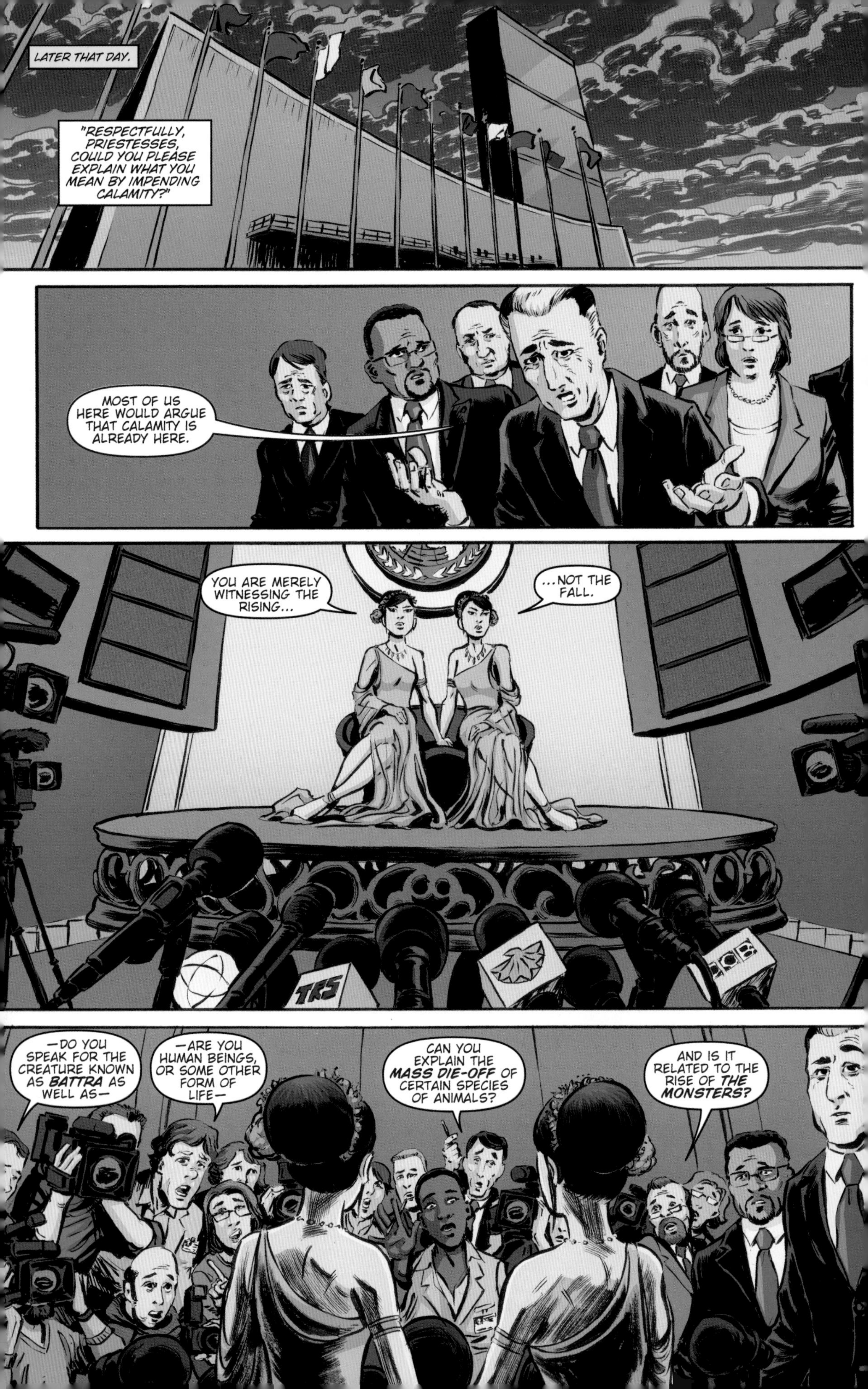
LATER THAT DAY.
"RESPECTFULLY, PRIESTESSES, COULD YOU PLEASE EXPLAIN WHAT YOU MEAN BY IMPENDING CALAMITY?"
MOST OF US HERE WOULD ARGUE THAT CALAMITY IS ALREADY HERE.
YOU ARE MERELY WITNESSING THE RISING...
...NOT THE FALL.
TRS
—DO YOU SPEAK FOR THE CREATURE KNOWN AS BATTRA AS WELL AS—
—ARE YOU HUMAN BEINGS, OR SOME OTHER FORM OF LIFE—
CAN YOU EXPLAIN THE MASS DIE-OFF OF CERTAIN SPECIES OF ANIMALS?
AND IS IT RELATED TO THE RISE OF THE MONSTERS?

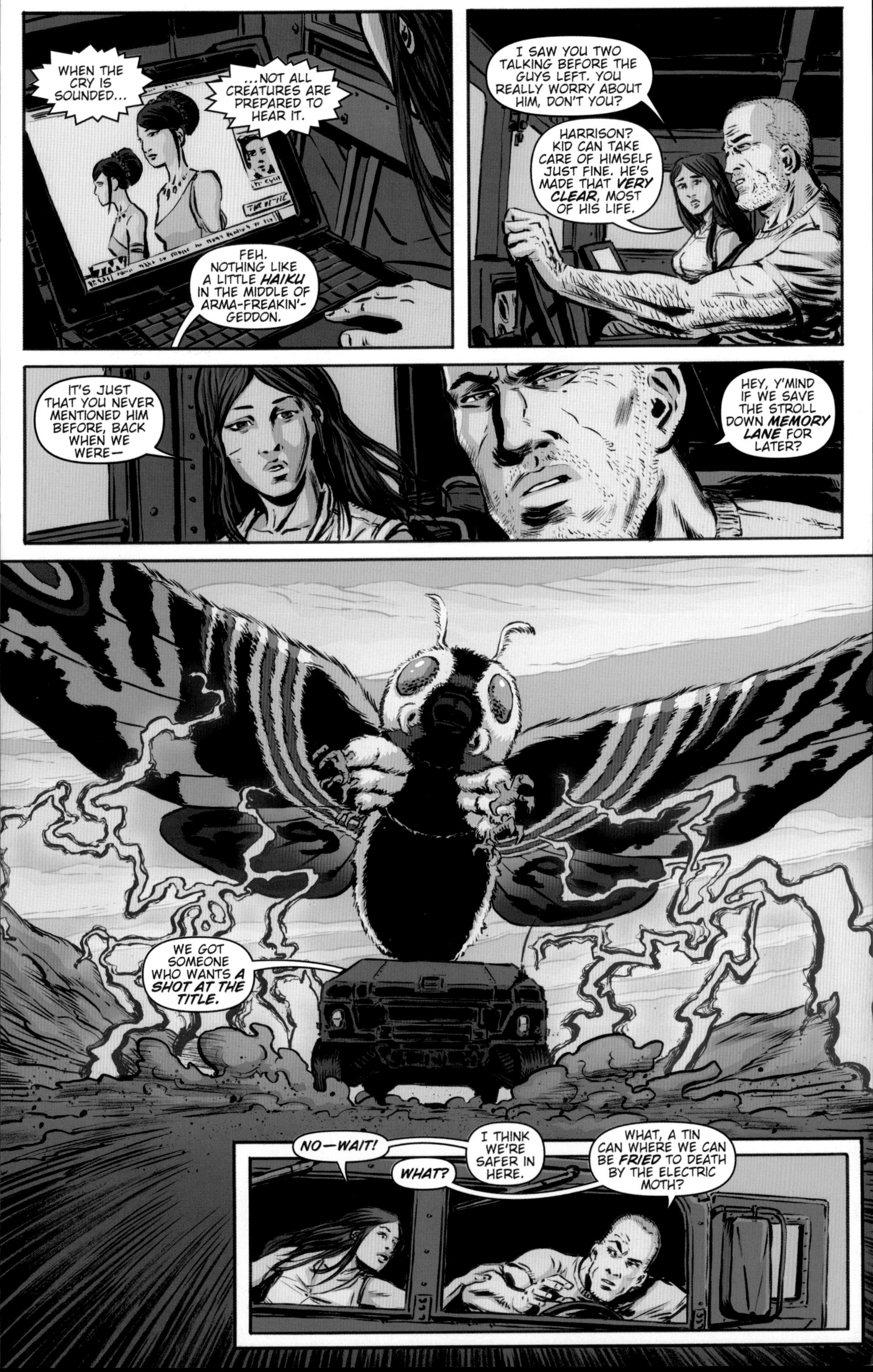
WHEN THE CRY IS SOUNDED...
...NOT ALL CREATURES ARE PREPARED TO HEAR IT.
FEH. NOTHING LIKE A LITTLE HAIKU IN THE MIDDLE OF ARMA-FREAKIN'-GEDDON.
I SAW YOU TWO TALKING BEFORE THE GUYS LEFT. YOU REALLY WORRY ABOUT HIM, DON'T YOU?
HARRISON? KID CAN TAKE CARE OF HIMSELF JUST FINE. HE'S MADE THAT VERY CLEAR, MOST OF HIS LIFE.
IT'S JUST THAT YOU NEVER MENTIONED HIM BEFORE, BACK WHEN WE WERE—
HEY, Y'MIND IF WE SAVE THE STROLL DOWN MEMORY LANE FOR LATER?
WE GOT SOMEONE WHO WANTS A SHOT AT THE TITLE.
NO—WAIT!
I THINK WE'RE SAFER IN HERE.
WHAT?
WHAT, A TIN CAN WHERE WE CAN BE FRIED TO DEATH BY THE ELECTRIC MOTH?

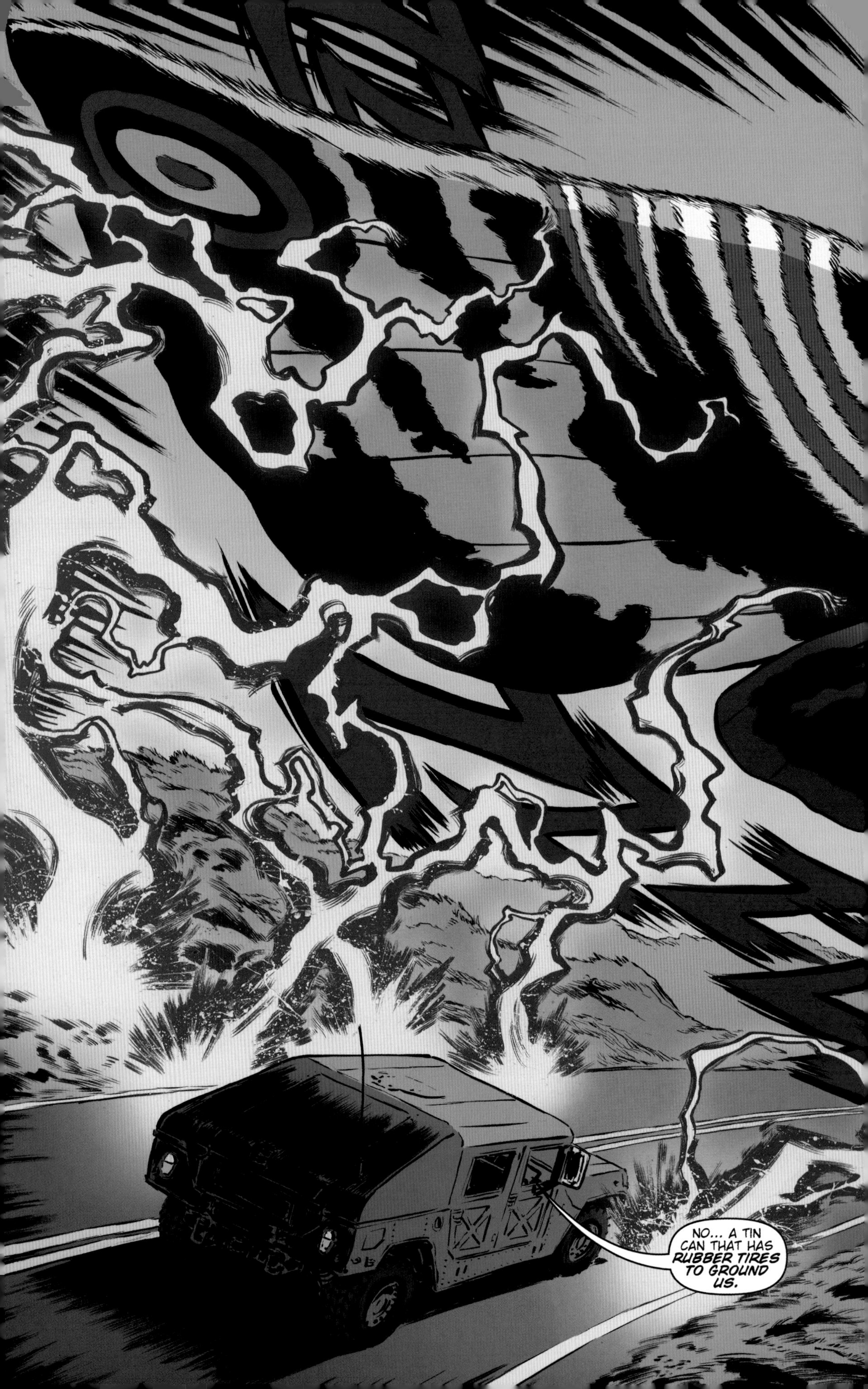
NO... A TIN CAN THAT HAS RUBBER TIRES TO GROUND US.

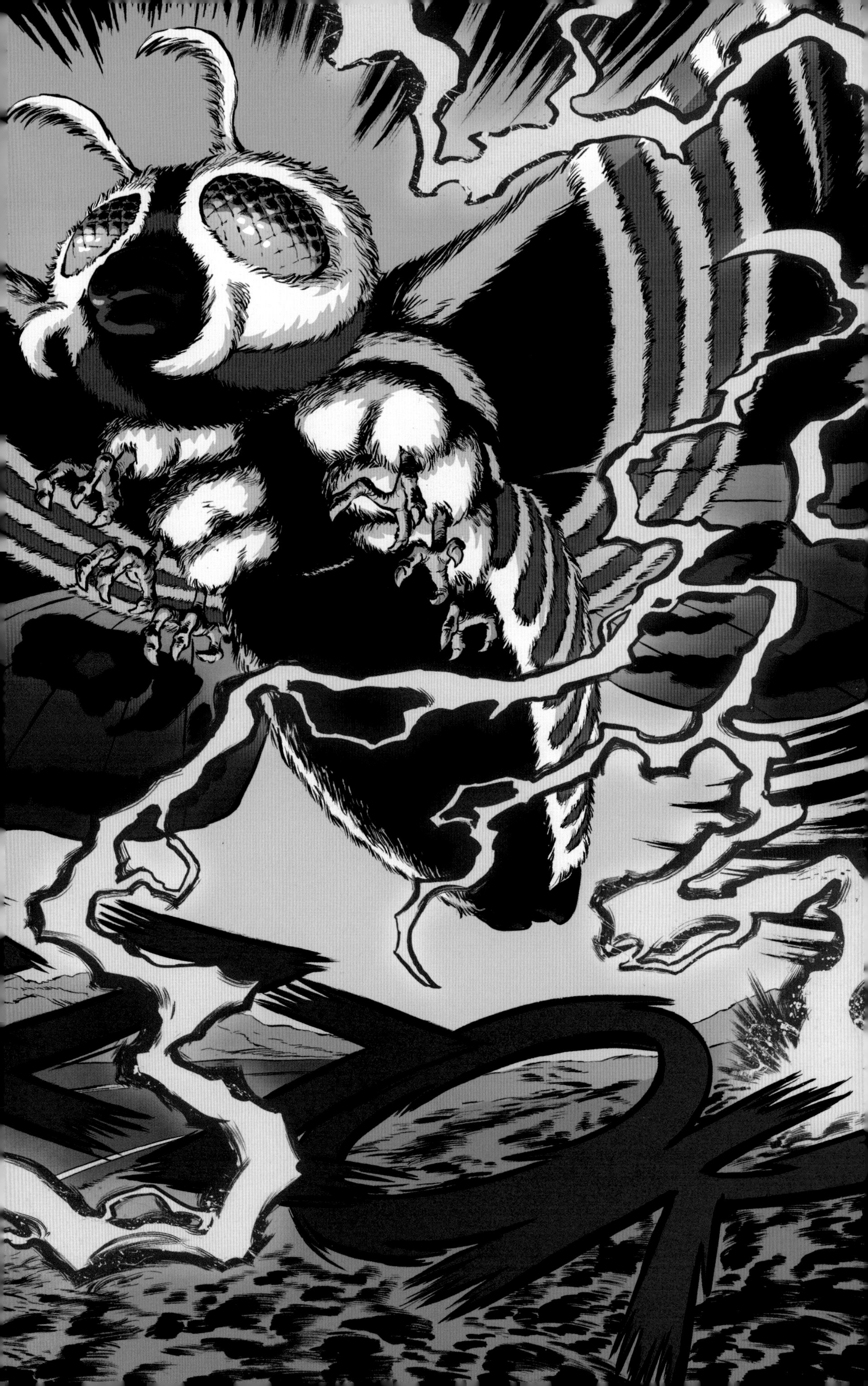

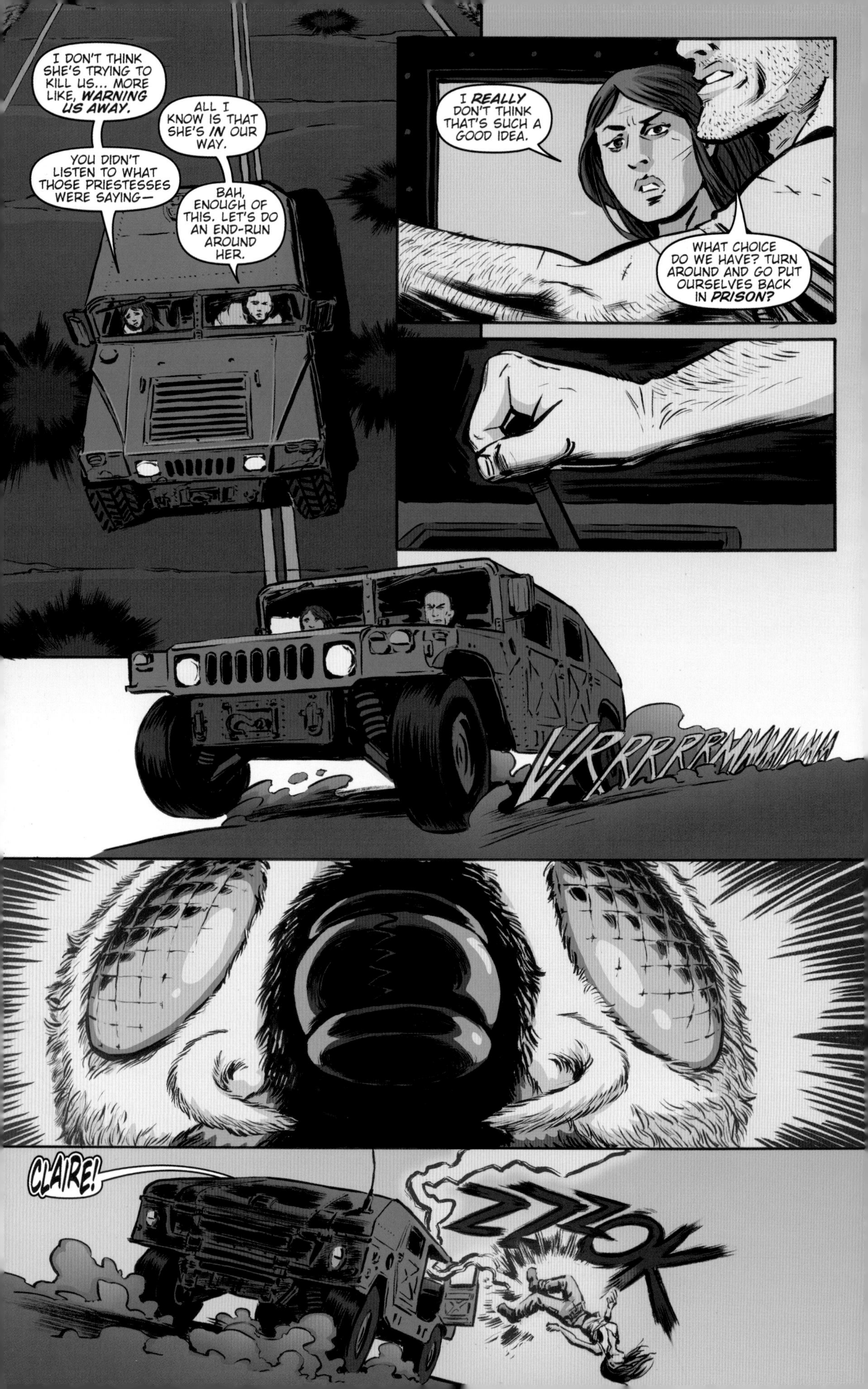

I DON'T THINK SHE'S TRYING TO KILL US... MORE LIKE, WARNING US AWAY.
ALL I KNOW IS THAT SHE'S IN OUR WAY.
YOU DIDN'T LISTEN TO WHAT THOSE PRIESTESSES WERE SAYING—
BAH, ENOUGH OF THIS. LET'S DO AN END-RUN AROUND HER.
I REALLY DON'T THINK THAT'S SUCH A GOOD IDEA.
WHAT CHOICE DO WE HAVE? TURN AROUND AND GO PUT OURSELVES BACK IN PRISON?
VRRRRRRMMMMMM
CLAIRE!
ZZZOK

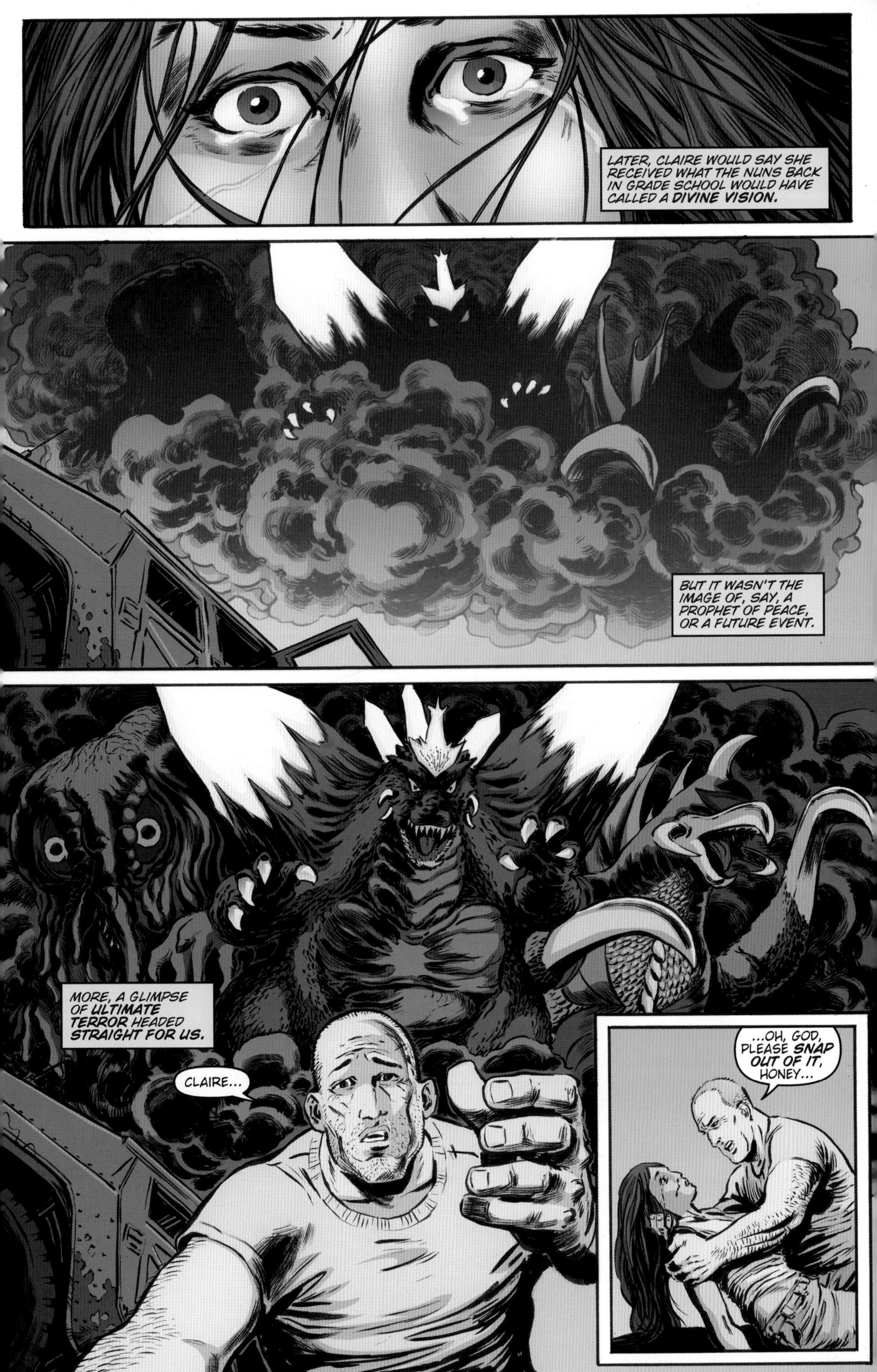
LATER, CLAIRE WOULD SAY SHE RECEIVED WHAT THE NUNS BACK IN GRADE SCHOOL WOULD HAVE CALLED A DIVINE VISION.
BUT IT WASN'T THE IMAGE OF, SAY, A PROPHET OF PEACE, OR A FUTURE EVENT.
MORE, A GLIMPSE OF ULTIMATE TERROR HEADED STRAIGHT FOR US.
CLAIRE...
...OH, GOD, PLEASE SNAP OUT OF IT, HONEY...

GAH!

ALRIGHT, YA BIG MOTH.

GET YER KICKS IN WHILE YOU CAN.

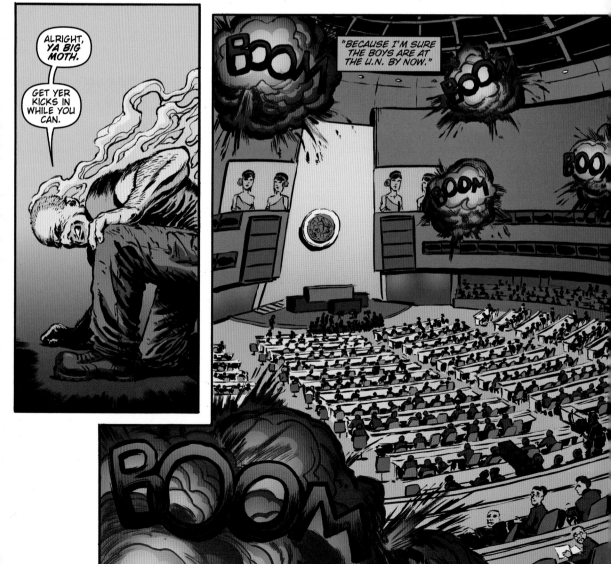

BOO

"BECAUSE I'M SURE THE BOYS ARE AT THE U.N. BY NOW."

BOO

BOOM

BOOM

BOOM

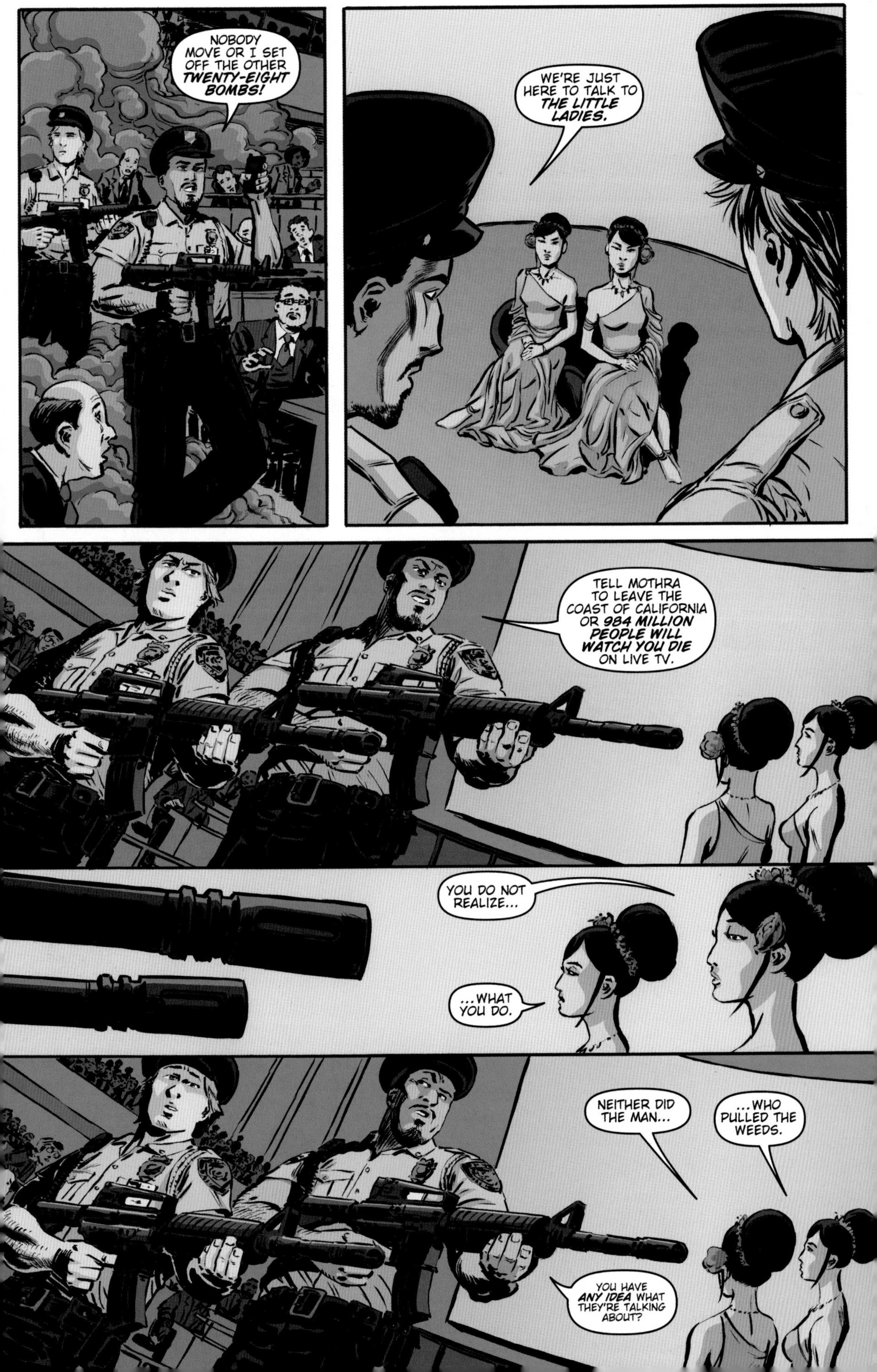
NOBODY MOVE OR I SET OFF THE OTHER *TWENTY-EIGHT BOMBS!*
WE'RE JUST HERE TO TALK TO *THE LITTLE LADIES.*
TELL MOTHRA TO LEAVE THE COAST OF CALIFORNIA OR *984 MILLION PEOPLE WILL WATCH YOU DIE* ON LIVE TV.
YOU DO NOT REALIZE...
...WHAT YOU DO.
NEITHER DID THE MAN...
...WHO PULLED THE WEEDS.
YOU HAVE *ANY IDEA* WHAT THEY'RE TALKING ABOUT?

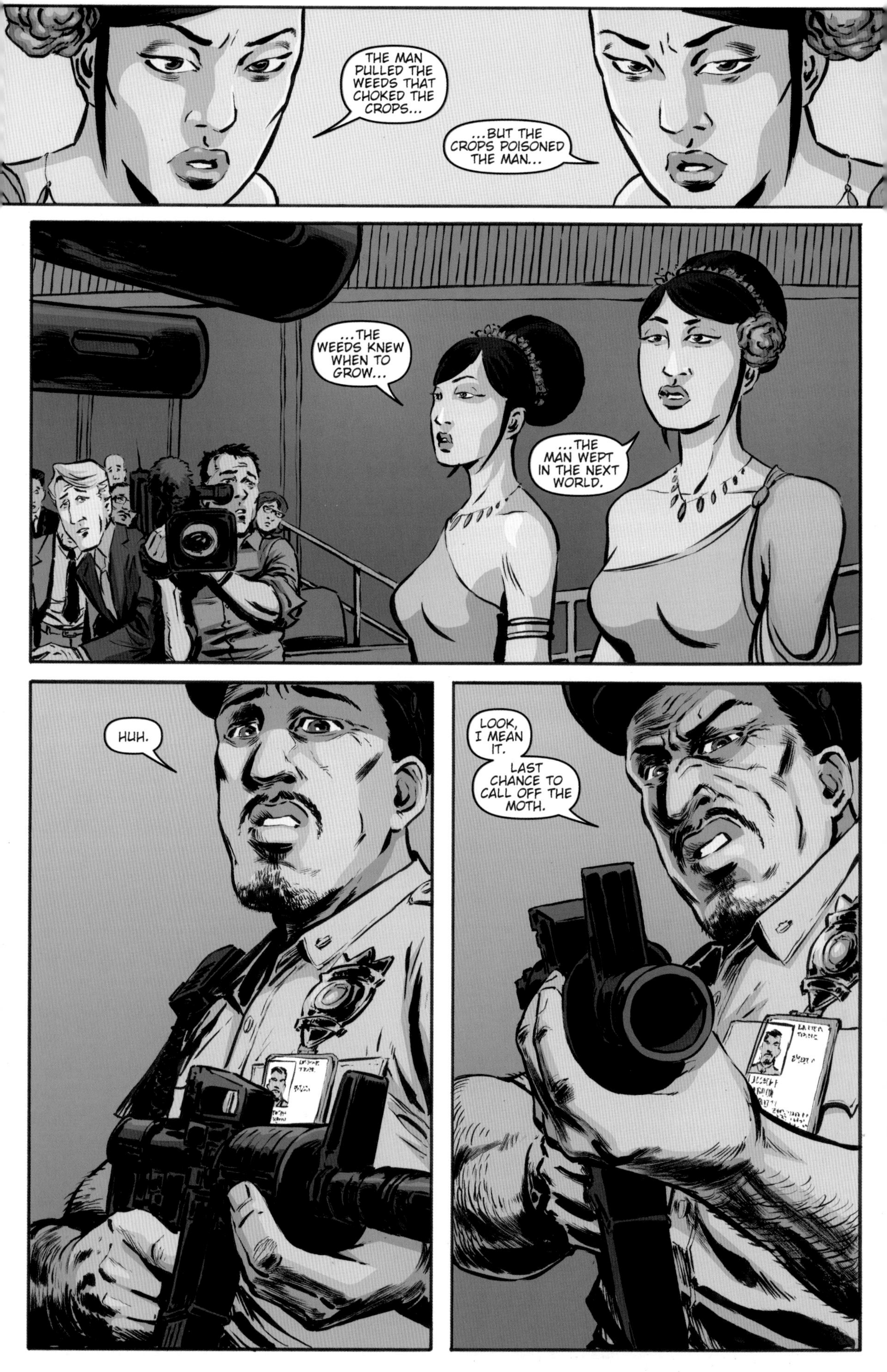
THE MAN PULLED THE WEEDS THAT CHOKED THE CROPS...
...BUT THE CROPS POISONED THE MAN...
...THE WEEDS KNEW WHEN TO GROW...
...THE MAN WEPT IN THE NEXT WORLD.
HUH.
LOOK, I MEAN IT.
LAST CHANCE TO CALL OFF THE MOTH.

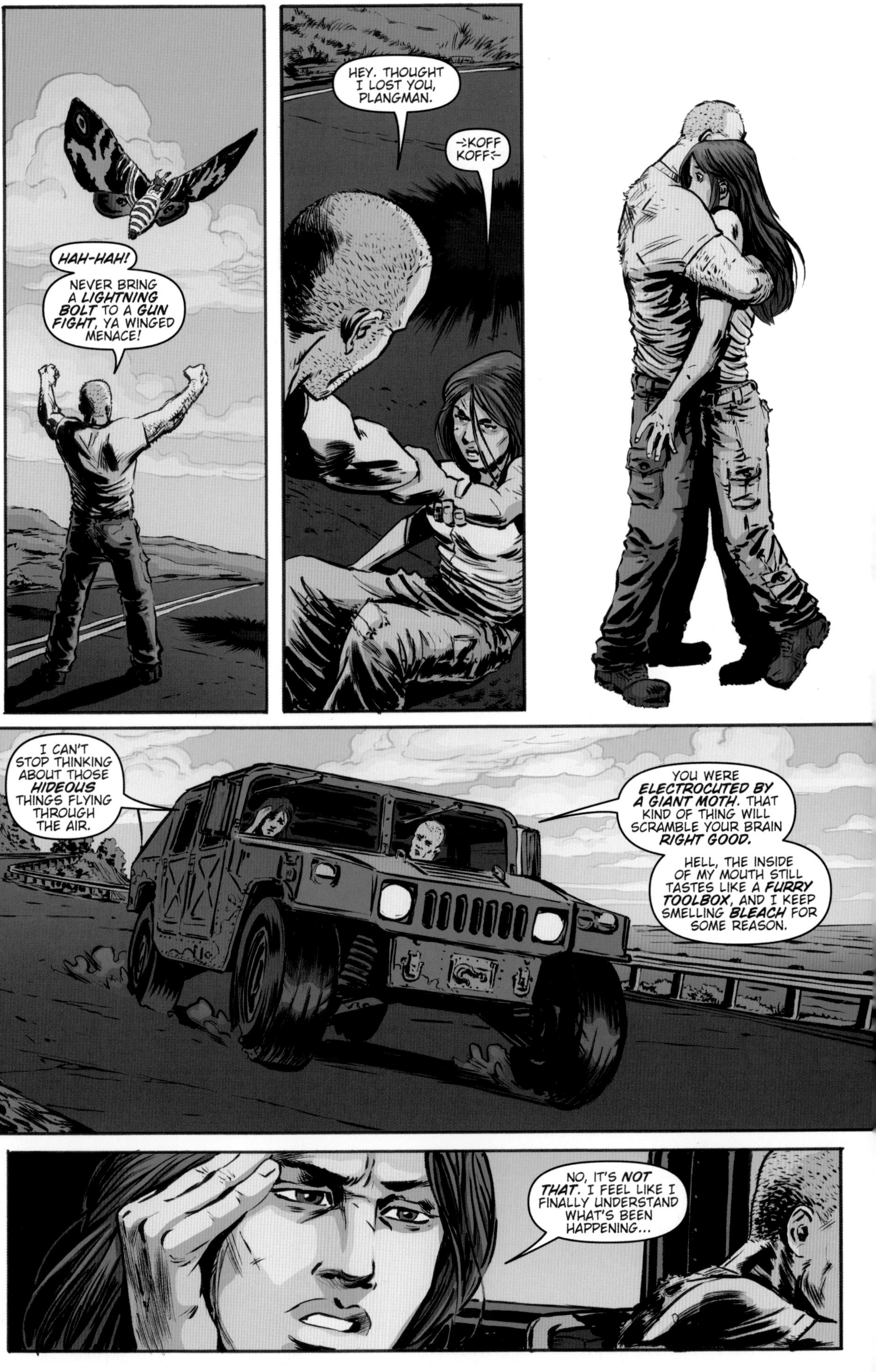
HAH-HAH!
NEVER BRING A LIGHTNING BOLT TO A GUN FIGHT, YA WINGED MENACE!
HEY. THOUGHT I LOST YOU, PLANGMAN.
-KOFF KOFF-
I CAN'T STOP THINKING ABOUT THOSE HIDEOUS THINGS FLYING THROUGH THE AIR.
YOU WERE ELECTROCUTED BY A GIANT MOTH. THAT KIND OF THING WILL SCRAMBLE YOUR BRAIN RIGHT GOOD.
HELL, THE INSIDE OF MY MOUTH STILL TASTES LIKE A FURRY TOOLBOX, AND I KEEP SMELLING BLEACH FOR SOME REASON.
NO, IT'S NOT THAT. I FEEL LIKE I FINALLY UNDERSTAND WHAT'S BEEN HAPPENING...

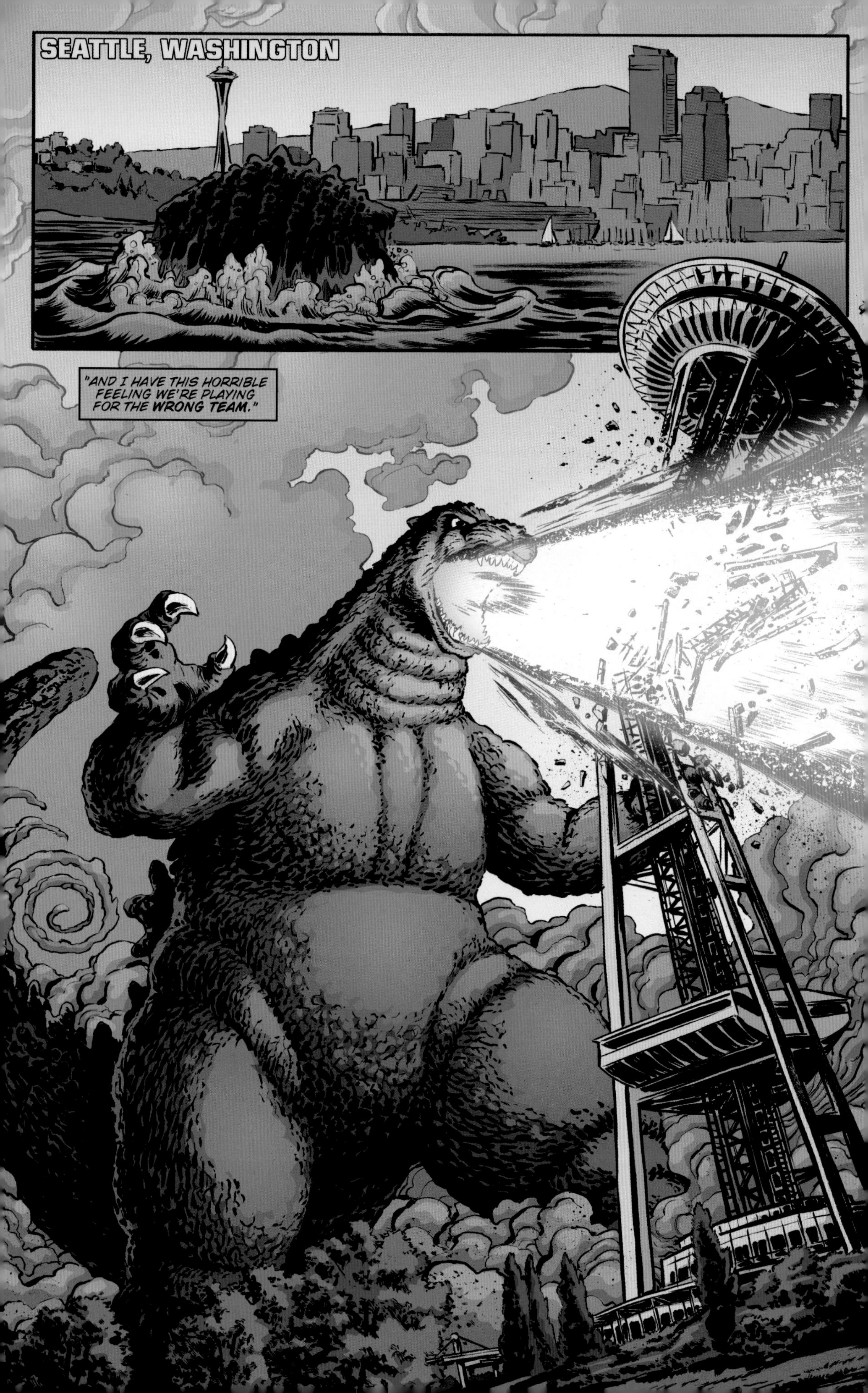
SEATTLE, WASHINGTON
"AND I HAVE THIS HORRIBLE FEELING WE'RE PLAYING FOR THE **WRONG TEAM**."

ART BY MATT FRANK

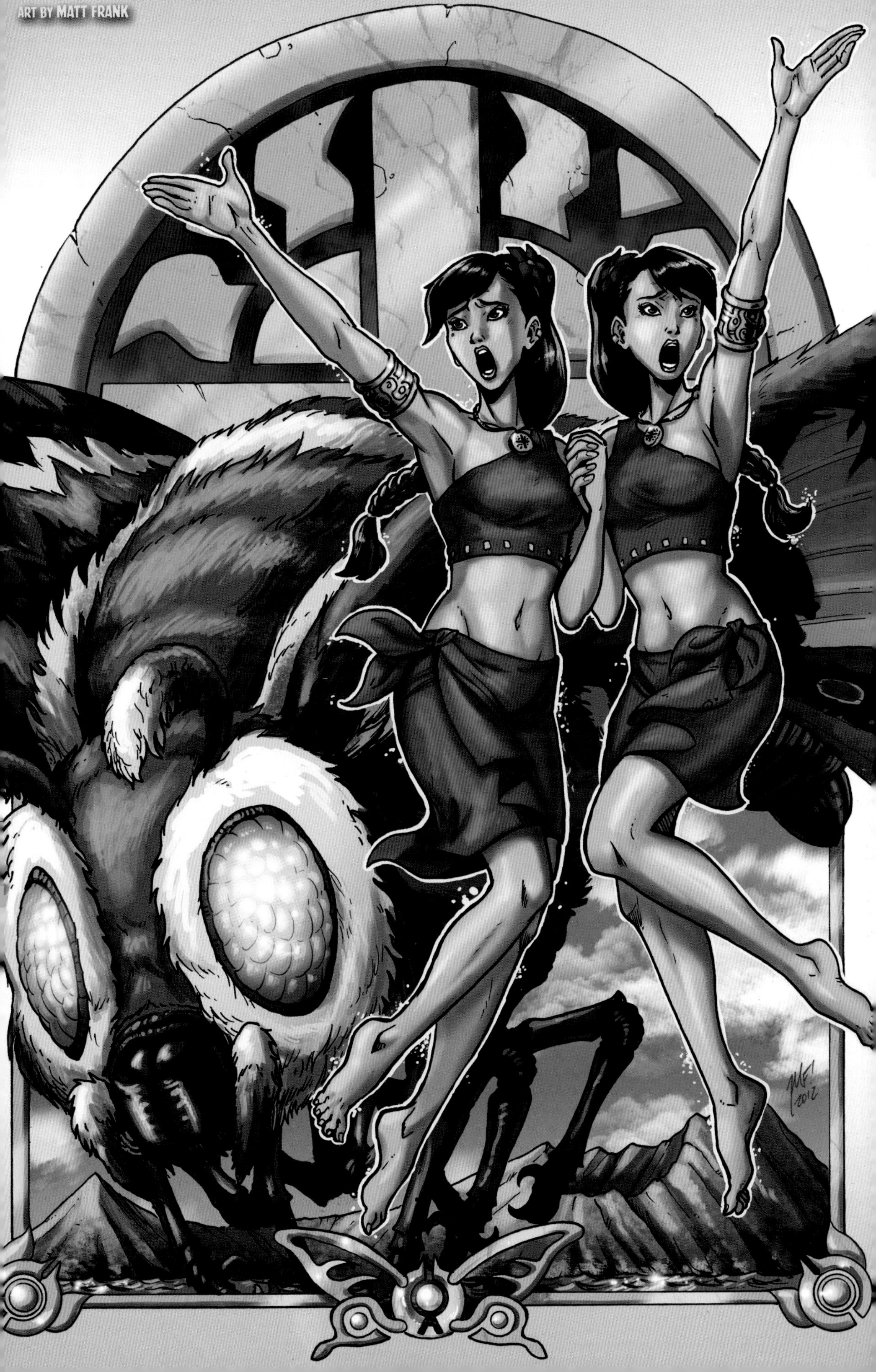

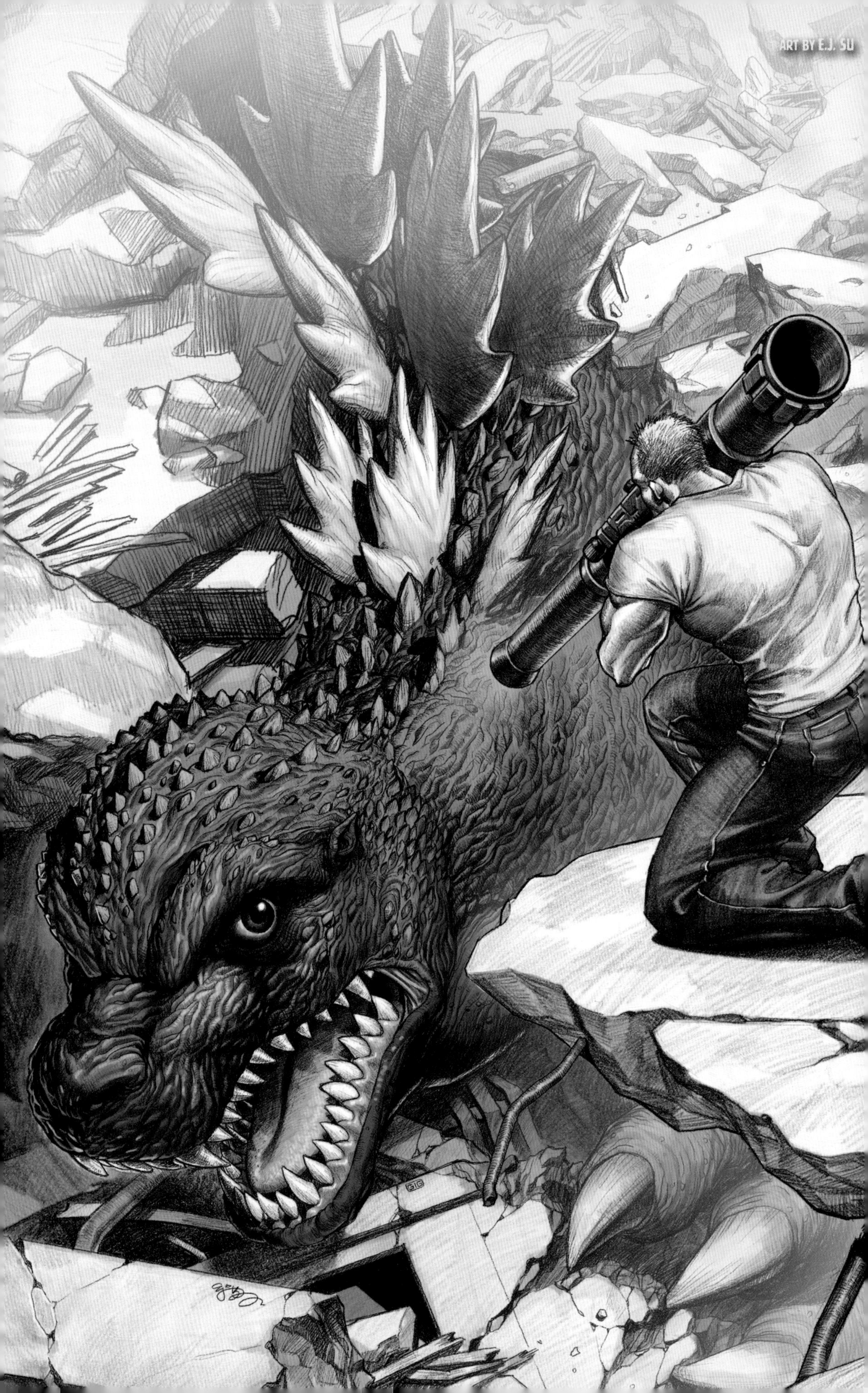
ART BY E.J. SU

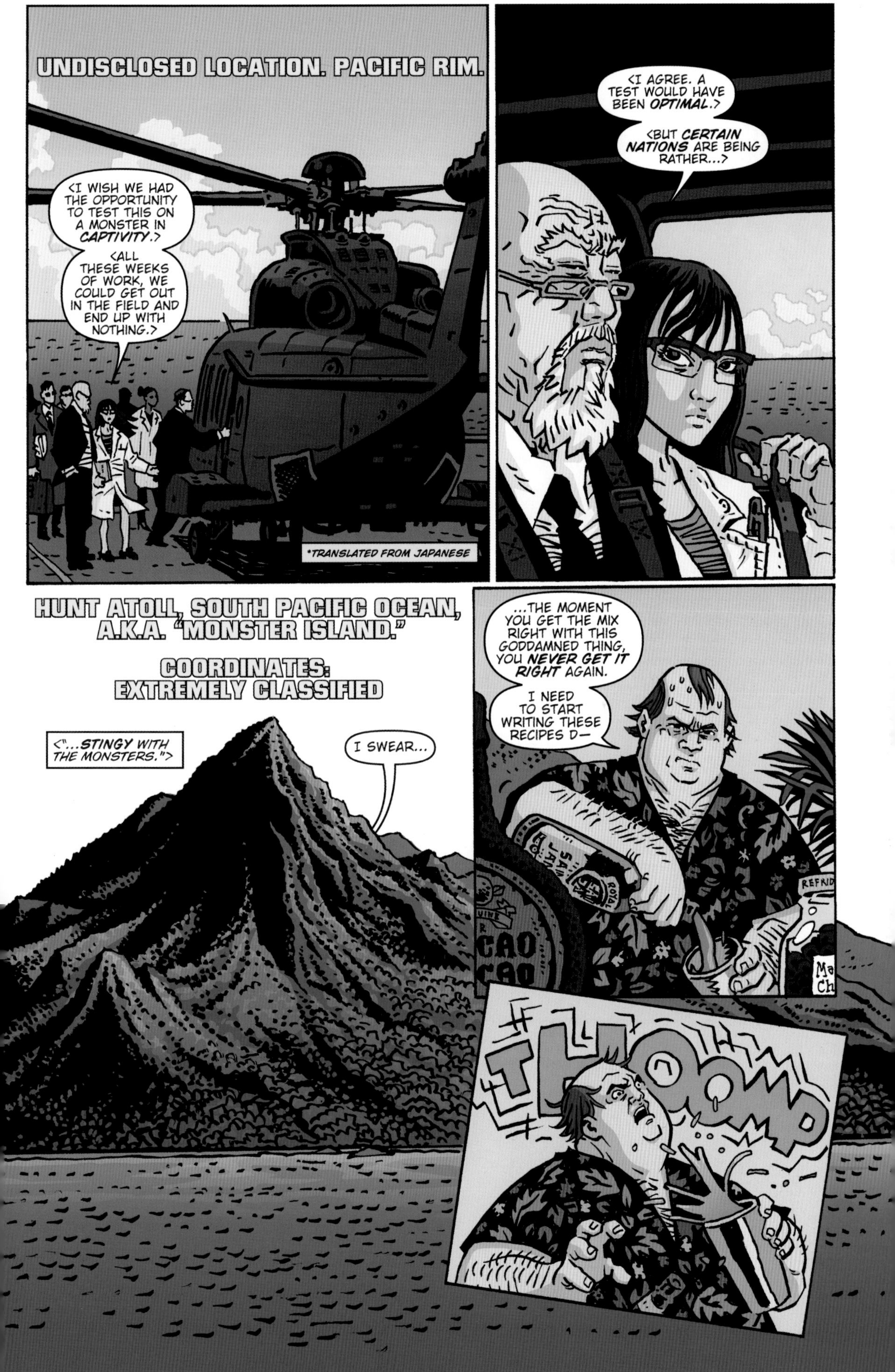
UNDISCLOSED LOCATION. PACIFIC RIM.
<I WISH WE HAD THE OPPORTUNITY TO TEST THIS ON A MONSTER IN *CAPTIVITY*.>
<ALL THESE WEEKS OF WORK, WE COULD GET OUT IN THE FIELD AND END UP WITH NOTHING.>
*TRANSLATED FROM JAPANESE
<I AGREE. A TEST WOULD HAVE BEEN *OPTIMAL*.>
<BUT *CERTAIN NATIONS* ARE BEING RATHER...>
HUNT ATOLL, SOUTH PACIFIC OCEAN, A.K.A. "MONSTER ISLAND."
COORDINATES: EXTREMELY CLASSIFIED
<"...*STINGY* WITH THE MONSTERS.">
I SWEAR...
...THE MOMENT YOU GET THE MIX RIGHT WITH THIS GODDAMNED THING, YOU ***NEVER GET IT RIGHT*** AGAIN.
I NEED TO START WRITING THESE RECIPES D—
THOOMP

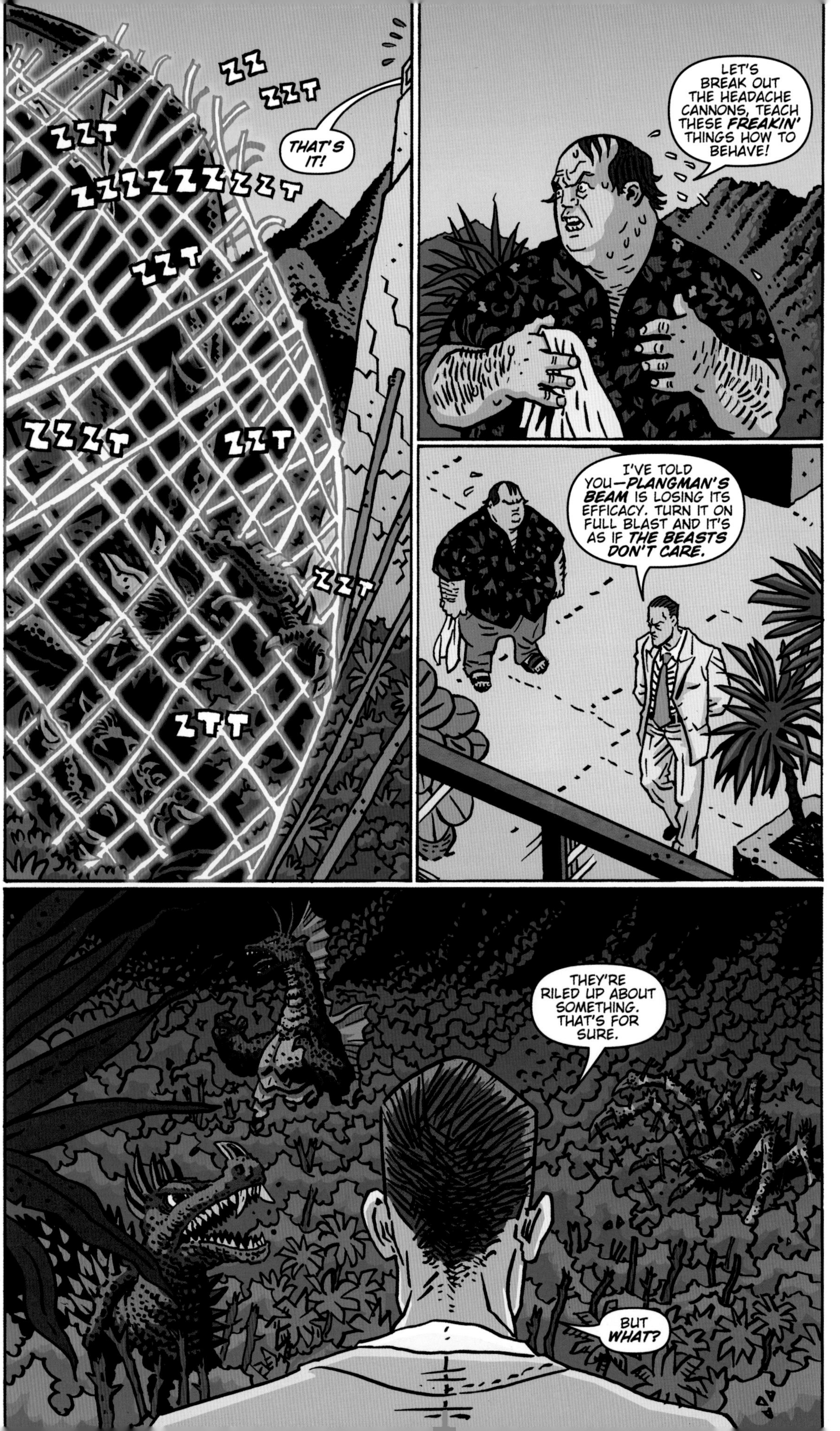
ZZ
ZZT
ZZT
ZZZZZZZZZZZT
THAT'S IT!
ZZT
ZZZT
ZZT
ZZT
ZTT
LET'S BREAK OUT THE HEADACHE CANNONS, TEACH THESE FREAKIN' THINGS HOW TO BEHAVE!
I'VE TOLD YOU—PLANGMAN'S BEAM IS LOSING ITS EFFICACY. TURN IT ON FULL BLAST AND IT'S AS IF THE BEASTS DON'T CARE.
THEY'RE RILED UP ABOUT SOMETHING. THAT'S FOR SURE.
BUT WHAT?

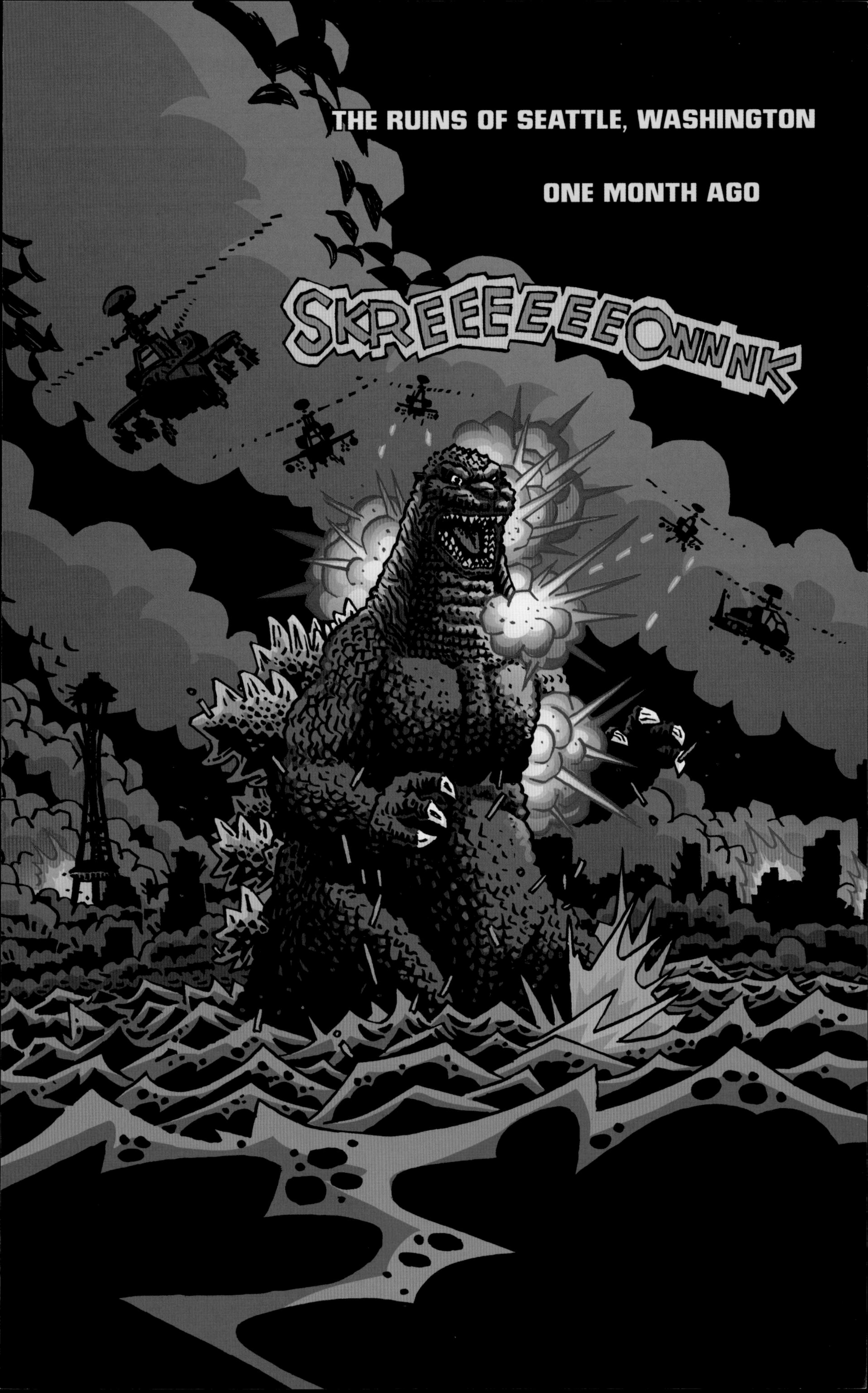
THE RUINS OF SEATTLE, WASHINGTON
ONE MONTH AGO
SKREEEEEEEONNNNK

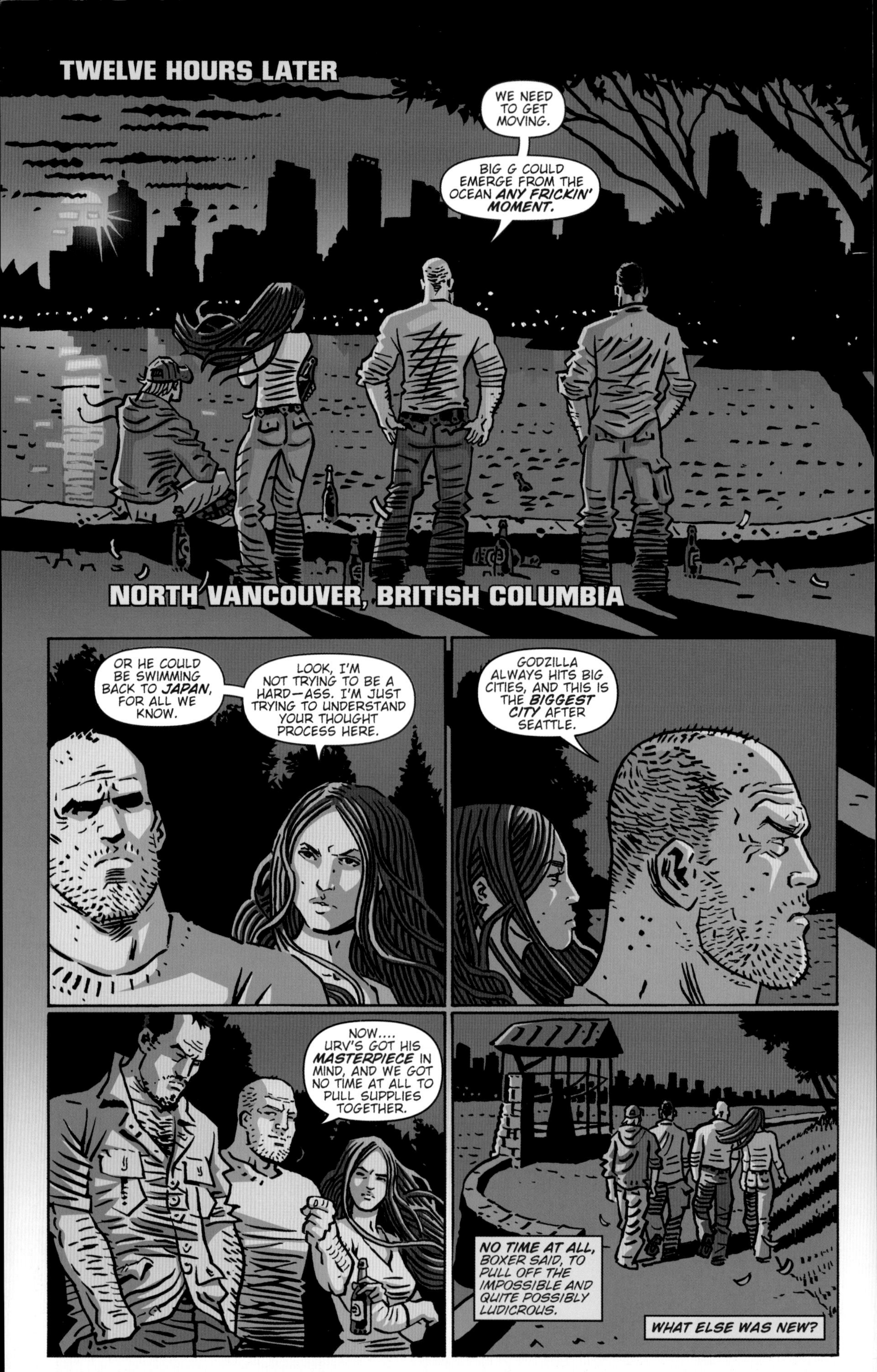
TWELVE HOURS LATER
WE NEED TO GET MOVING.
BIG G COULD EMERGE FROM THE OCEAN ANY FRICKIN' MOMENT.
NORTH VANCOUVER, BRITISH COLUMBIA
OR HE COULD BE SWIMMING BACK TO JAPAN, FOR ALL WE KNOW.
LOOK, I'M NOT TRYING TO BE A HARD—ASS. I'M JUST TRYING TO UNDERSTAND YOUR THOUGHT PROCESS HERE.
GODZILLA ALWAYS HITS BIG CITIES, AND THIS IS THE BIGGEST CITY AFTER SEATTLE.
NOW.... URV'S GOT HIS MASTERPIECE IN MIND, AND WE GOT NO TIME AT ALL TO PULL SUPPLIES TOGETHER.
NO TIME AT ALL, BOXER SAID, TO PULL OFF THE IMPOSSIBLE AND QUITE POSSIBLY LUDICROUS.
WHAT ELSE WAS NEW?

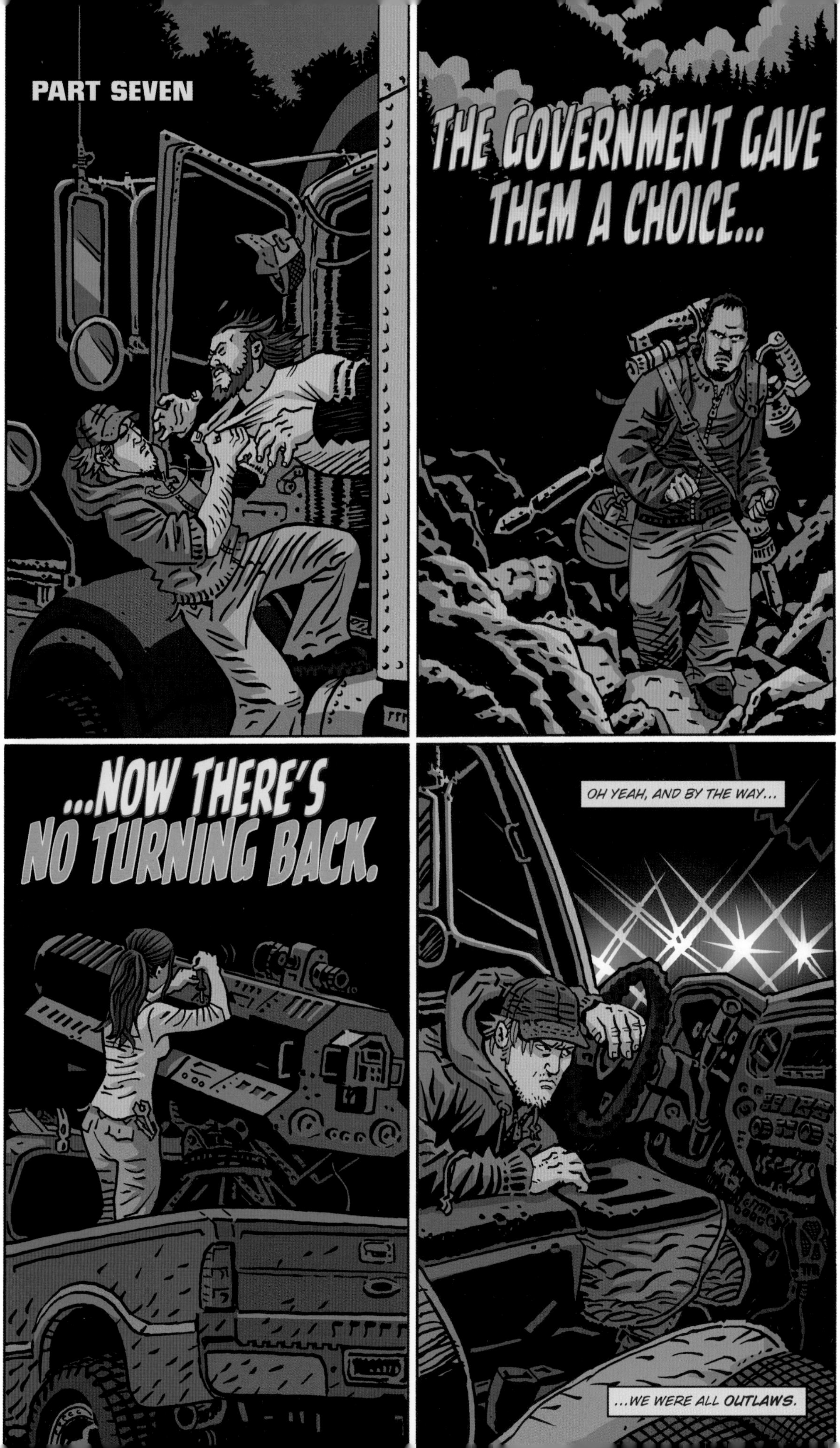
PART SEVEN
THE GOVERNMENT GAVE THEM A CHOICE...
...NOW THERE'S NO TURNING BACK.
OH YEAH, AND BY THE WAY...
...WE WERE ALL OUTLAWS.

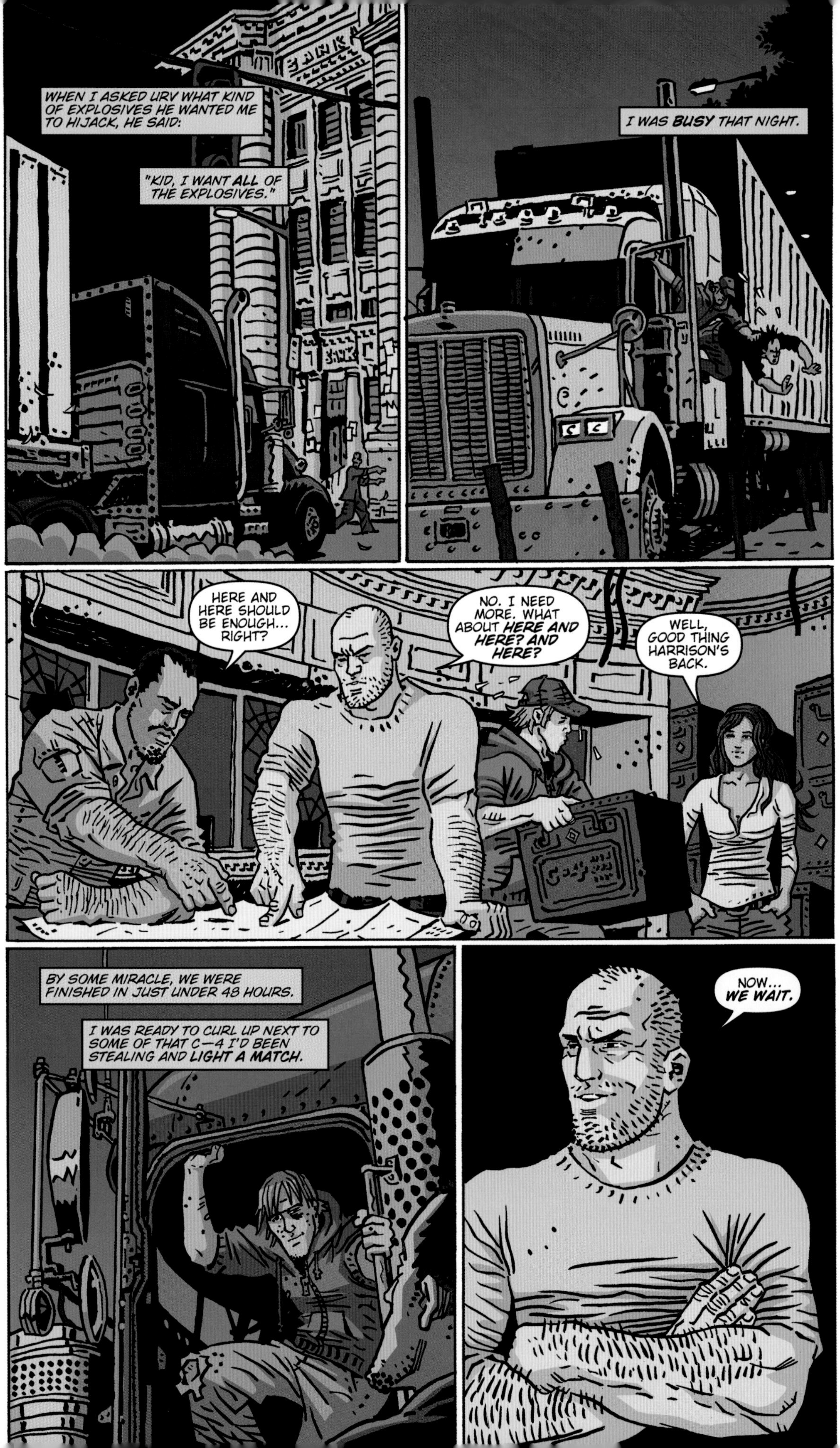
WHEN I ASKED URV WHAT KIND OF EXPLOSIVES HE WANTED ME TO HIJACK, HE SAID:
"KID, I WANT ALL OF THE EXPLOSIVES."
I WAS BUSY THAT NIGHT.
HERE AND HERE SHOULD BE ENOUGH... RIGHT?
NO. I NEED MORE. WHAT ABOUT HERE AND HERE? AND HERE?
WELL, GOOD THING HARRISON'S BACK.
BY SOME MIRACLE, WE WERE FINISHED IN JUST UNDER 48 HOURS.
I WAS READY TO CURL UP NEXT TO SOME OF THAT C—4 I'D BEEN STEALING AND LIGHT A MATCH.
NOW... WE WAIT.

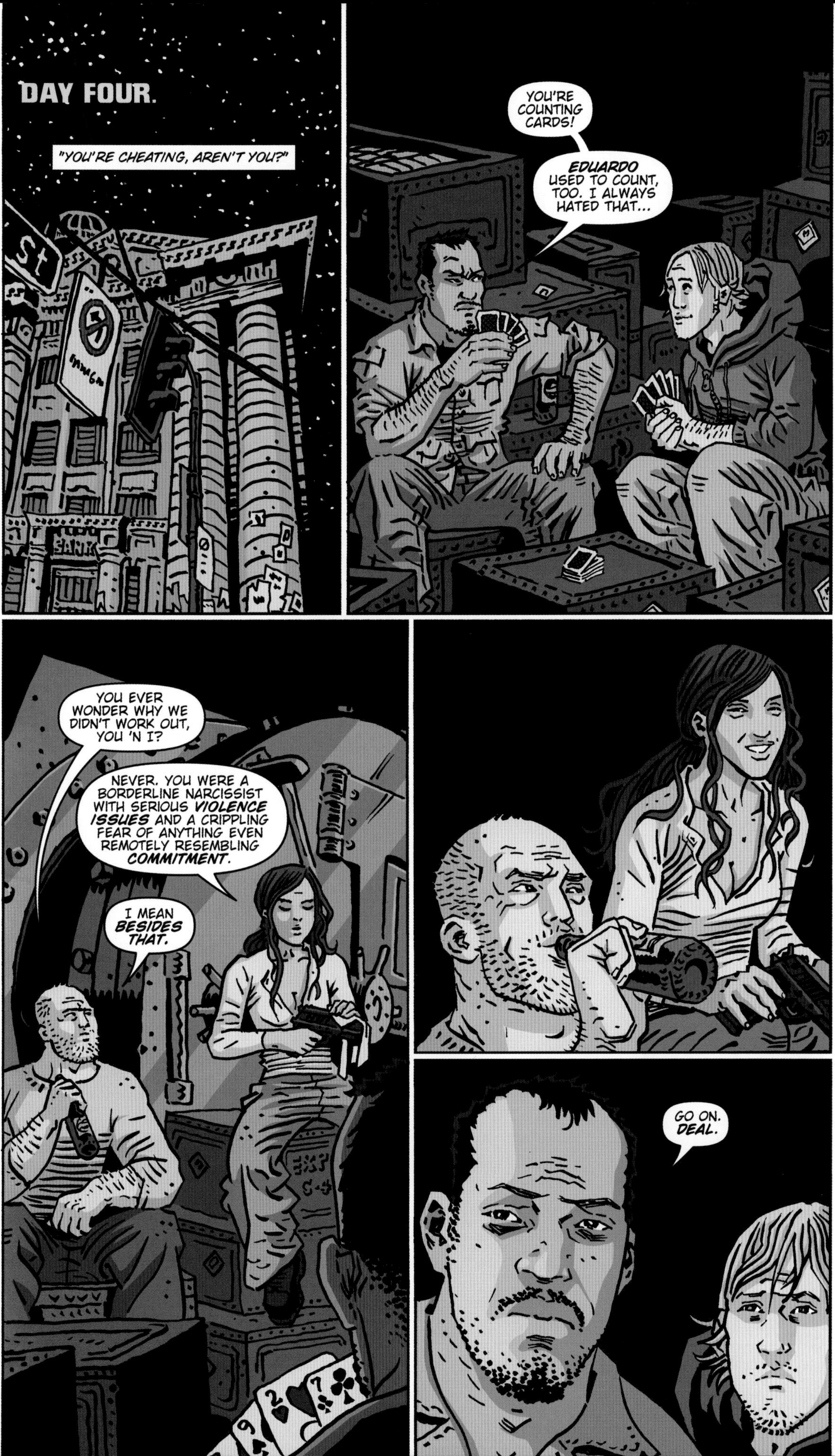

DAY FOUR.
"YOU'RE CHEATING, AREN'T YOU?"
YOU'RE COUNTING CARDS!
EDUARDO USED TO COUNT, TOO. I ALWAYS HATED THAT...
YOU EVER WONDER WHY WE DIDN'T WORK OUT, YOU 'N I?
NEVER. YOU WERE A BORDERLINE NARCISSIST WITH SERIOUS VIOLENCE ISSUES AND A CRIPPLING FEAR OF ANYTHING EVEN REMOTELY RESEMBLING COMMITMENT.
I MEAN BESIDES THAT.
GO ON. DEAL.

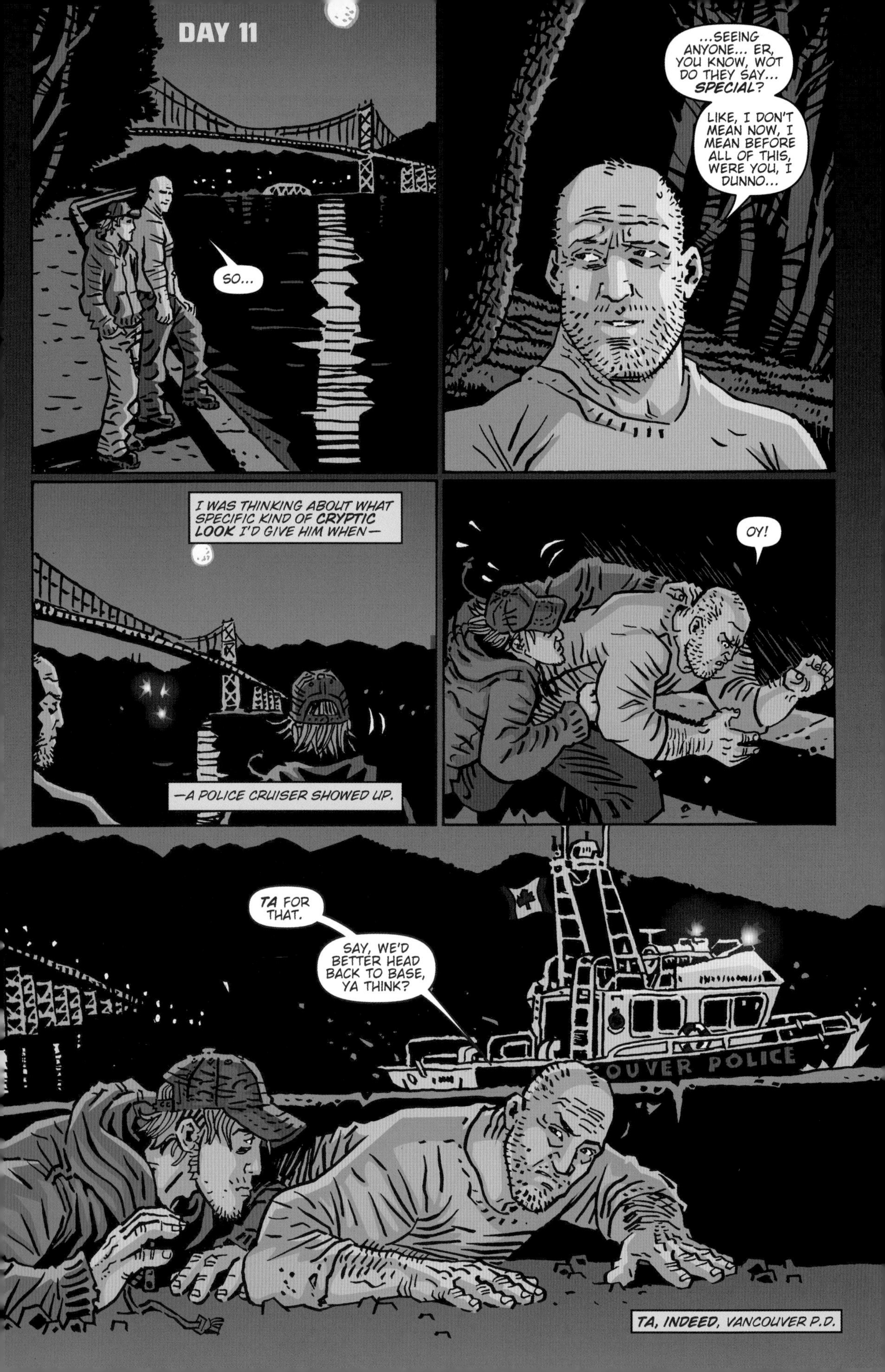
DAY 11
SO...
...SEEING ANYONE... ER, YOU KNOW, WOT DO THEY SAY... SPECIAL?
LIKE, I DON'T MEAN NOW, I MEAN BEFORE ALL OF THIS, WERE YOU, I DUNNO...
I WAS THINKING ABOUT WHAT SPECIFIC KIND OF CRYPTIC LOOK I'D GIVE HIM WHEN—
—A POLICE CRUISER SHOWED UP.
OY!
TA FOR THAT.
SAY, WE'D BETTER HEAD BACK TO BASE, YA THINK?
COUVER POLICE
TA, INDEED, VANCOUVER P.D.

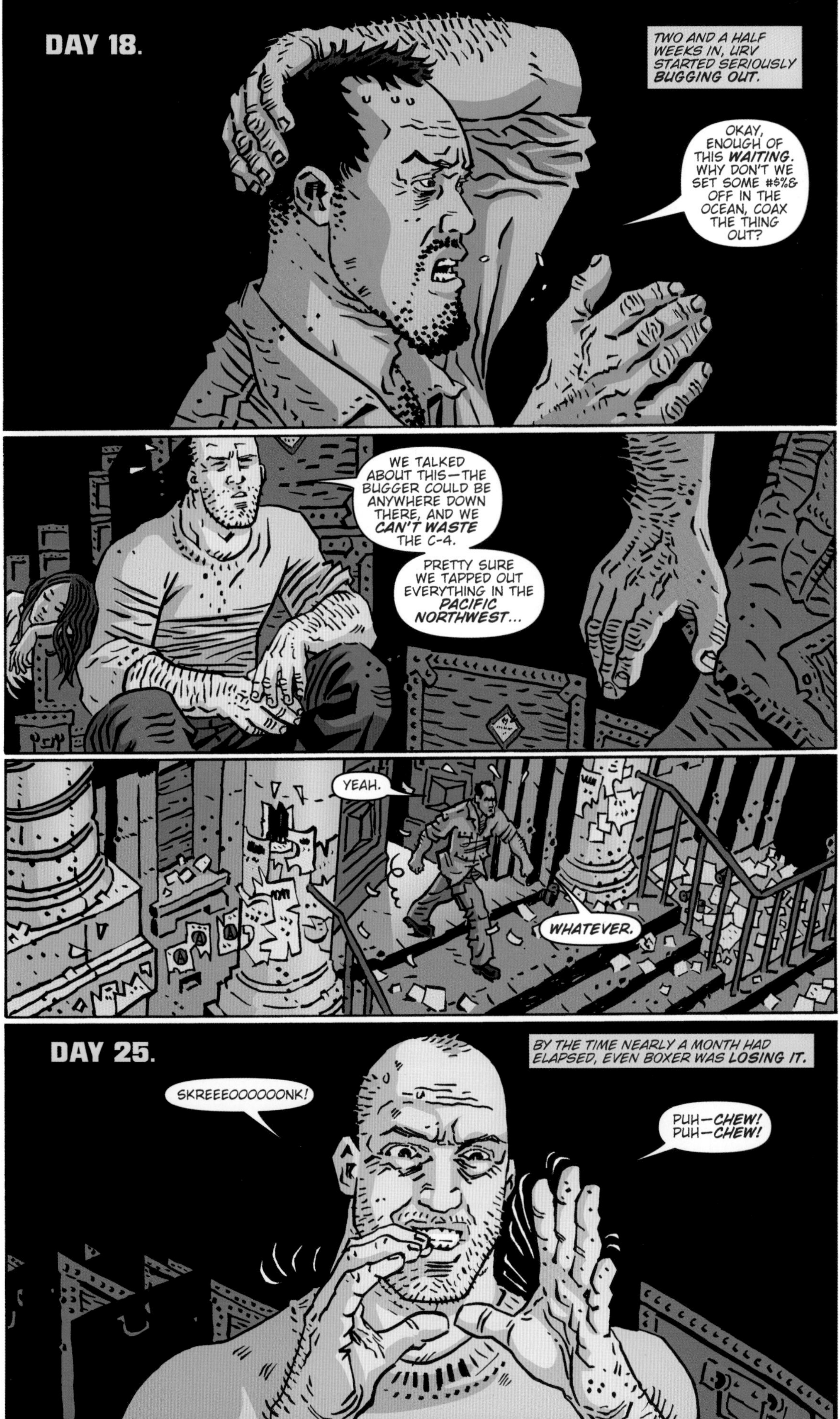
DAY 18.
TWO AND A HALF WEEKS IN, URV STARTED SERIOUSLY BUGGING OUT.
OKAY, ENOUGH OF THIS WAITING. WHY DON'T WE SET SOME #$%& OFF IN THE OCEAN, COAX THE THING OUT?
WE TALKED ABOUT THIS—THE BUGGER COULD BE ANYWHERE DOWN THERE, AND WE CAN'T WASTE THE C-4.
PRETTY SURE WE TAPPED OUT EVERYTHING IN THE PACIFIC NORTHWEST...
YEAH.
WHATEVER.
DAY 25.
BY THE TIME NEARLY A MONTH HAD ELAPSED, EVEN BOXER WAS LOSING IT.
SKREEEOOOOOONK!
PUH—CHEW! PUH—CHEW!

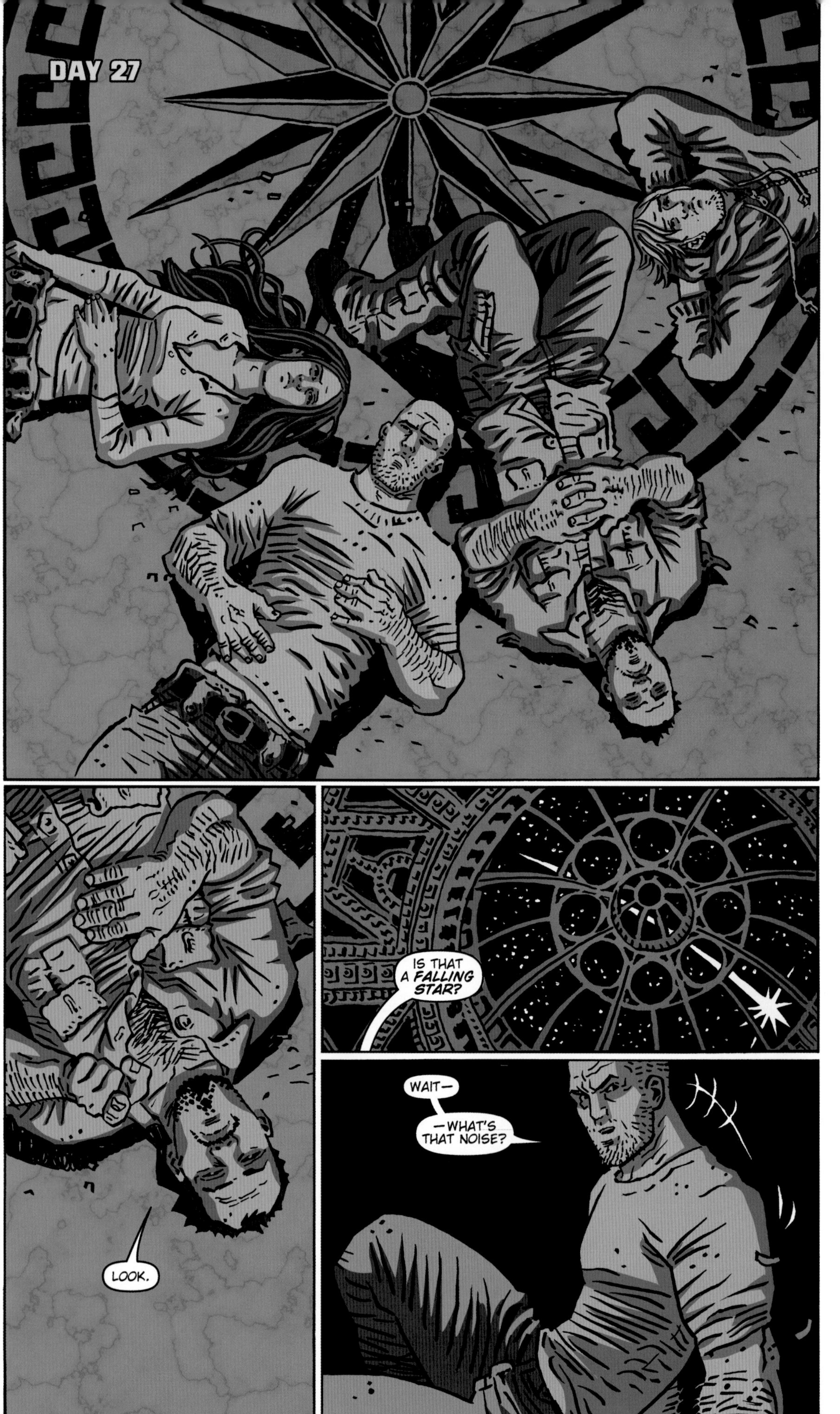
DAY 27
LOOK.
IS THAT A FALLING STAR?
WAIT—
—WHAT'S THAT NOISE?

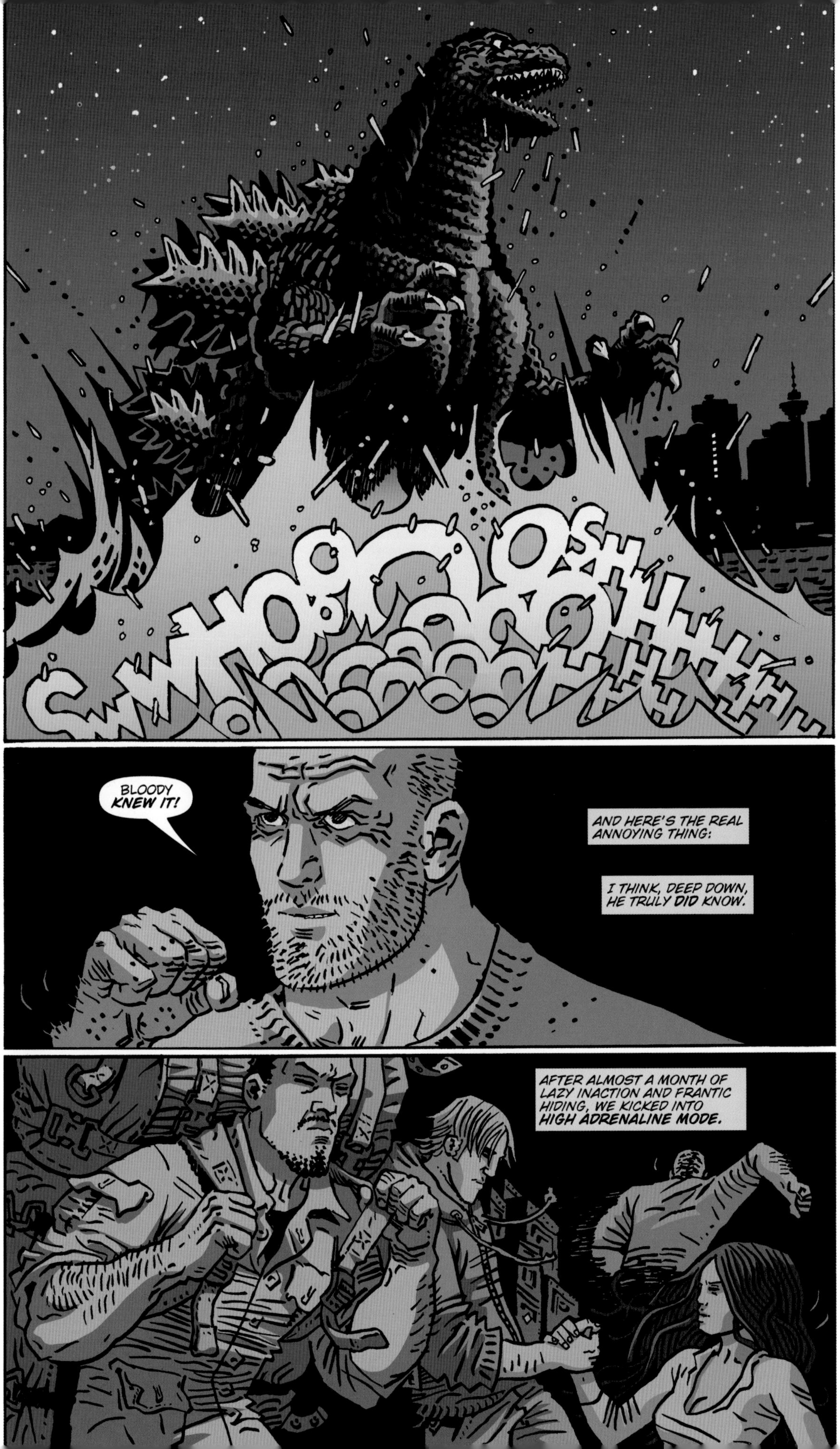
BLOODY KNEW IT!
AND HERE'S THE REAL ANNOYING THING:
I THINK, DEEP DOWN, HE TRULY DID KNOW.
AFTER ALMOST A MONTH OF LAZY INACTION AND FRANTIC HIDING, WE KICKED INTO HIGH ADRENALINE MODE.

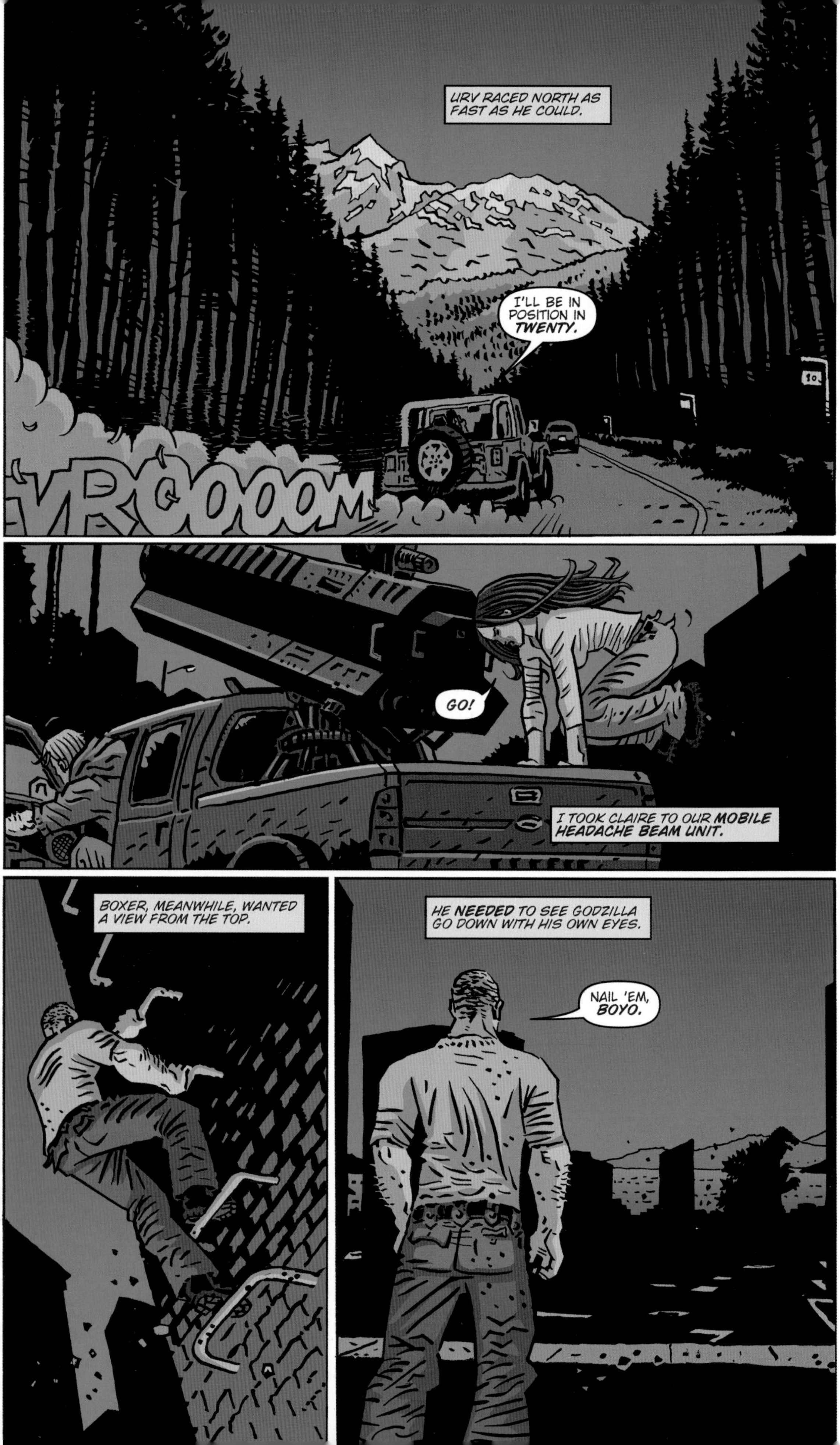
URV RACED NORTH AS FAST AS HE COULD.
I'LL BE IN POSITION IN TWENTY.
VROOOOM
GO!
I TOOK CLAIRE TO OUR MOBILE HEADACHE BEAM UNIT.
BOXER, MEANWHILE, WANTED A VIEW FROM THE TOP.
HE NEEDED TO SEE GODZILLA GO DOWN WITH HIS OWN EYES.
NAIL 'EM, BOYO.

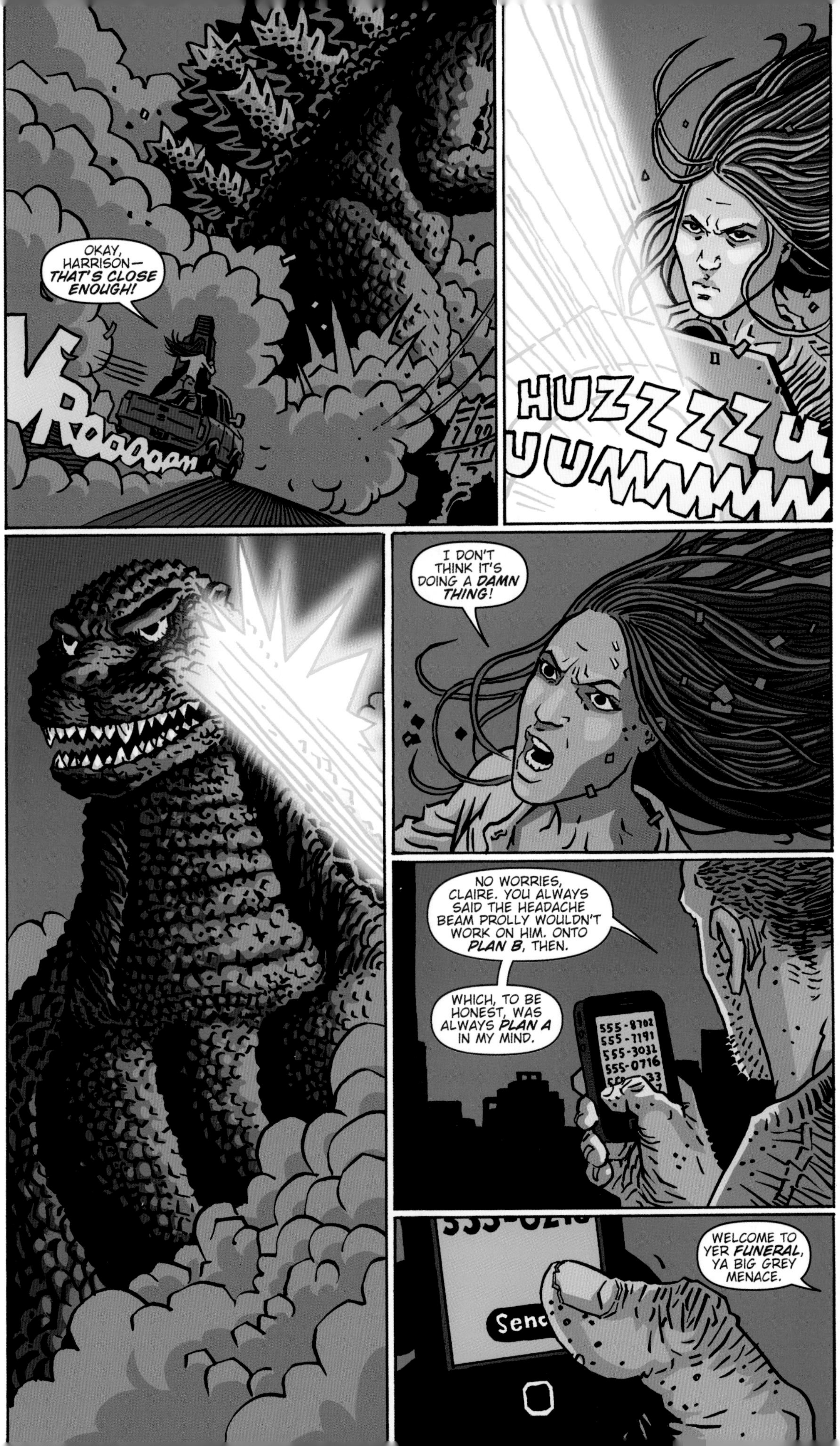
OKAY, HARRISON— THAT'S CLOSE ENOUGH!
VROOOOOOM
HUZZZZUUUMMMMM
I DON'T THINK IT'S DOING A DAMN THING!
NO WORRIES, CLAIRE. YOU ALWAYS SAID THE HEADACHE BEAM PROLLY WOULDN'T WORK ON HIM. ONTO PLAN B, THEN.
WHICH, TO BE HONEST, WAS ALWAYS PLAN A IN MY MIND.
555-8702
555-7191
555-3032
555-0716
WELCOME TO YER FUNERAL, YA BIG GREY MENACE.

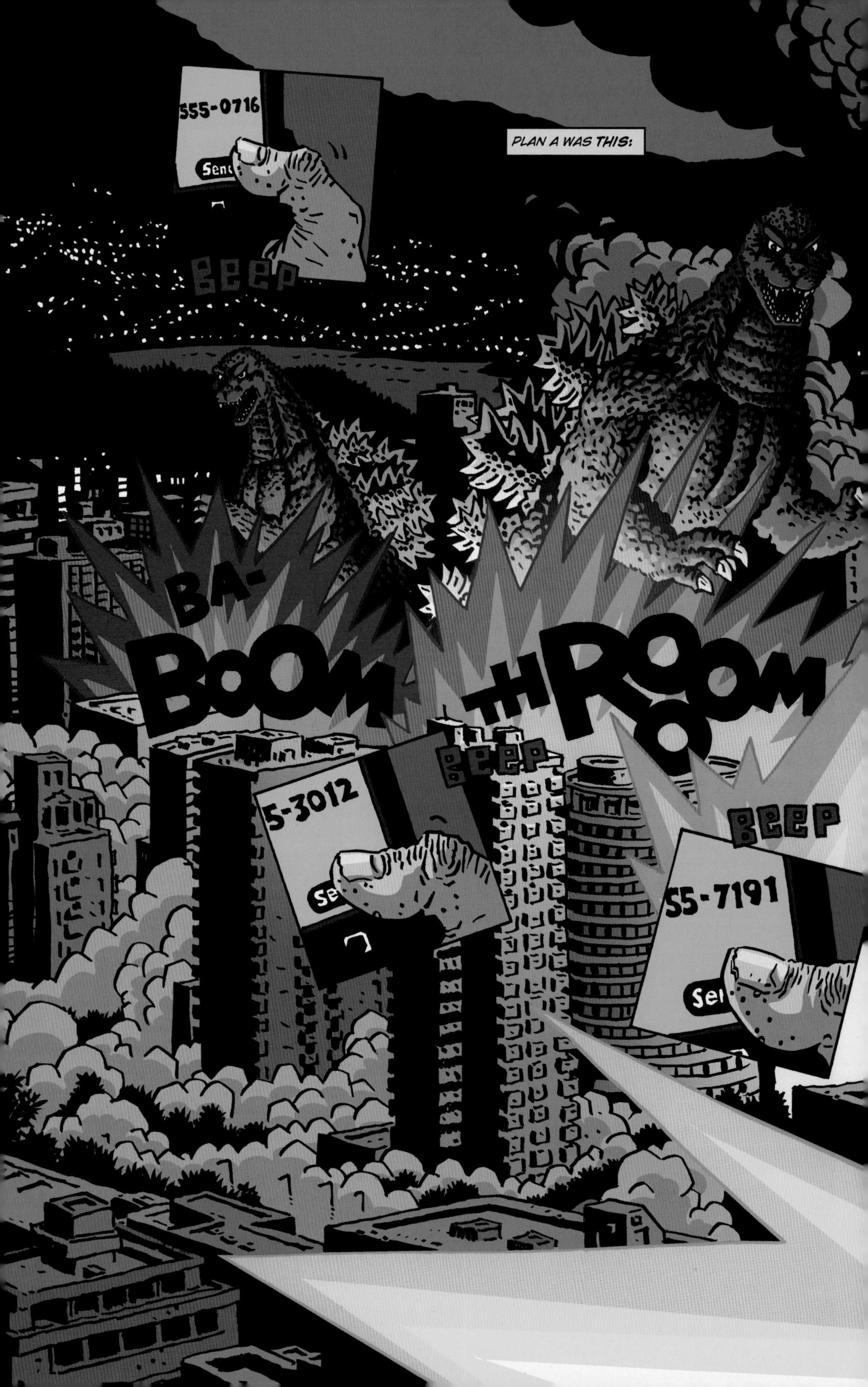
PLAN A WAS THIS:
555-0716
Sen
BEEP
BA-
BOOM
THROOOM
5-3012
BEEP
Se
BEEP
55-7191
Sei

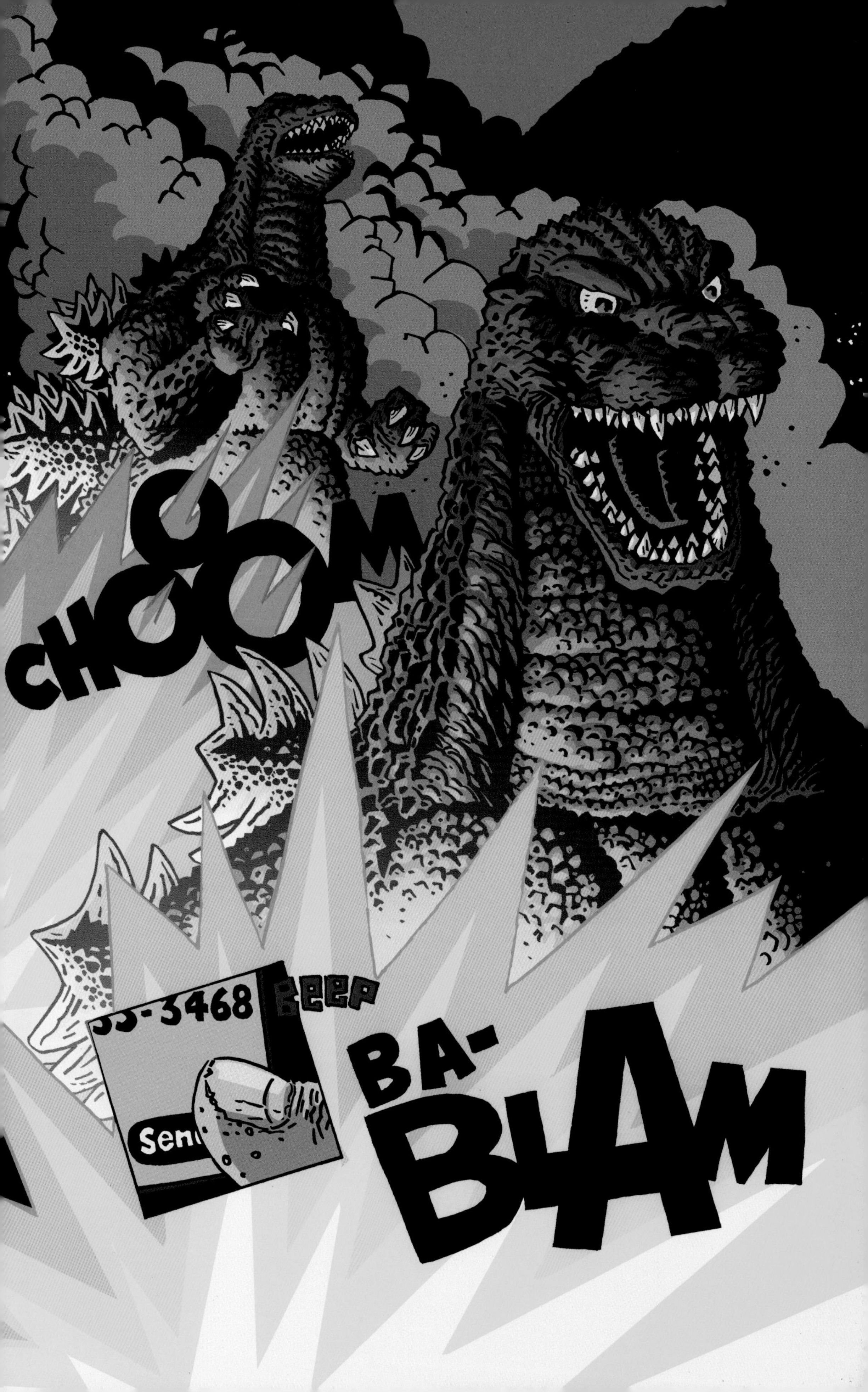
CHOOOOM
55-3468
BEEP
Send
BA-
BLAM

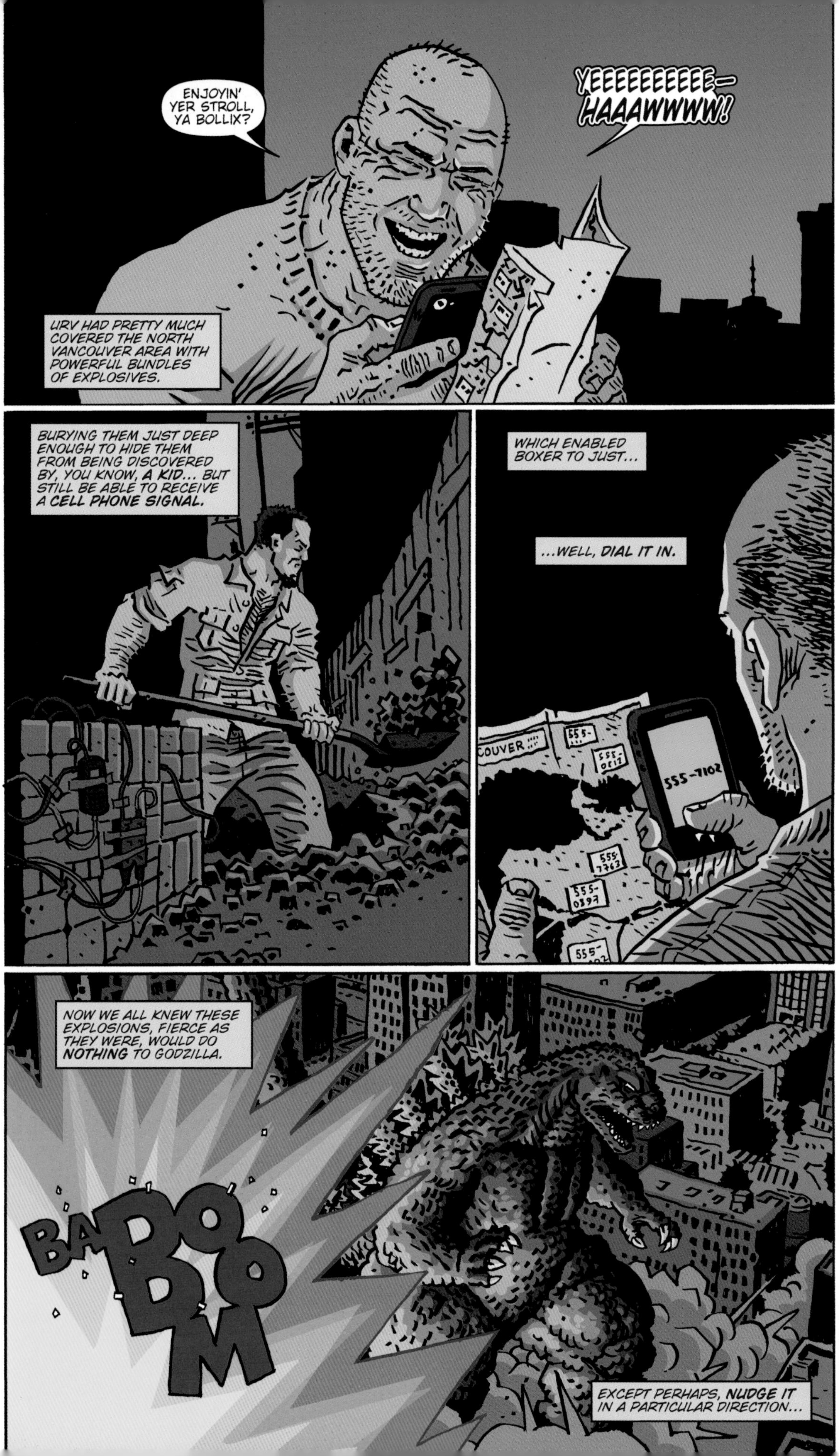
ENJOYIN' YER STROLL, YA BOLLIX?
YEEEEEEEEEE— HAAAWWWW!
URV HAD PRETTY MUCH COVERED THE NORTH VANCOUVER AREA WITH POWERFUL BUNDLES OF EXPLOSIVES.
BURYING THEM JUST DEEP ENOUGH TO HIDE THEM FROM BEING DISCOVERED BY, YOU KNOW, A KID... BUT STILL BE ABLE TO RECEIVE A CELL PHONE SIGNAL.
WHICH ENABLED BOXER TO JUST...
...WELL, DIAL IT IN.
555-7102
NOW WE ALL KNEW THESE EXPLOSIONS, FIERCE AS THEY WERE, WOULD DO NOTHING TO GODZILLA.
BADOOOM
EXCEPT PERHAPS, NUDGE IT IN A PARTICULAR DIRECTION...

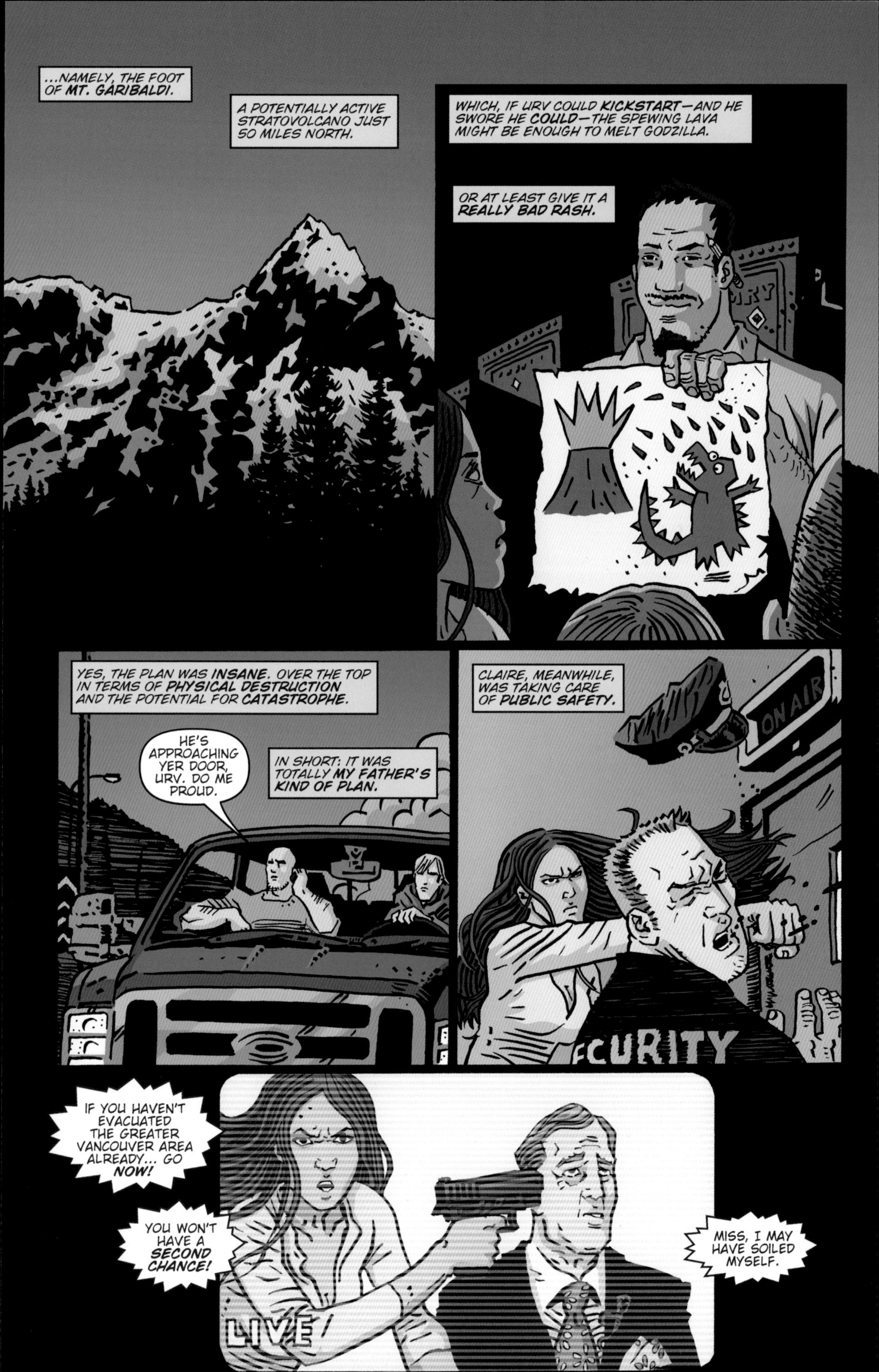
...NAMELY, THE FOOT OF MT. GARIBALDI.
A POTENTIALLY ACTIVE STRATOVOLCANO JUST 50 MILES NORTH.
WHICH, IF URV COULD KICKSTART—AND HE SWORE HE COULD—THE SPEWING LAVA MIGHT BE ENOUGH TO MELT GODZILLA.
OR AT LEAST GIVE IT A REALLY BAD RASH.
YES, THE PLAN WAS INSANE. OVER THE TOP IN TERMS OF PHYSICAL DESTRUCTION AND THE POTENTIAL FOR CATASTROPHE.
HE'S APPROACHING YER DOOR, URV. DO ME PROUD.
IN SHORT: IT WAS TOTALLY MY FATHER'S KIND OF PLAN.
CLAIRE, MEANWHILE, WAS TAKING CARE OF PUBLIC SAFETY.
ON AIR
ECURITY
IF YOU HAVEN'T EVACUATED THE GREATER VANCOUVER AREA ALREADY... GO NOW!
YOU WON'T HAVE A SECOND CHANCE!
MISS, I MAY HAVE SOILED MYSELF.
LIVE

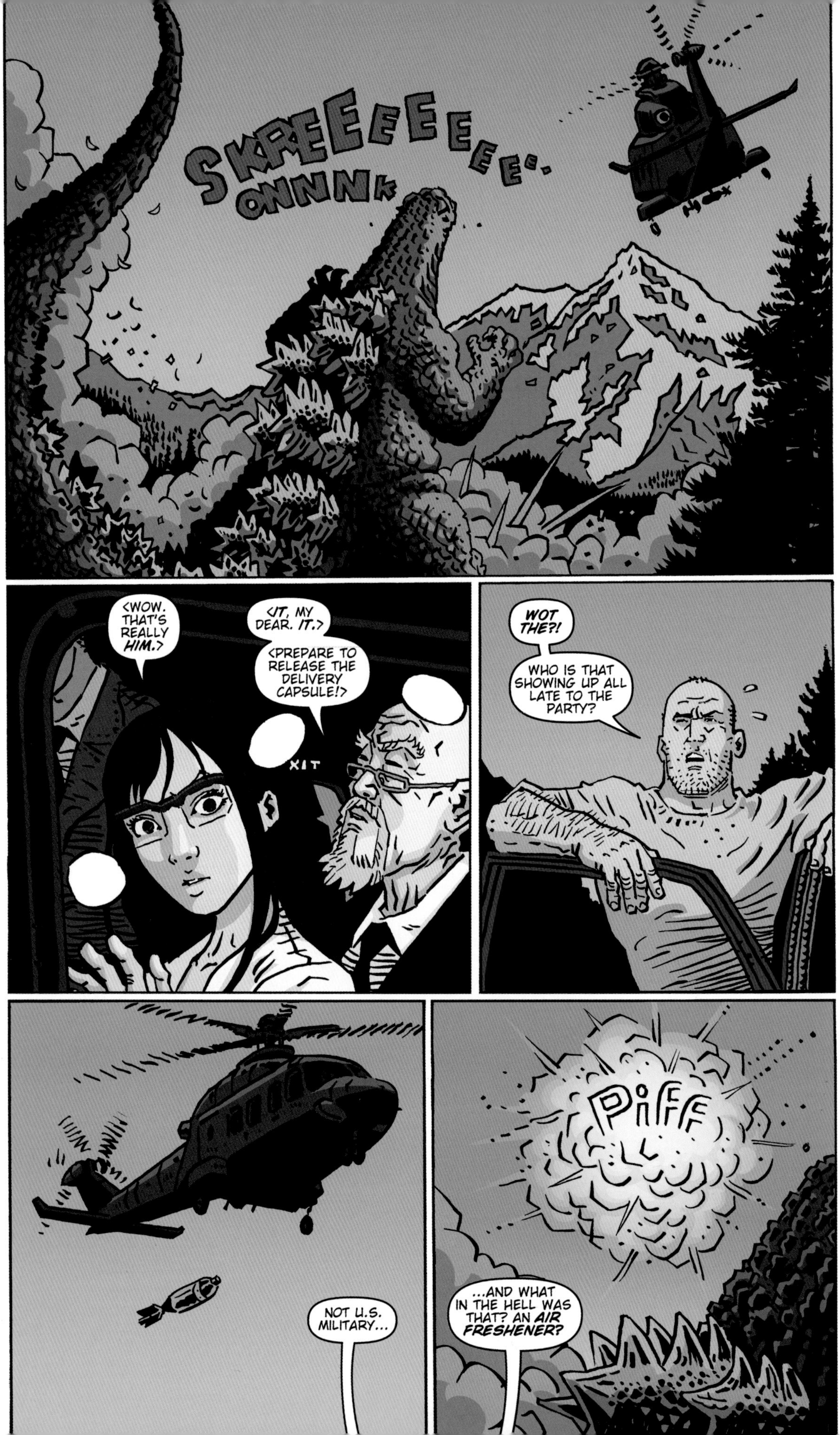
SKREEEEEEEe.
ONNNK
<WOW. THAT'S REALLY *HIM.*>
<*IT,* MY DEAR. *IT.*>
<PREPARE TO RELEASE THE DELIVERY CAPSULE!>
WOT THE?!
WHO IS THAT SHOWING UP ALL LATE TO THE PARTY?
NOT U.S. MILITARY...
PIFF
...AND WHAT IN THE HELL WAS THAT? AN *AIR FRESHENER?*

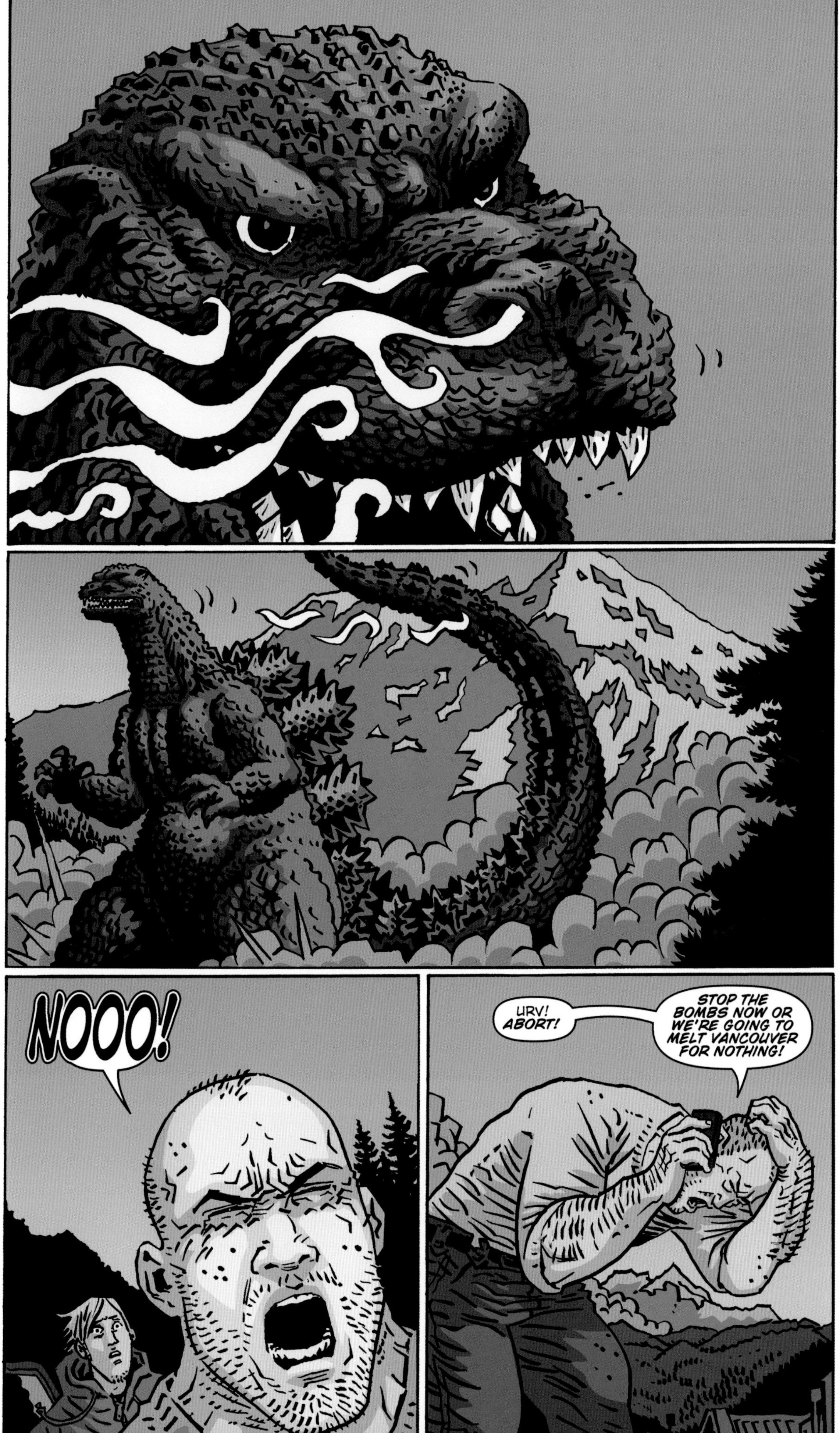
NOOO!
URV! ABORT!
STOP THE BOMBS NOW OR WE'RE GOING TO MELT VANCOUVER FOR NOTHING!

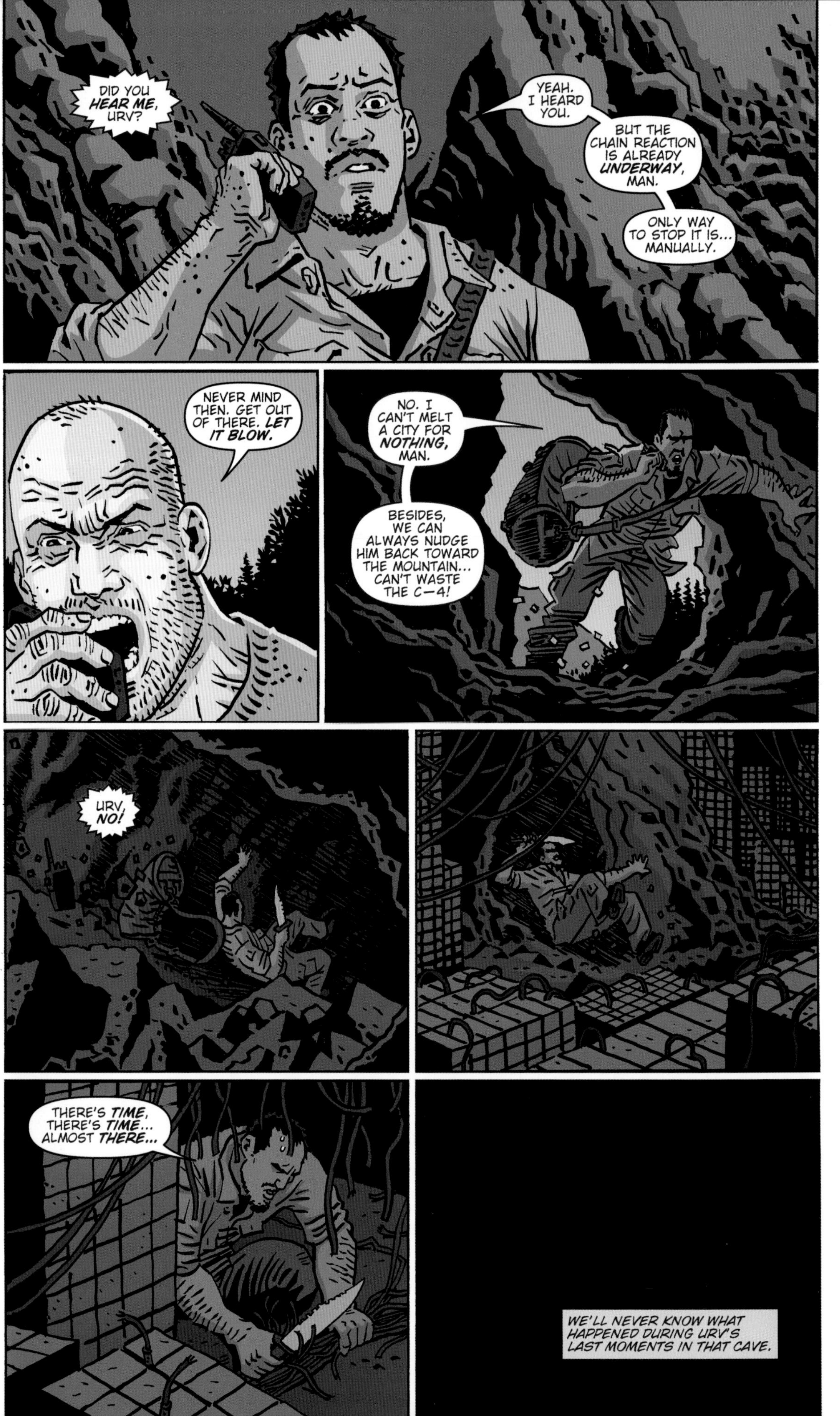
DID YOU HEAR ME, URV?
YEAH. I HEARD YOU.
BUT THE CHAIN REACTION IS ALREADY UNDERWAY, MAN.
ONLY WAY TO STOP IT IS... MANUALLY.
NEVER MIND THEN. GET OUT OF THERE. LET IT BLOW.
NO. I CAN'T MELT A CITY FOR NOTHING, MAN.
BESIDES, WE CAN ALWAYS NUDGE HIM BACK TOWARD THE MOUNTAIN... CAN'T WASTE THE C-4!
URV, NO!
THERE'S TIME, THERE'S TIME... ALMOST THERE...
WE'LL NEVER KNOW WHAT HAPPENED DURING URV'S LAST MOMENTS IN THAT CAVE.

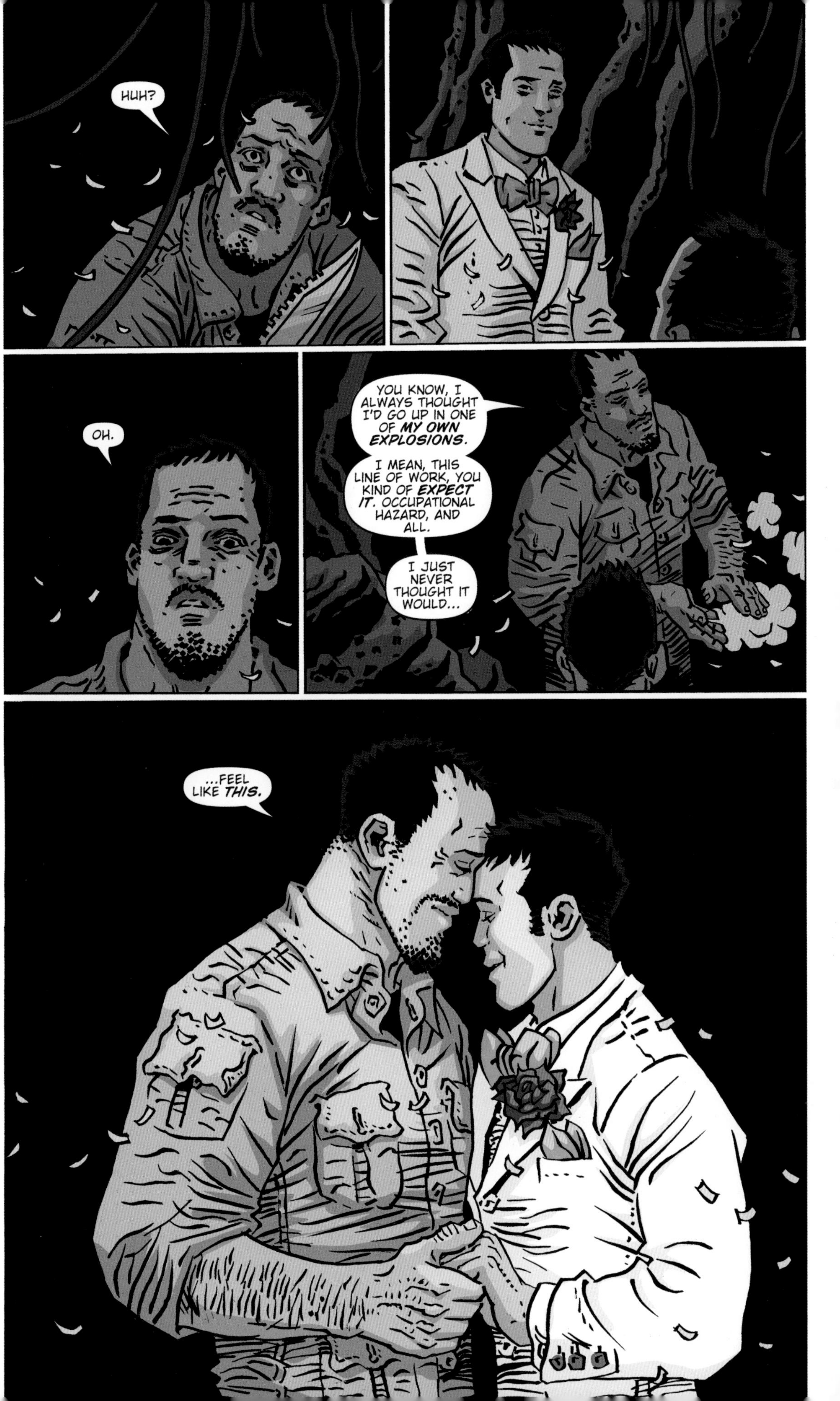
HUH?
OH.
YOU KNOW, I ALWAYS THOUGHT I'D GO UP IN ONE OF MY OWN EXPLOSIONS.
I MEAN, THIS LINE OF WORK, YOU KIND OF EXPECT IT. OCCUPATIONAL HAZARD, AND ALL.
I JUST NEVER THOUGHT IT WOULD...
...FEEL LIKE THIS.

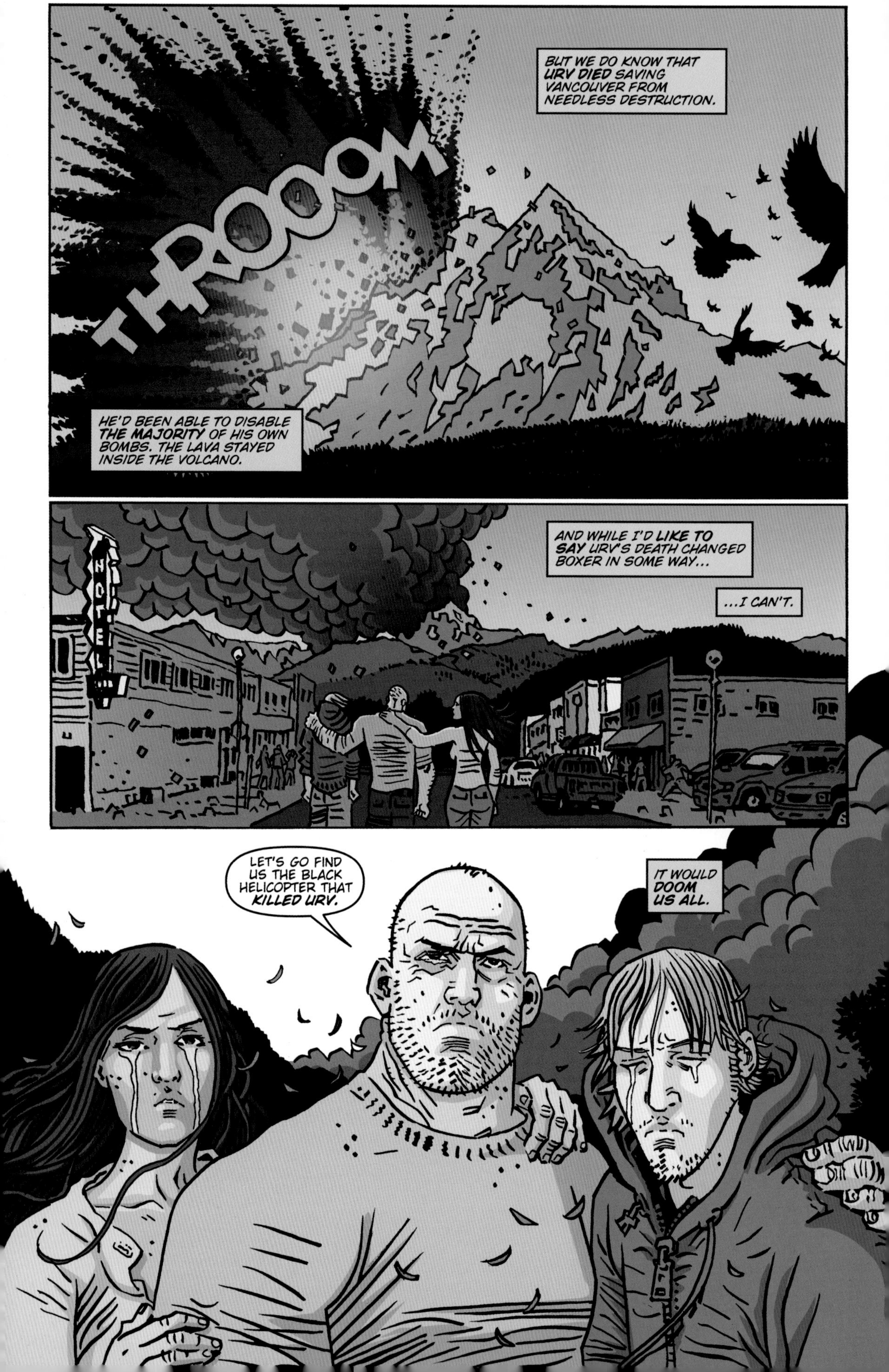
BUT WE DO KNOW THAT URV DIED SAVING VANCOUVER FROM NEEDLESS DESTRUCTION.
THROOOM
HE'D BEEN ABLE TO DISABLE THE MAJORITY OF HIS OWN BOMBS. THE LAVA STAYED INSIDE THE VOLCANO.
HOTEL
AND WHILE I'D LIKE TO SAY URV'S DEATH CHANGED BOXER IN SOME WAY...
...I CAN'T.
LET'S GO FIND US THE BLACK HELICOPTER THAT KILLED URV.
IT WOULD DOOM US ALL.

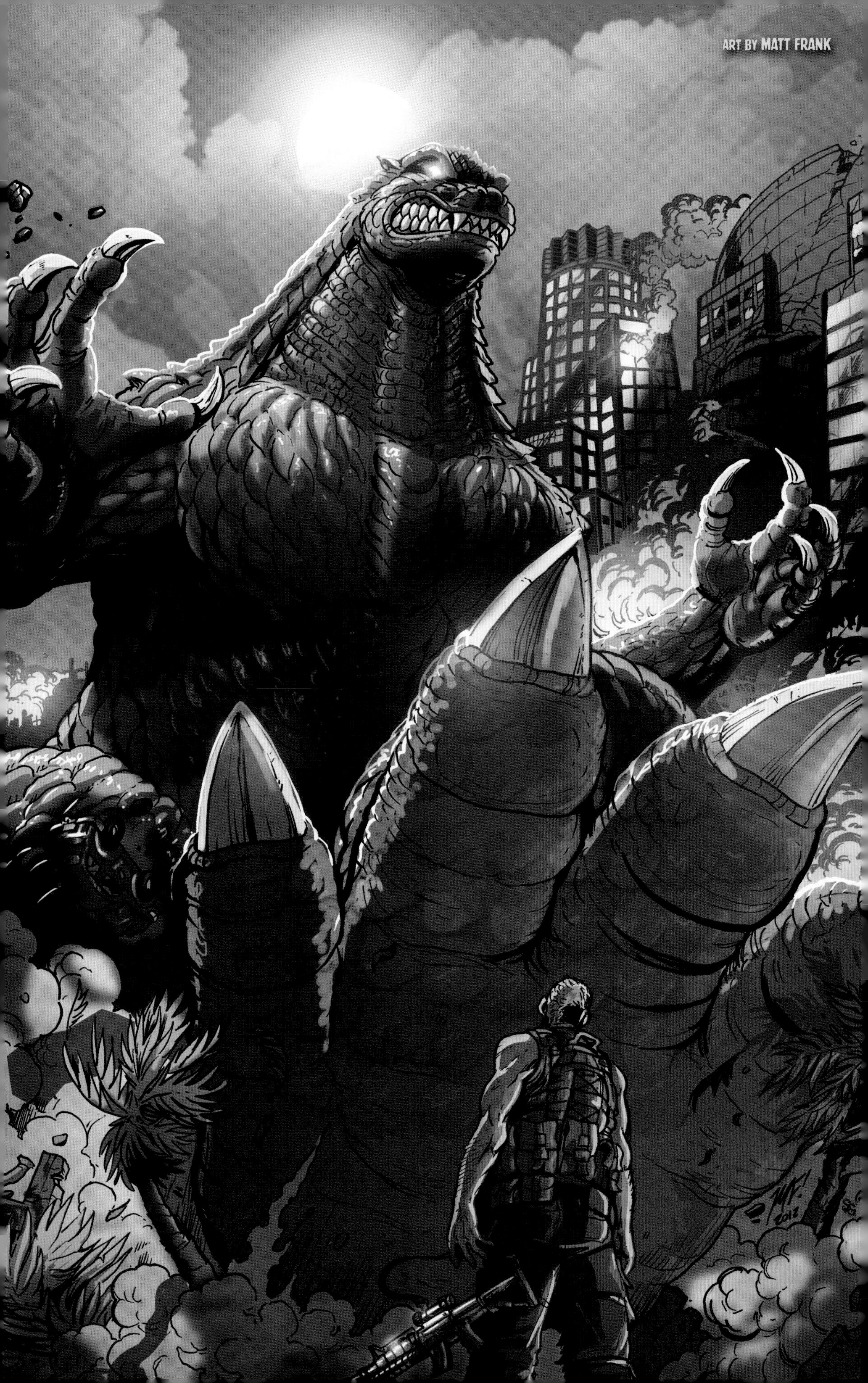

ART BY MATT FRANK

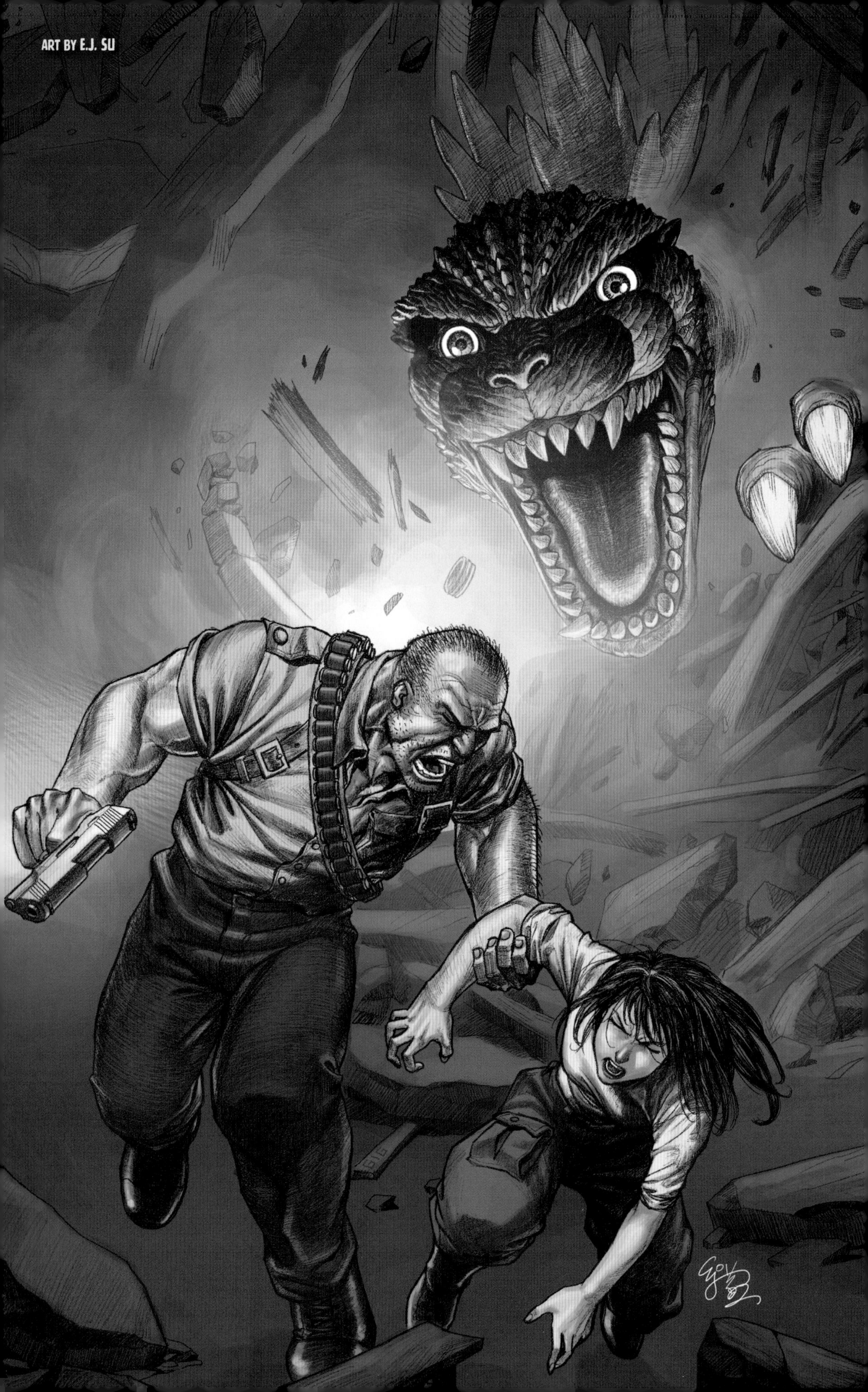
ART BY E.J. SU

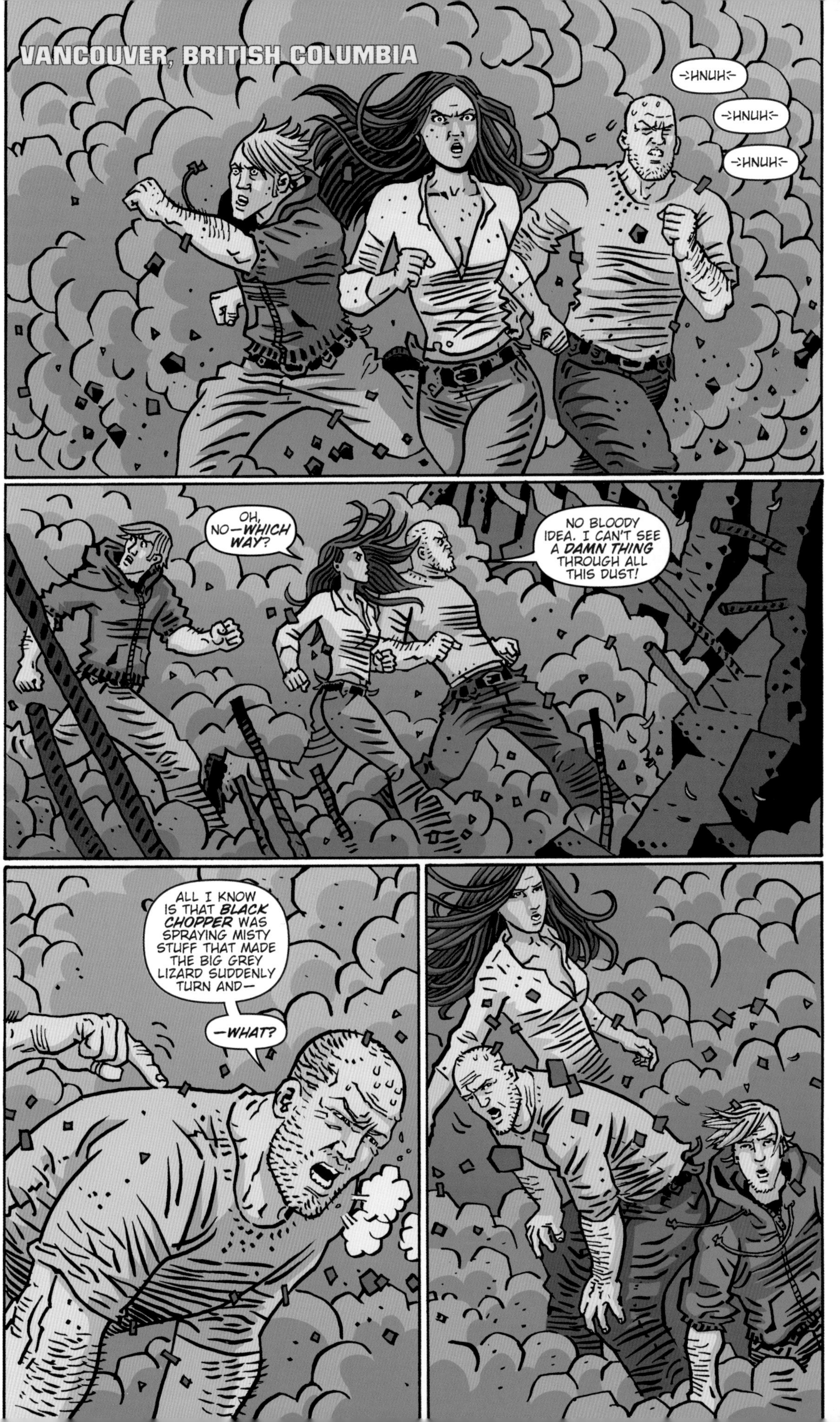
VANCOUVER, BRITISH COLUMBIA
HNUH
HNUH
HNUH
OH, NO—WHICH WAY?
NO BLOODY IDEA. I CAN'T SEE A DAMN THING THROUGH ALL THIS DUST!
ALL I KNOW IS THAT BLACK CHOPPER WAS SPRAYING MISTY STUFF THAT MADE THE BIG GREY LIZARD SUDDENLY TURN AND—
—WHAT?

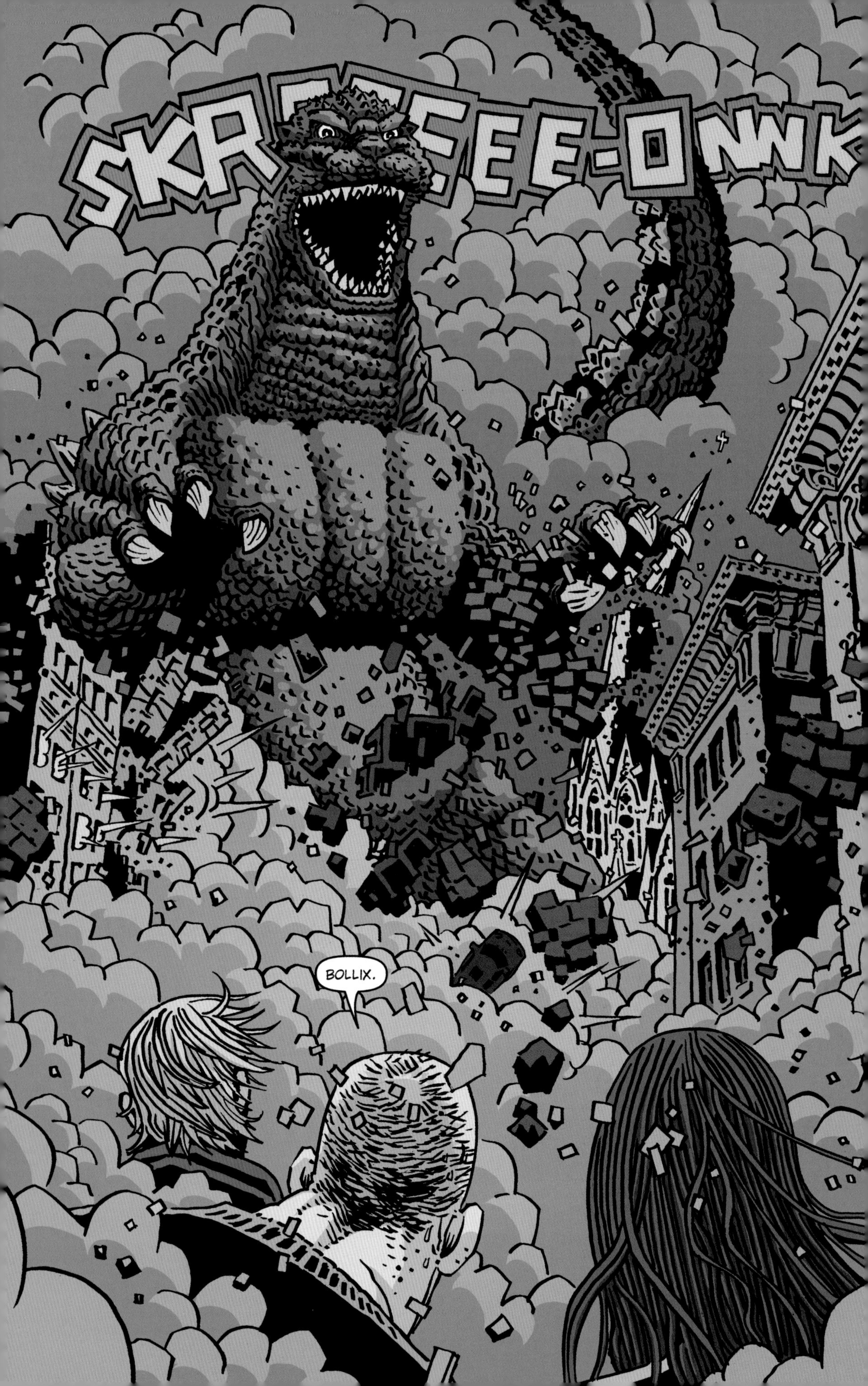
SKR
EEE-ONWK
BOLLIX.

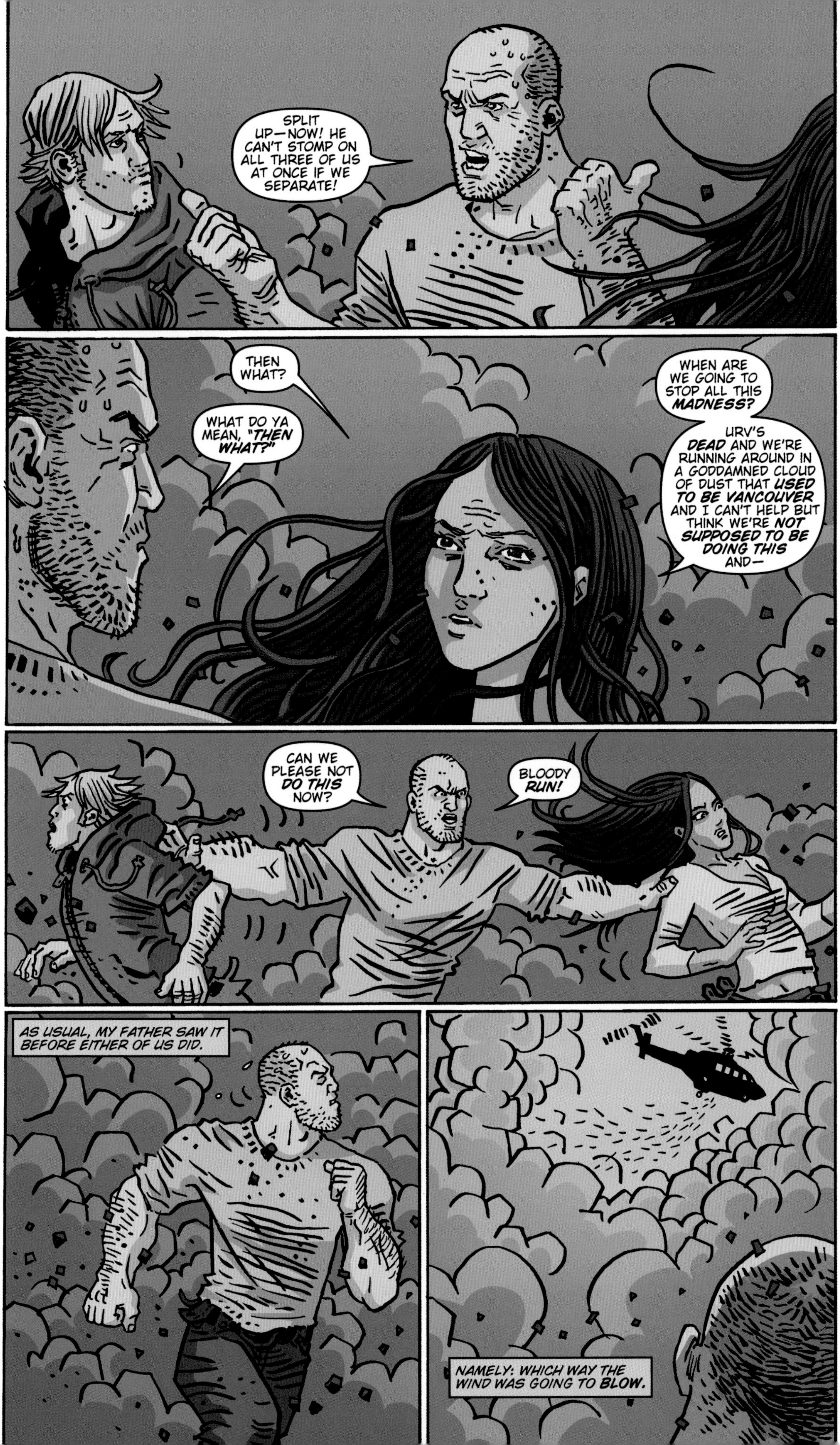

SPLIT UP—NOW! HE CAN'T STOMP ON ALL THREE OF US AT ONCE IF WE SEPARATE!
THEN WHAT?
WHAT DO YA MEAN, "THEN WHAT?"
WHEN ARE WE GOING TO STOP ALL THIS MADNESS?
URV'S DEAD AND WE'RE RUNNING AROUND IN A GODDAMNED CLOUD OF DUST THAT USED TO BE VANCOUVER AND I CAN'T HELP BUT THINK WE'RE NOT SUPPOSED TO BE DOING THIS AND—
CAN WE PLEASE NOT DO THIS NOW?
BLOODY RUN!
AS USUAL, MY FATHER SAW IT BEFORE EITHER OF US DID.
NAMELY: WHICH WAY THE WIND WAS GOING TO BLOW.

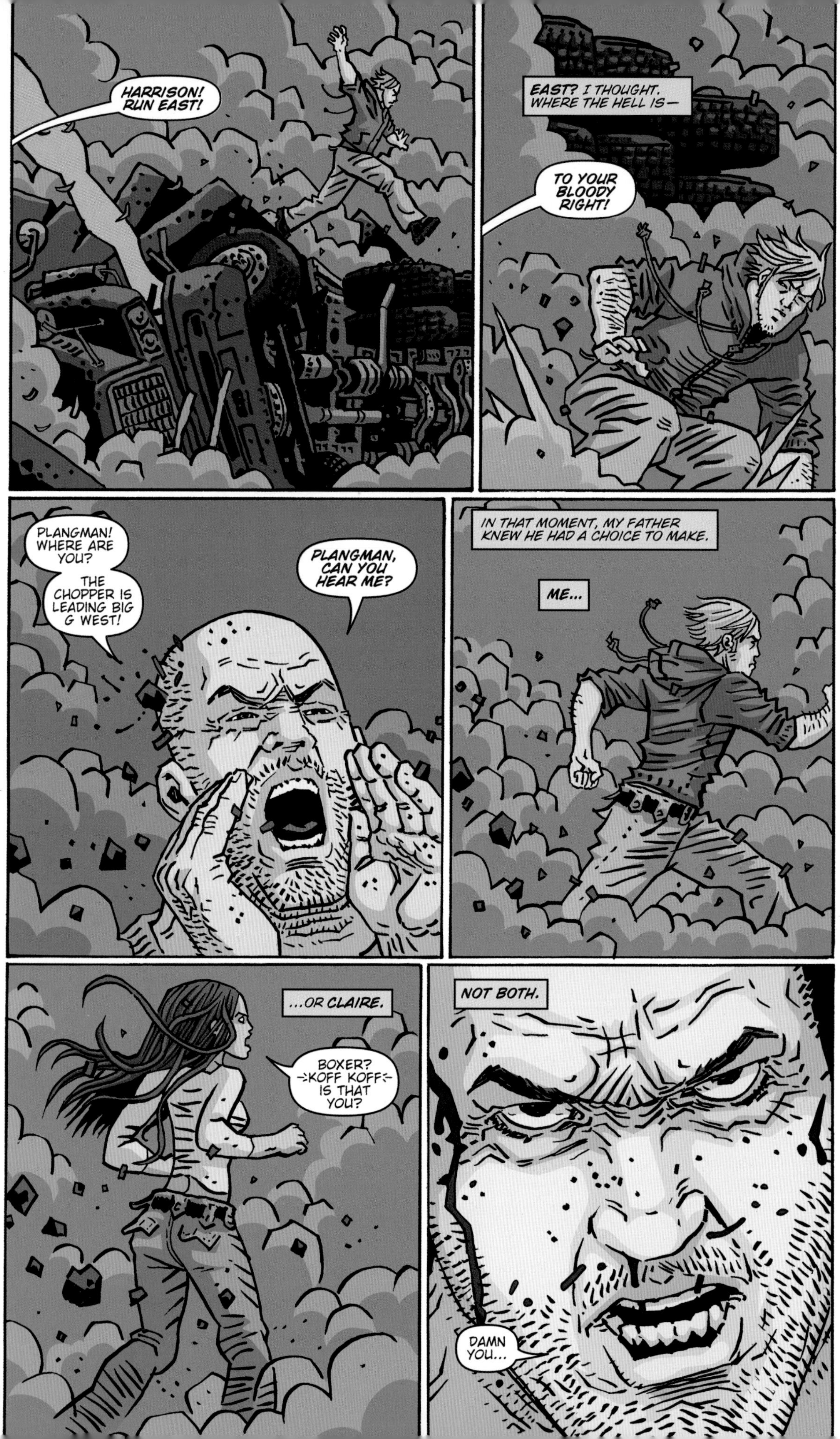

HARRISON! RUN EAST!
EAST? I THOUGHT. WHERE THE HELL IS—
TO YOUR BLOODY RIGHT!
PLANGMAN! WHERE ARE YOU?
THE CHOPPER IS LEADING BIG G WEST!
PLANGMAN, CAN YOU HEAR ME?
IN THAT MOMENT, MY FATHER KNEW HE HAD A CHOICE TO MAKE.
ME...
...OR CLAIRE.
BOXER? -KOFF KOFF- IS THAT YOU?
NOT BOTH.
DAMN YOU...

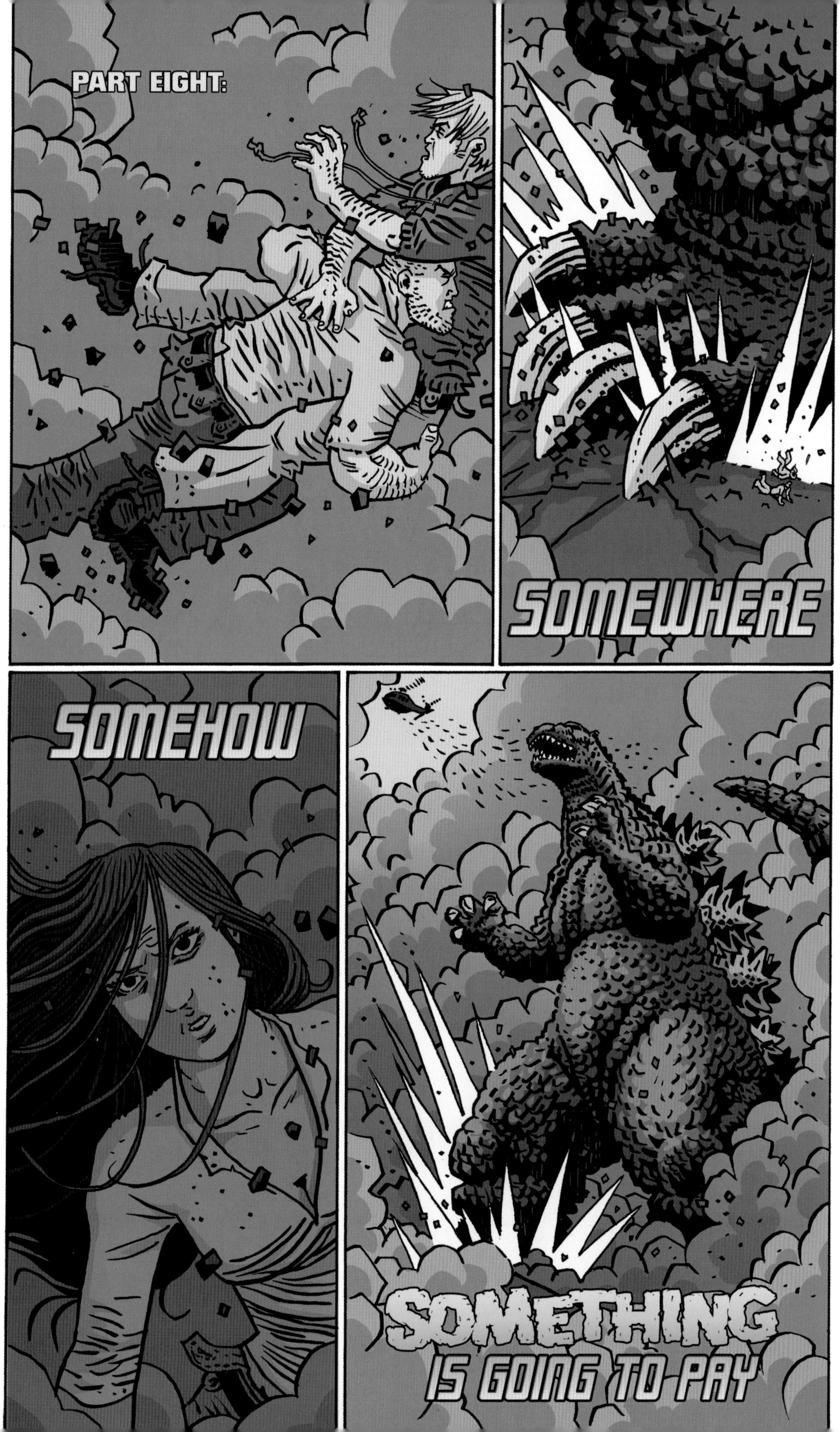
PART EIGHT:
SOMEWHERE
SOMEHOW
SOMETHING
IS GOING TO PAY

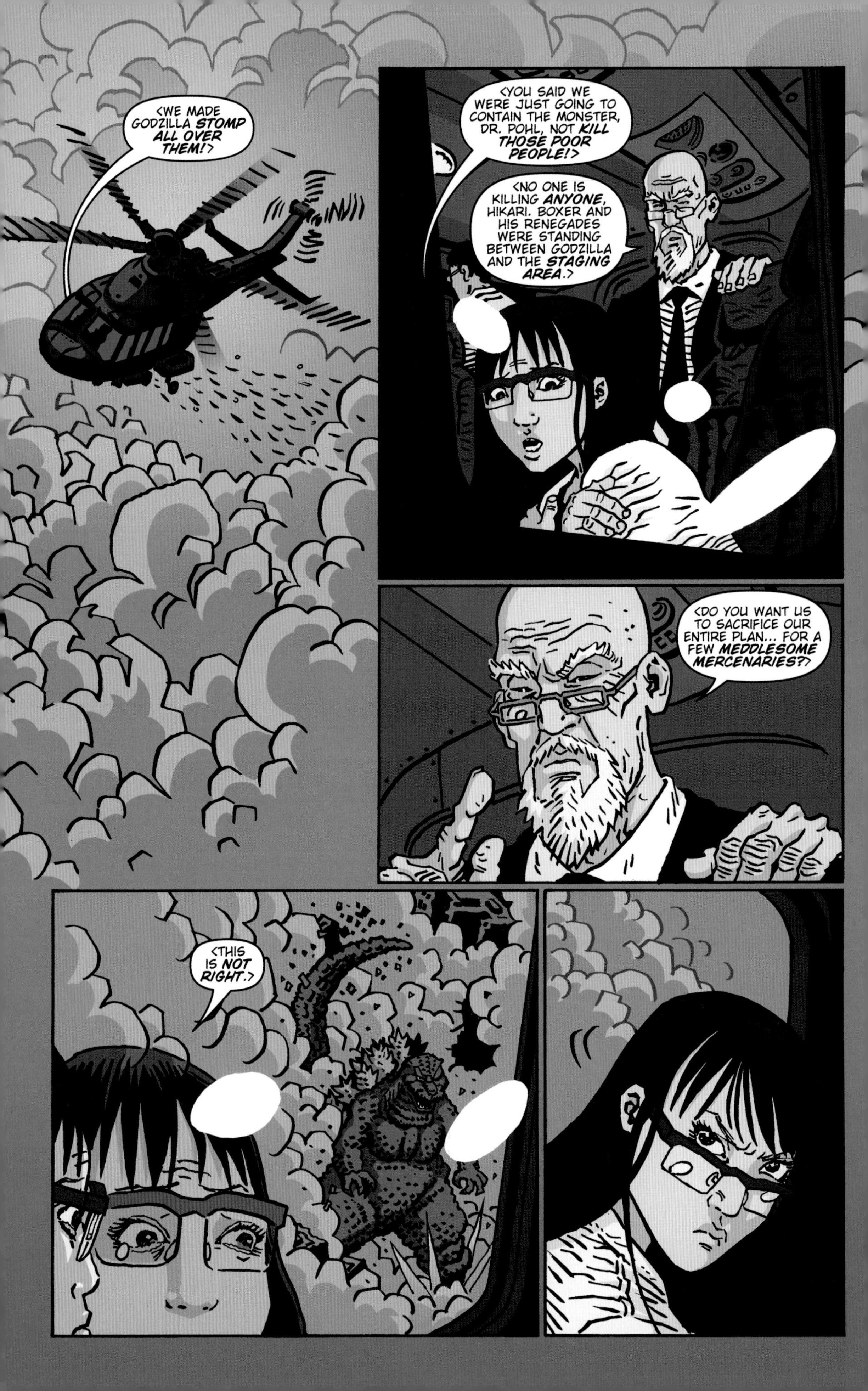

<WE MADE GODZILLA STOMP ALL OVER THEM!>
<YOU SAID WE WERE JUST GOING TO CONTAIN THE MONSTER, DR. POHL, NOT KILL THOSE POOR PEOPLE!>
<NO ONE IS KILLING ANYONE, HIKARI. BOXER AND HIS RENEGADES WERE STANDING BETWEEN GODZILLA AND THE STAGING AREA.>
<DO YOU WANT US TO SACRIFICE OUR ENTIRE PLAN... FOR A FEW MEDDLESOME MERCENARIES?>
<THIS IS NOT RIGHT.>

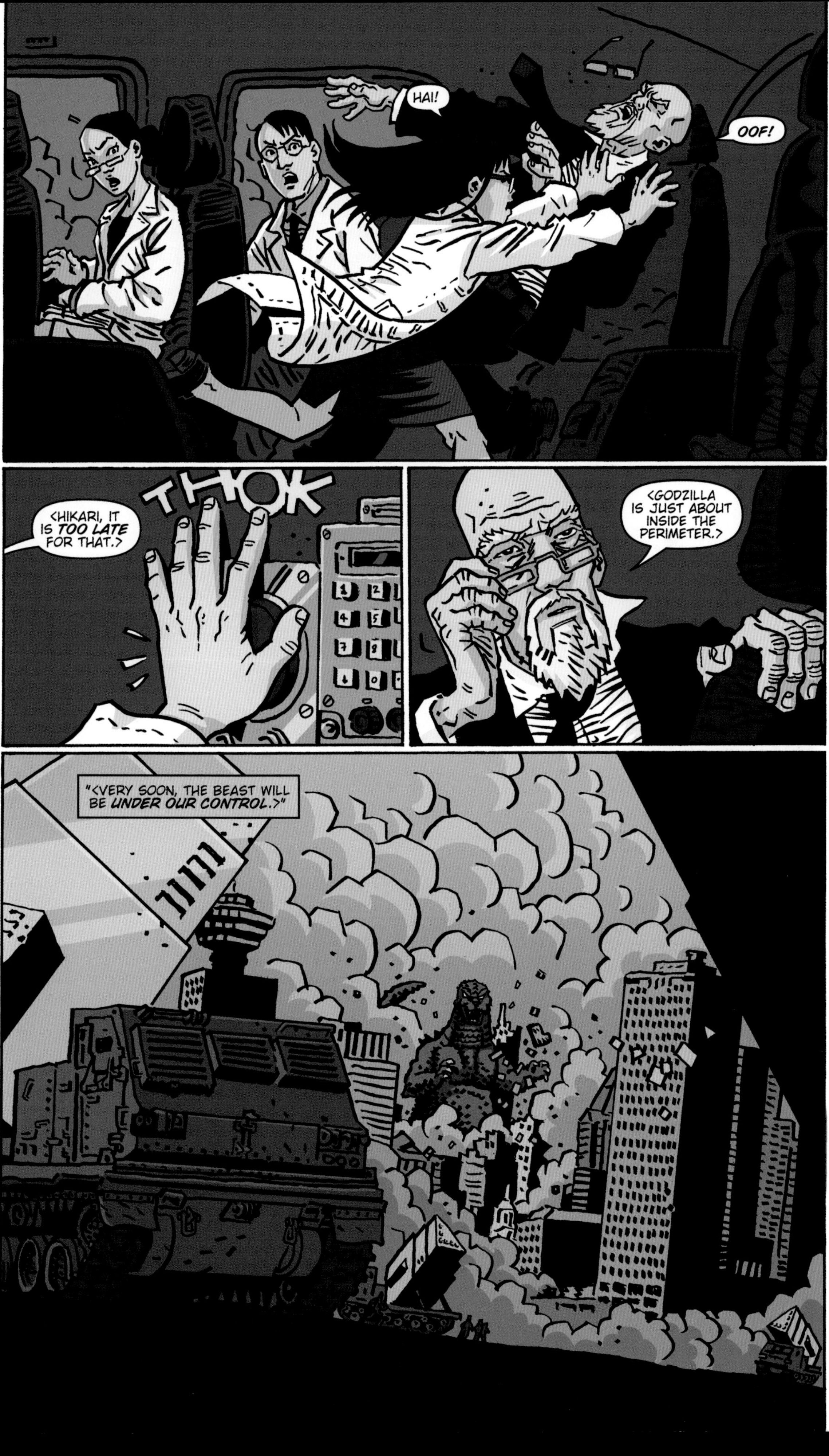
HAI!
OOF!
THOK
<HIKARI, IT IS *TOO LATE* FOR THAT.>
<GODZILLA IS JUST ABOUT INSIDE THE PERIMETER.>
"<VERY SOON, THE BEAST WILL BE ***UNDER OUR CONTROL***.>"

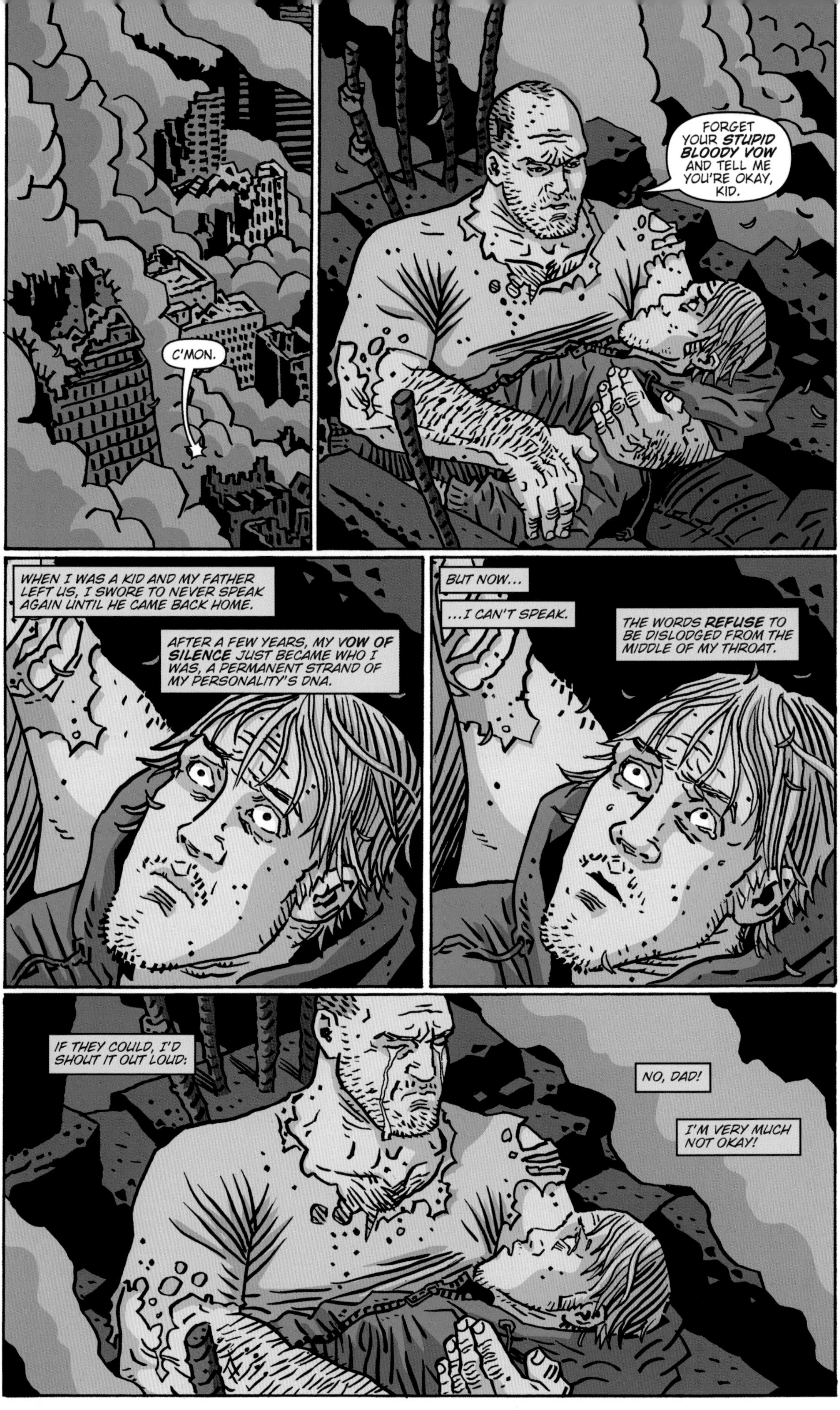
C'MON.
FORGET YOUR **STUPID BLOODY VOW** AND TELL ME YOU'RE OKAY, KID.
WHEN I WAS A KID AND MY FATHER LEFT US, I SWORE TO NEVER SPEAK AGAIN UNTIL HE CAME BACK HOME.
AFTER A FEW YEARS, MY **VOW OF SILENCE** JUST BECAME WHO I WAS, A PERMANENT STRAND OF MY PERSONALITY'S DNA.
BUT NOW...
...I CAN'T SPEAK.
THE WORDS **REFUSE** TO BE DISLODGED FROM THE MIDDLE OF MY THROAT.
IF THEY COULD, I'D SHOUT IT OUT LOUD:
NO, DAD!
I'M VERY MUCH NOT OKAY!

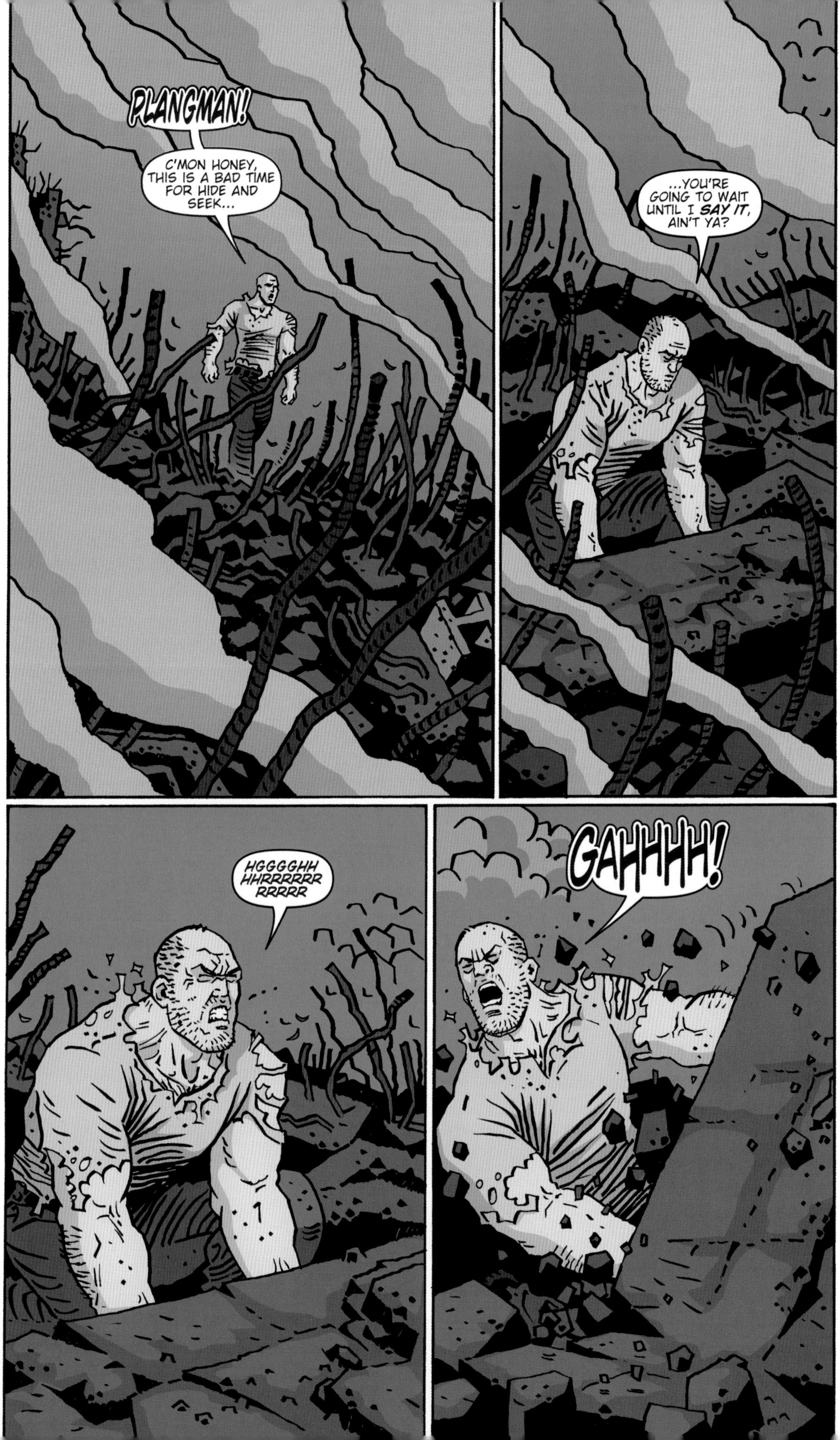
PLANGMAN!
C'MON HONEY, THIS IS A BAD TIME FOR HIDE AND SEEK...
...YOU'RE GOING TO WAIT UNTIL I SAY IT, AIN'T YA?
HGGGGHH HHRRRRRR RRRRR
GAHHHH!

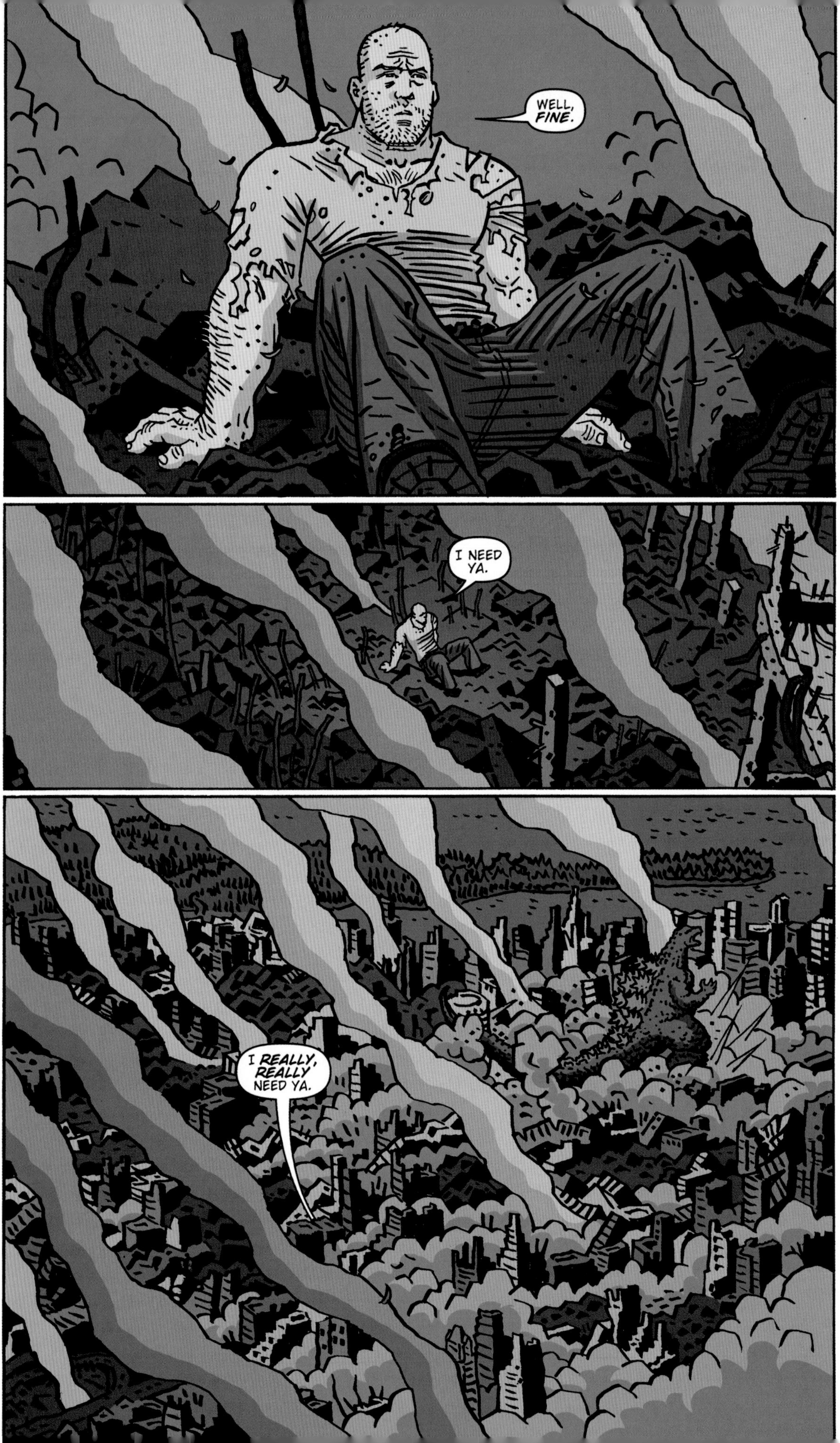
WELL, FINE.
I NEED YA.
I REALLY, REALLY NEED YA.

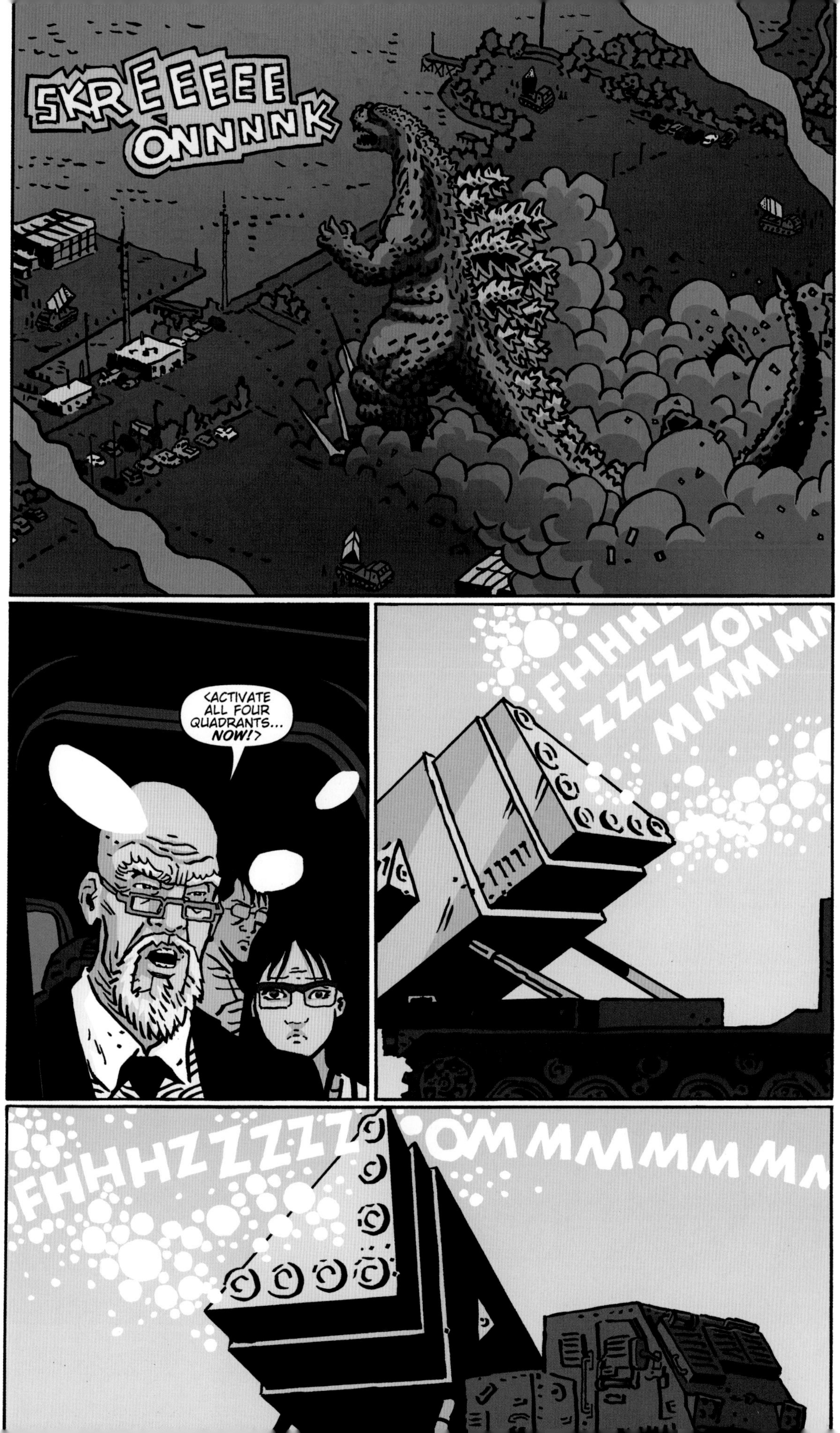
SKREEEEEE ONNNNK
<ACTIVATE ALL FOUR QUADRANTS... NOW!>
FHHHZ ZZZZZOM MMMMM
FHHHZZZZZOOMMMMMMM

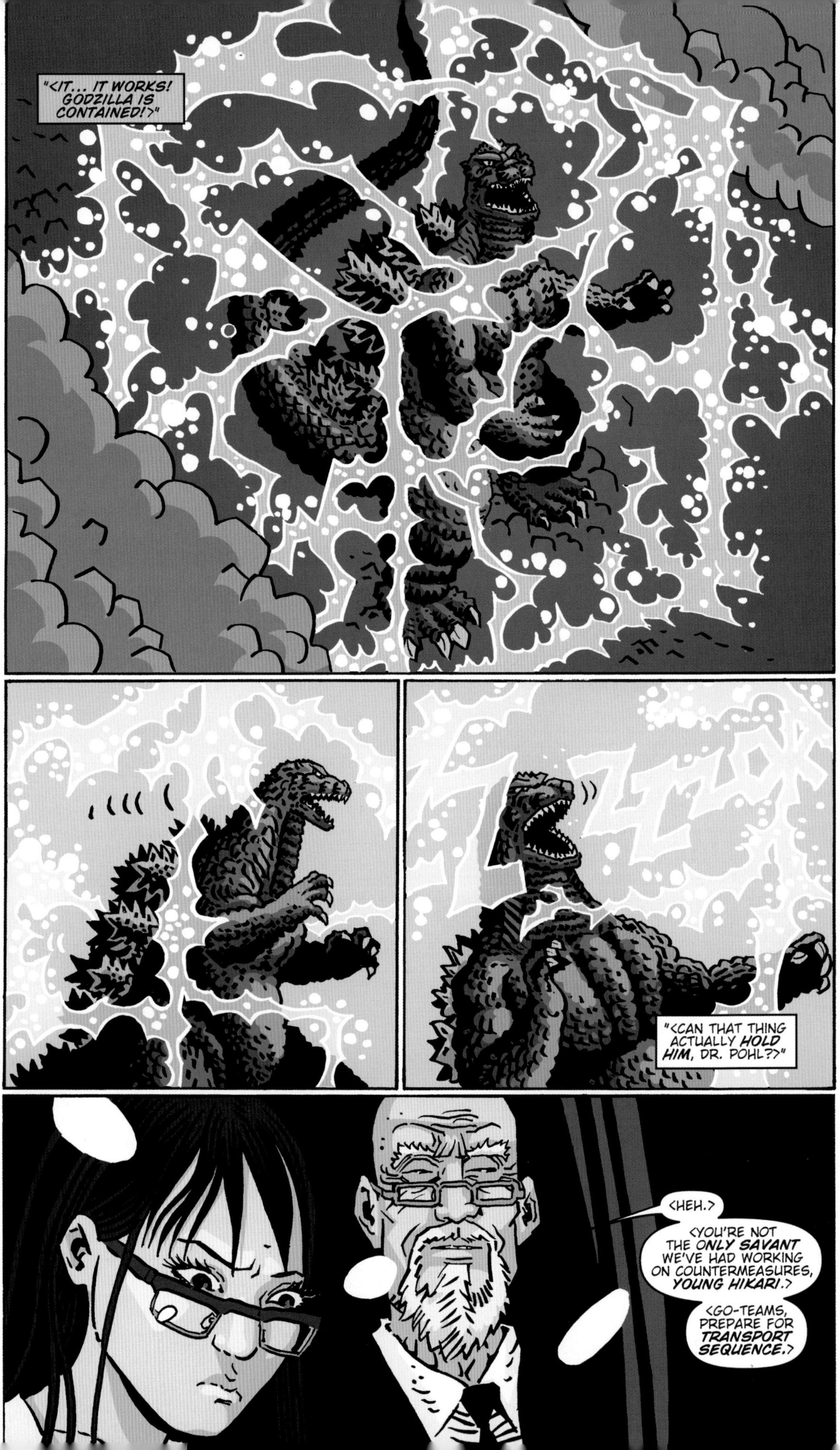
"<IT... IT WORKS! GODZILLA IS CONTAINED!>"
"<CAN THAT THING ACTUALLY HOLD HIM, DR. POHL?>"
<HEH.>
<YOU'RE NOT THE ONLY SAVANT WE'VE HAD WORKING ON COUNTERMEASURES, YOUNG HIKARI.>
<GO-TEAMS, PREPARE FOR TRANSPORT SEQUENCE.>

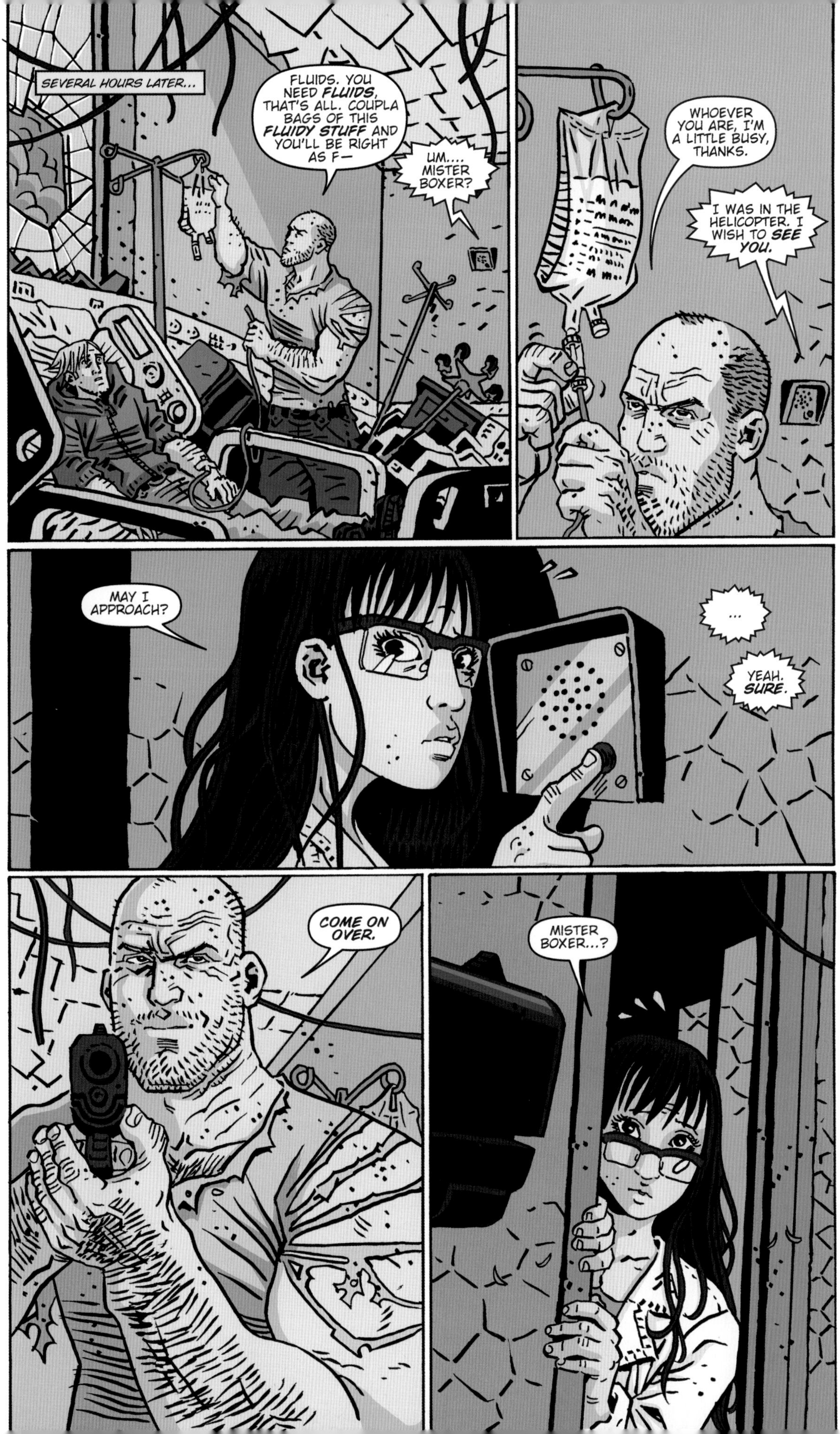
SEVERAL HOURS LATER...
FLUIDS. YOU NEED FLUIDS, THAT'S ALL. COUPLA BAGS OF THIS FLUIDY STUFF AND YOU'LL BE RIGHT AS F—
UM.... MISTER BOXER?
WHOEVER YOU ARE, I'M A LITTLE BUSY, THANKS.
I WAS IN THE HELICOPTER. I WISH TO SEE YOU.
MAY I APPROACH?
...
YEAH. SURE.
COME ON OVER.
MISTER BOXER...?

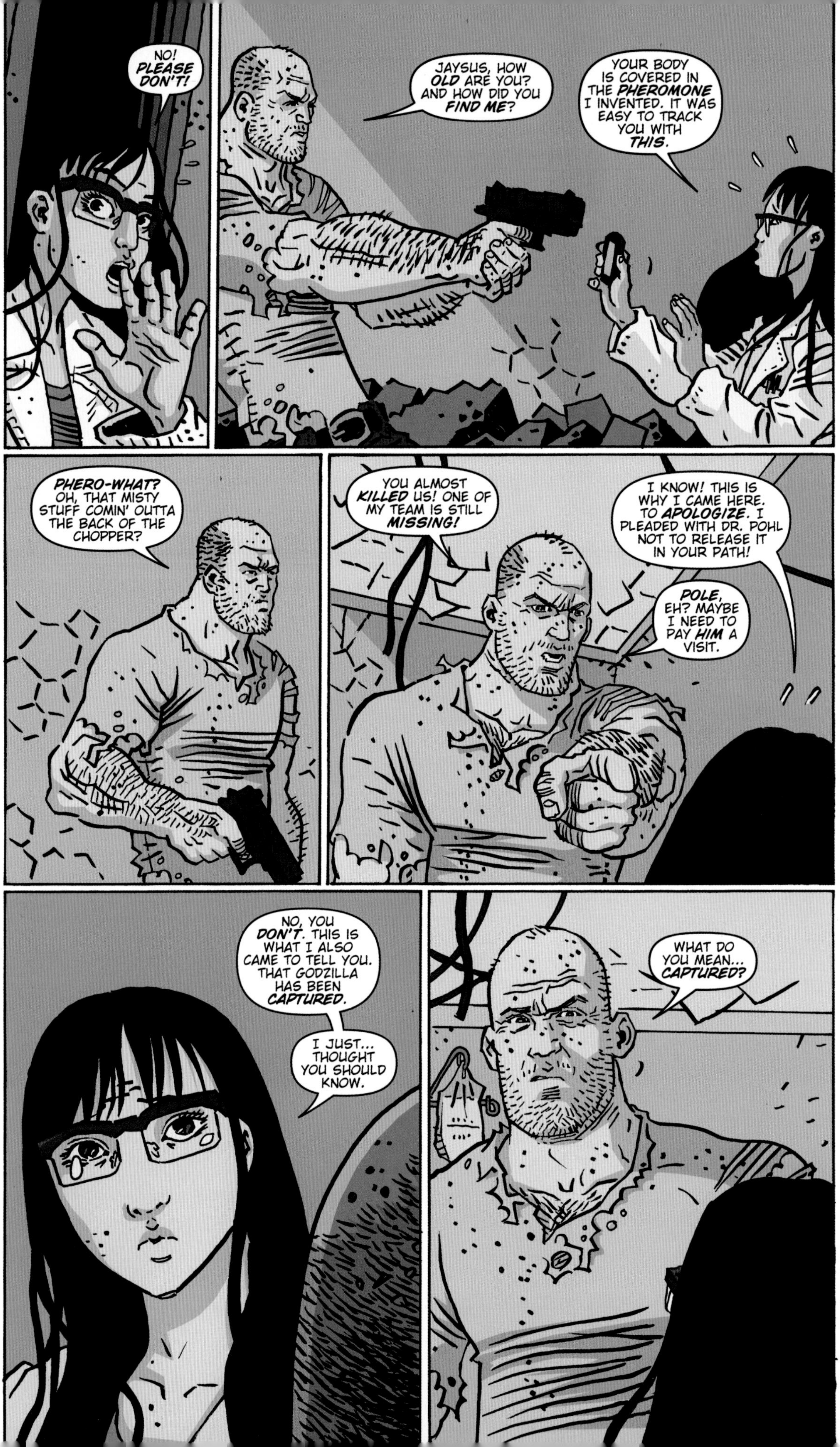
NO! PLEASE DON'T!
JAYSUS, HOW OLD ARE YOU? AND HOW DID YOU FIND ME?
YOUR BODY IS COVERED IN THE PHEROMONE I INVENTED. IT WAS EASY TO TRACK YOU WITH THIS.
PHERO-WHAT? OH, THAT MISTY STUFF COMIN' OUTTA THE BACK OF THE CHOPPER?
YOU ALMOST KILLED US! ONE OF MY TEAM IS STILL MISSING!
I KNOW! THIS IS WHY I CAME HERE. TO APOLOGIZE. I PLEADED WITH DR. POHL NOT TO RELEASE IT IN YOUR PATH!
POLE, EH? MAYBE I NEED TO PAY HIM A VISIT.
NO, YOU DON'T. THIS IS WHAT I ALSO CAME TO TELL YOU. THAT GODZILLA HAS BEEN CAPTURED.
I JUST... THOUGHT YOU SHOULD KNOW.
WHAT DO YOU MEAN... CAPTURED?

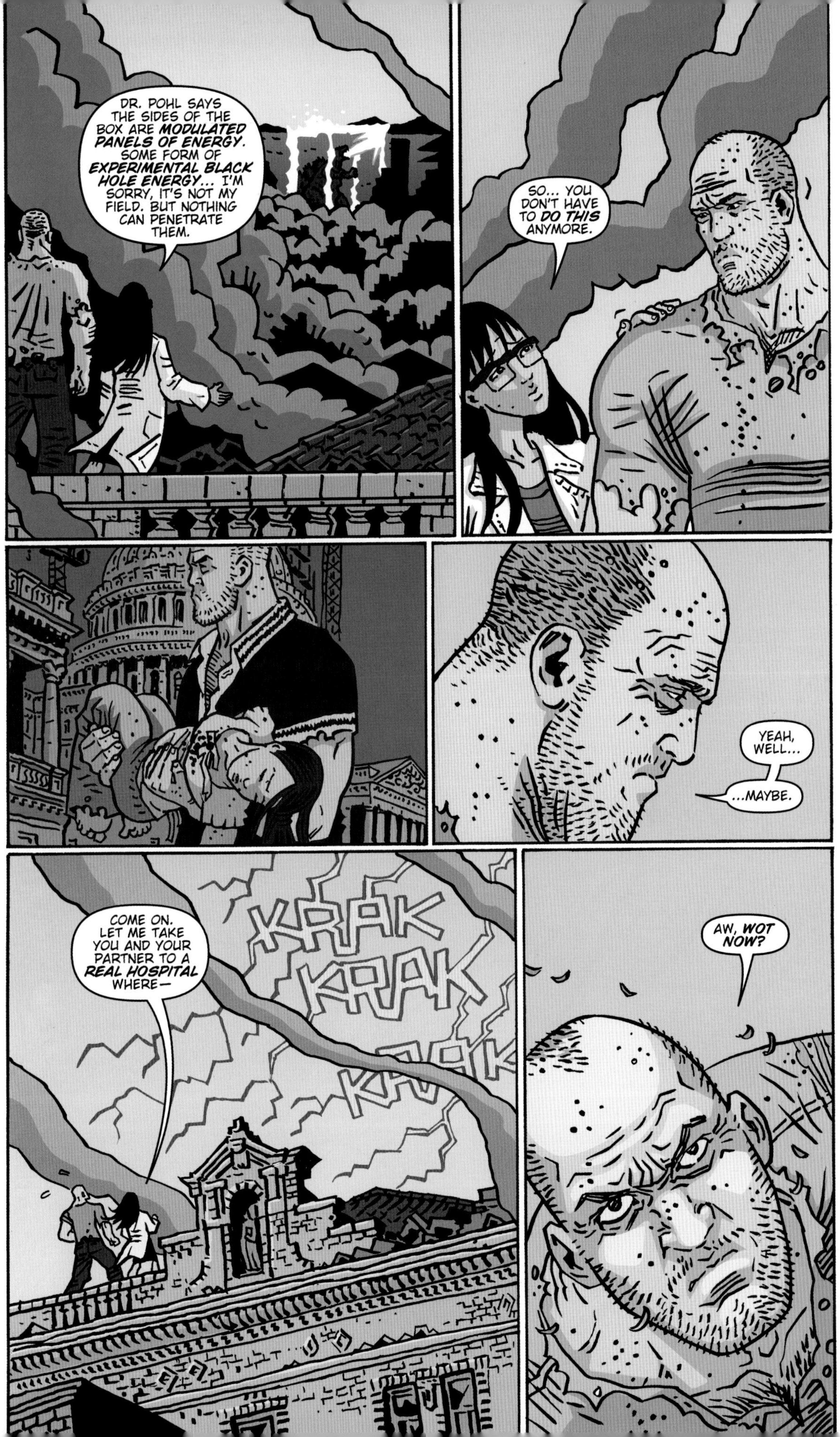

DR. POHL SAYS THE SIDES OF THE BOX ARE MODULATED PANELS OF ENERGY. SOME FORM OF EXPERIMENTAL BLACK HOLE ENERGY... I'M SORRY, IT'S NOT MY FIELD. BUT NOTHING CAN PENETRATE THEM.
SO... YOU DON'T HAVE TO DO THIS ANYMORE.
YEAH, WELL...
...MAYBE.
COME ON. LET ME TAKE YOU AND YOUR PARTNER TO A REAL HOSPITAL WHERE—
KRAK
KRAK
AW, WOT NOW?

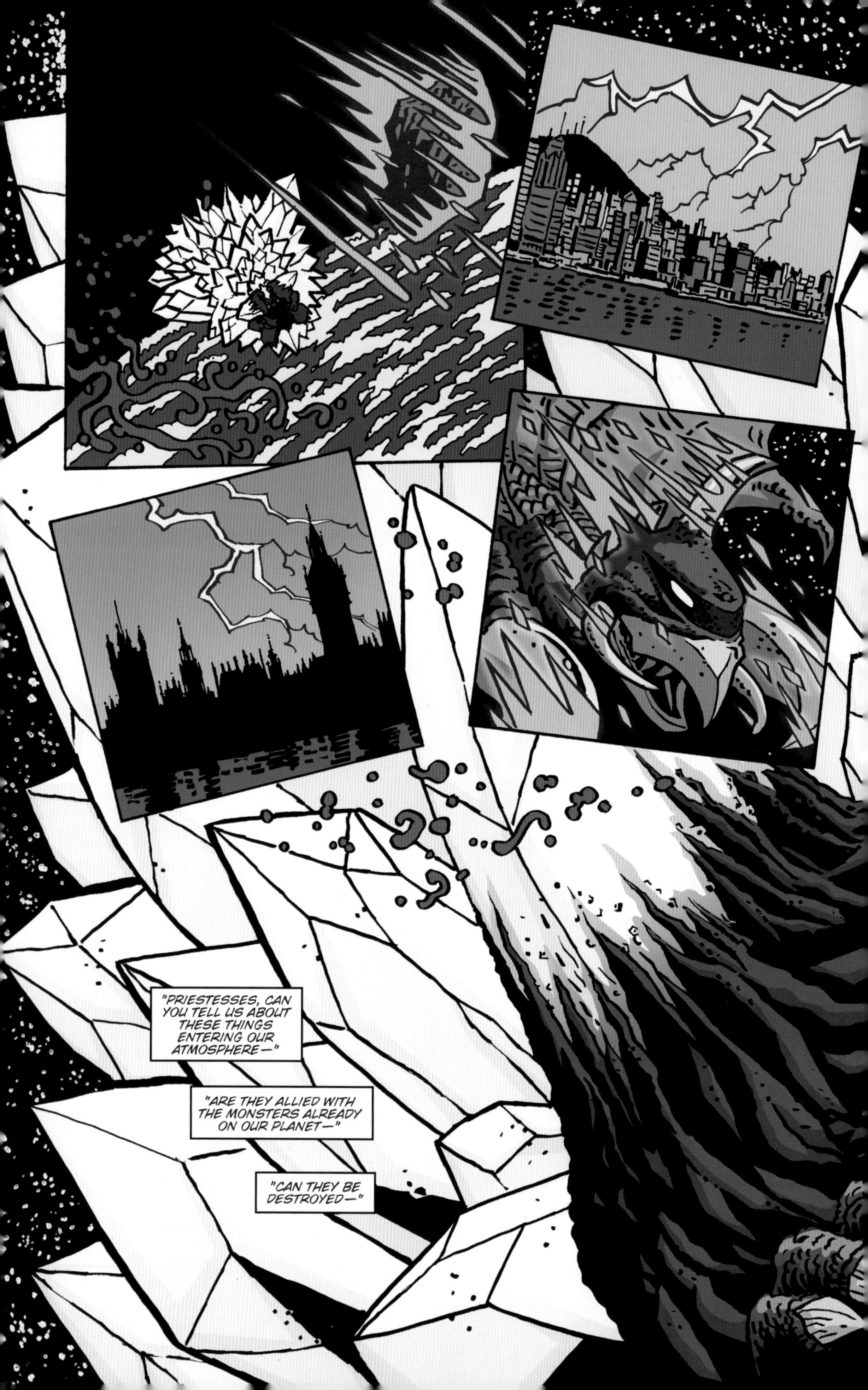
"PRIESTESSES, CAN YOU TELL US ABOUT THESE THINGS ENTERING OUR ATMOSPHERE—"
"ARE THEY ALLIED WITH THE MONSTERS ALREADY ON OUR PLANET—"
"CAN THEY BE DESTROYED—"

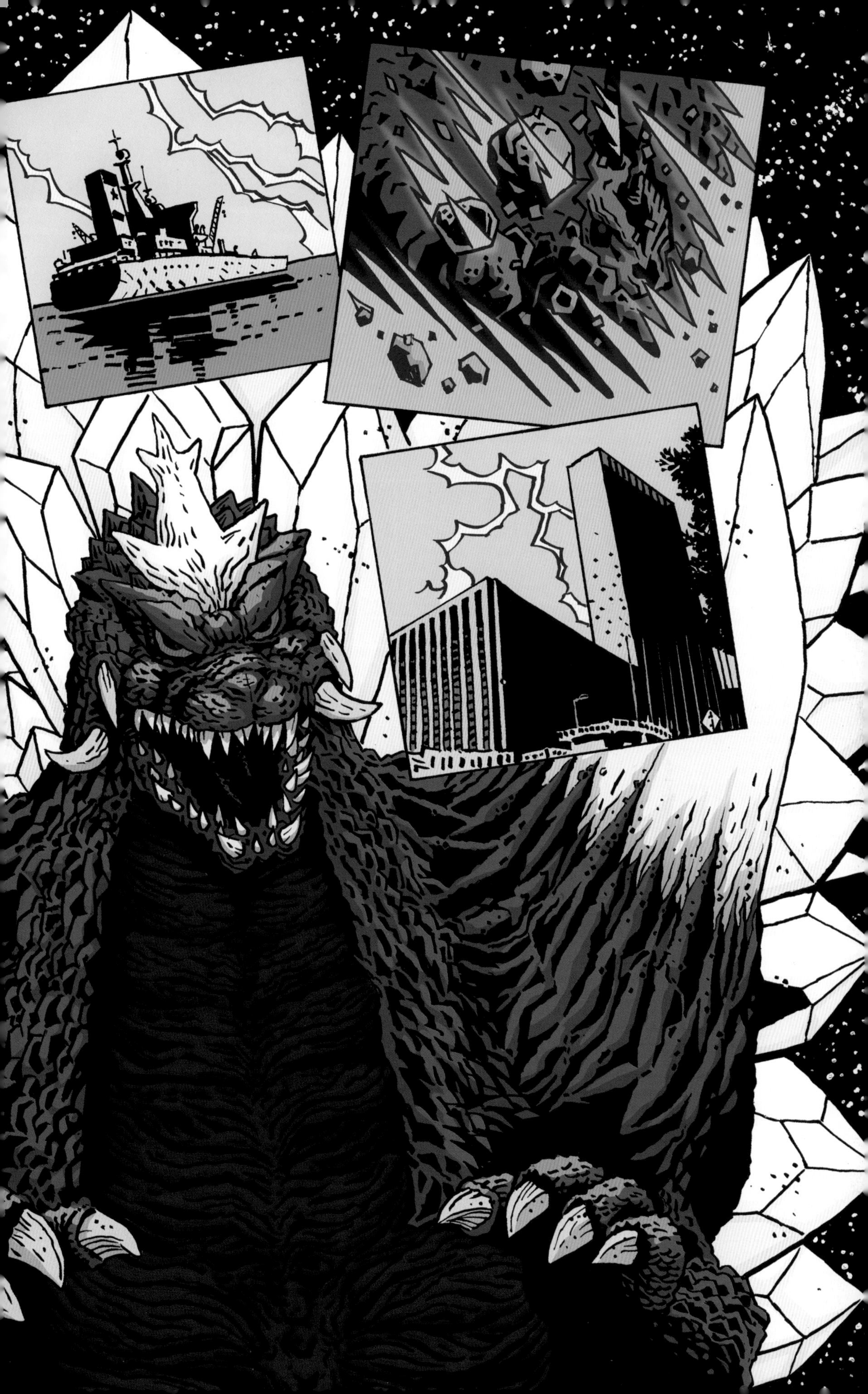

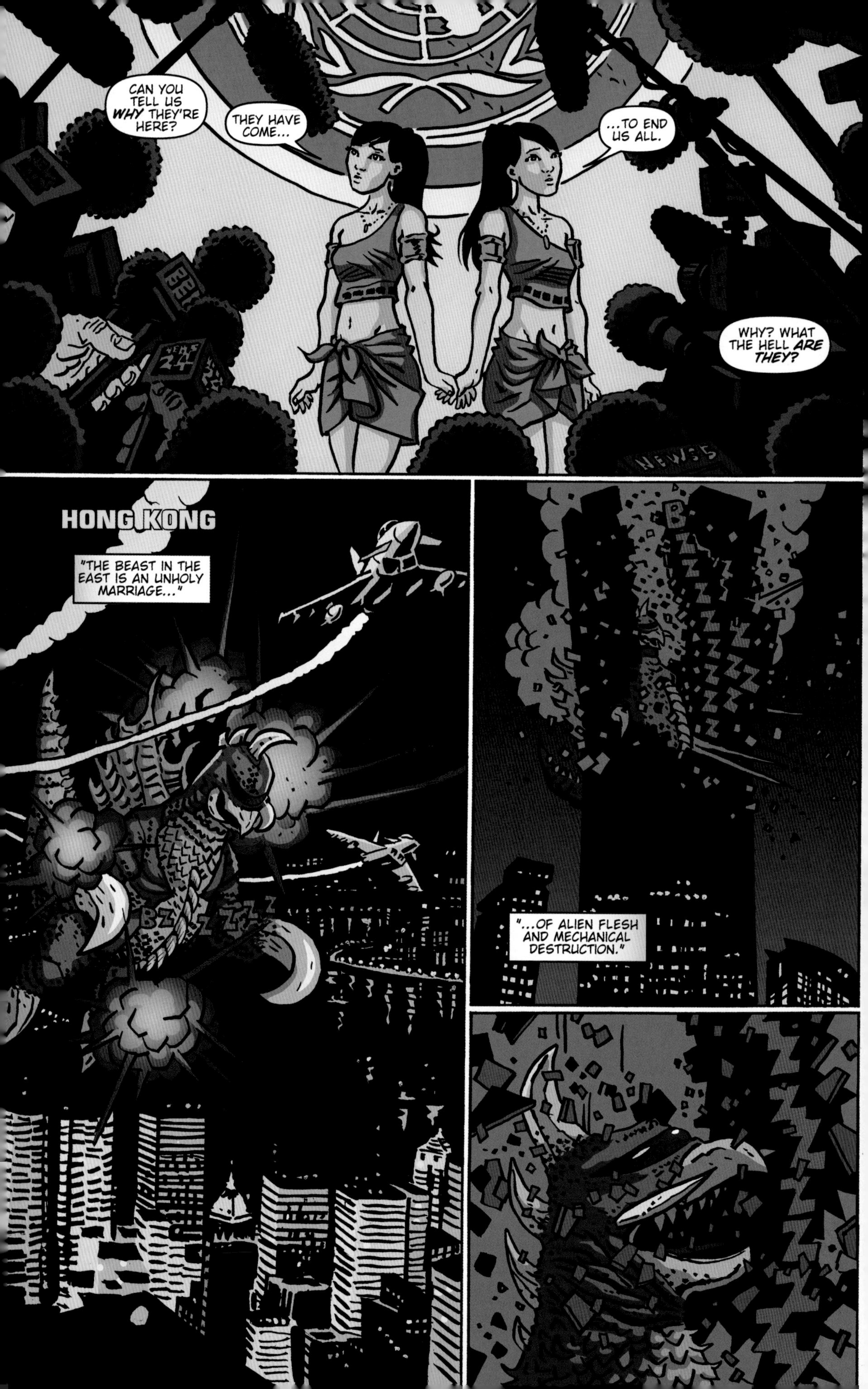
CAN YOU TELL US *WHY* THEY'RE HERE?
THEY HAVE COME...
...TO END US ALL.
NEWS 24
NEWS55
WHY? WHAT THE HELL *ARE THEY?*
HONG KONG
"THE BEAST IN THE EAST IS AN UNHOLY MARRIAGE..."
"...OF ALIEN FLESH AND MECHANICAL DESTRUCTION."

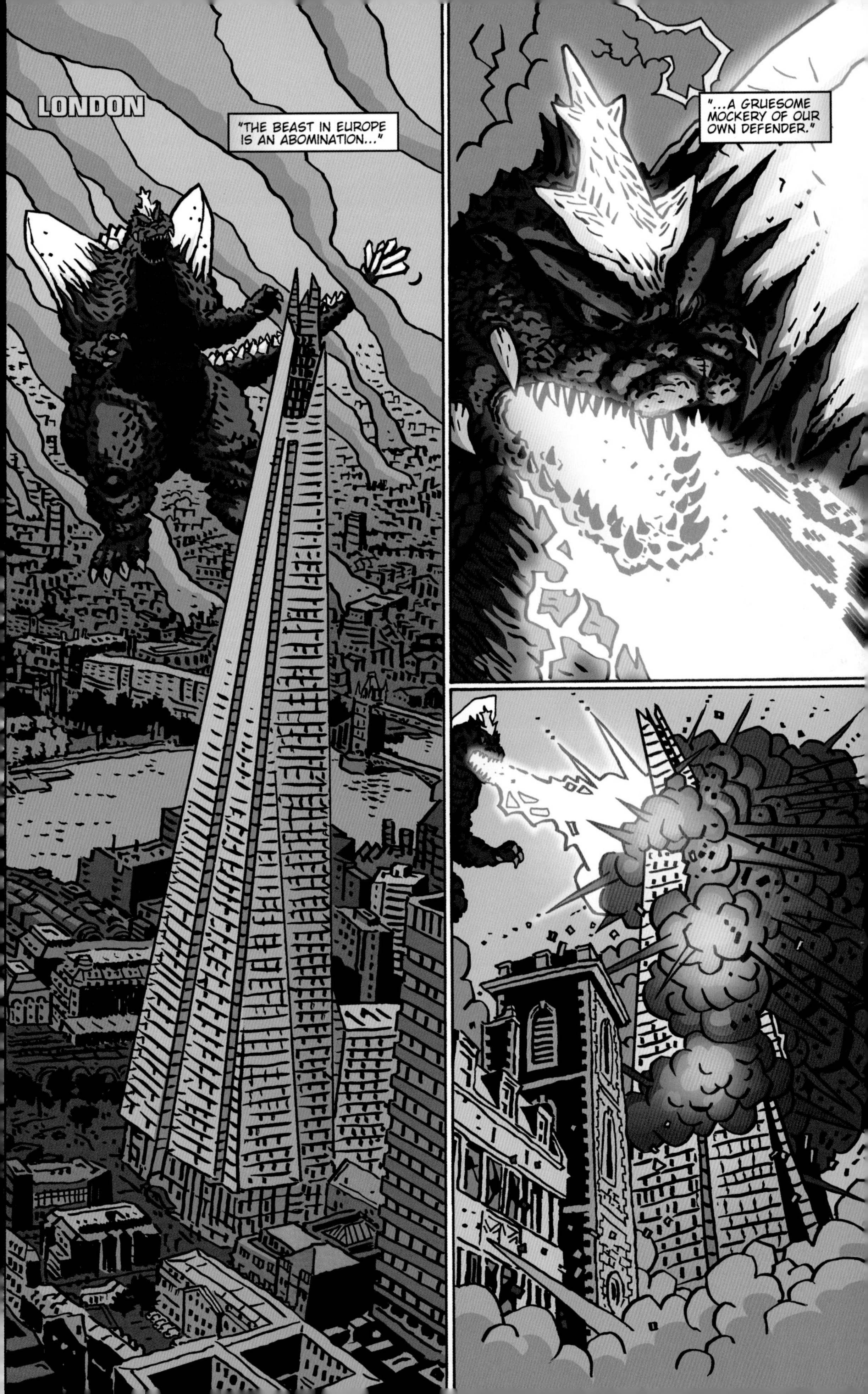
LONDON
"THE BEAST IN EUROPE IS AN ABOMINATION..."
"...A GRUESOME MOCKERY OF OUR OWN DEFENDER."

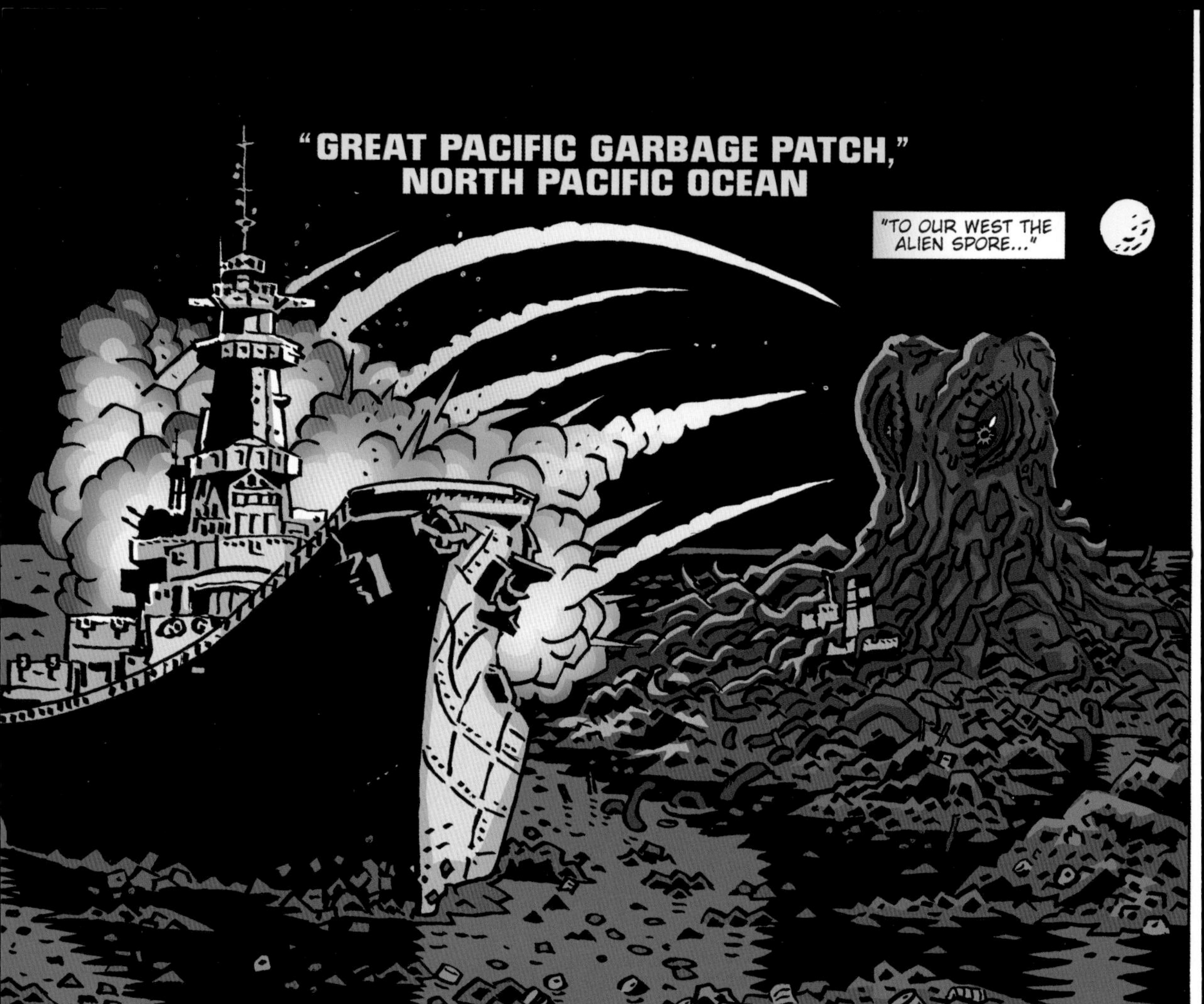
"GREAT PACIFIC GARBAGE PATCH,"
NORTH PACIFIC OCEAN
"TO OUR WEST THE ALIEN SPORE..."
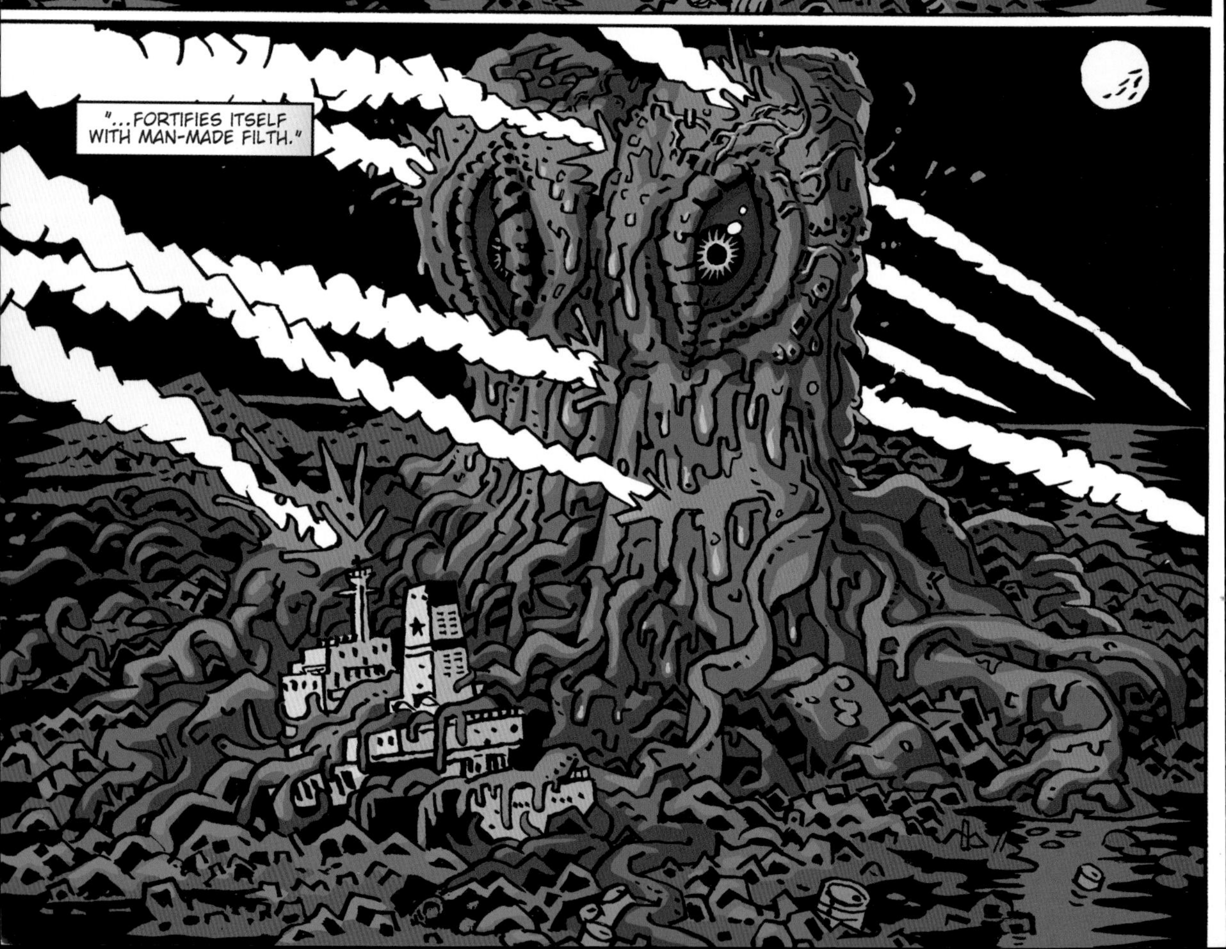
"...FORTIFIES ITSELF WITH MAN-MADE FILTH."

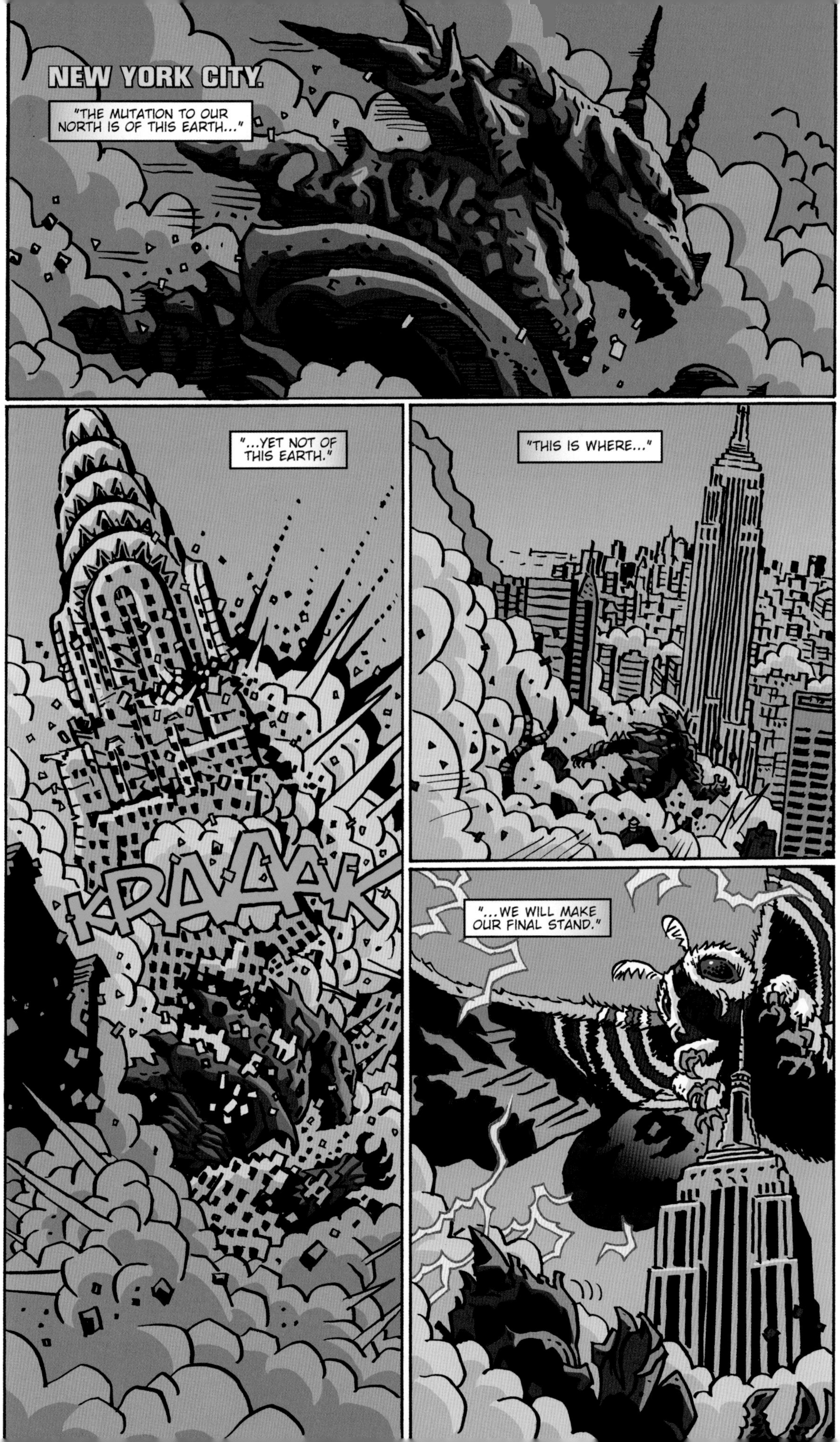
NEW YORK CITY.
"THE MUTATION TO OUR NORTH IS OF THIS EARTH..."
"...YET NOT OF THIS EARTH."
KRAAAK
"THIS IS WHERE..."
"...WE WILL MAKE OUR FINAL STAND."

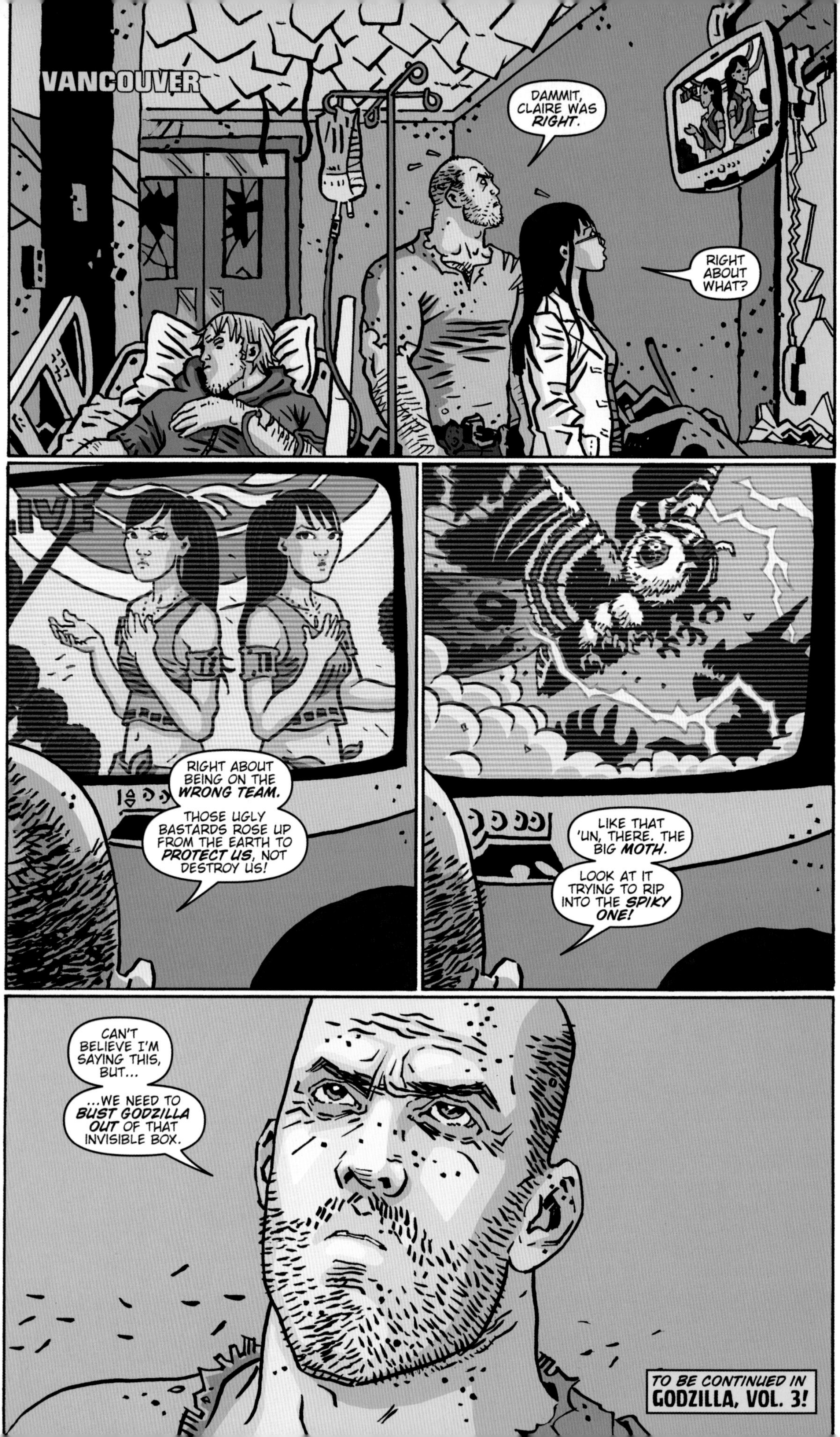
VANCOUVER
DAMMIT, CLAIRE WAS RIGHT.
RIGHT ABOUT WHAT?
RIGHT ABOUT BEING ON THE WRONG TEAM.
THOSE UGLY BASTARDS ROSE UP FROM THE EARTH TO PROTECT US, NOT DESTROY US!
LIKE THAT 'UN, THERE. THE BIG MOTH.
LOOK AT IT TRYING TO RIP INTO THE SPIKY ONE!
CAN'T BELIEVE I'M SAYING THIS, BUT...
...WE NEED TO BUST GODZILLA OUT OF THAT INVISIBLE BOX.
TO BE CONTINUED IN GODZILLA, VOL. 3!

ART BY MATT FRANK

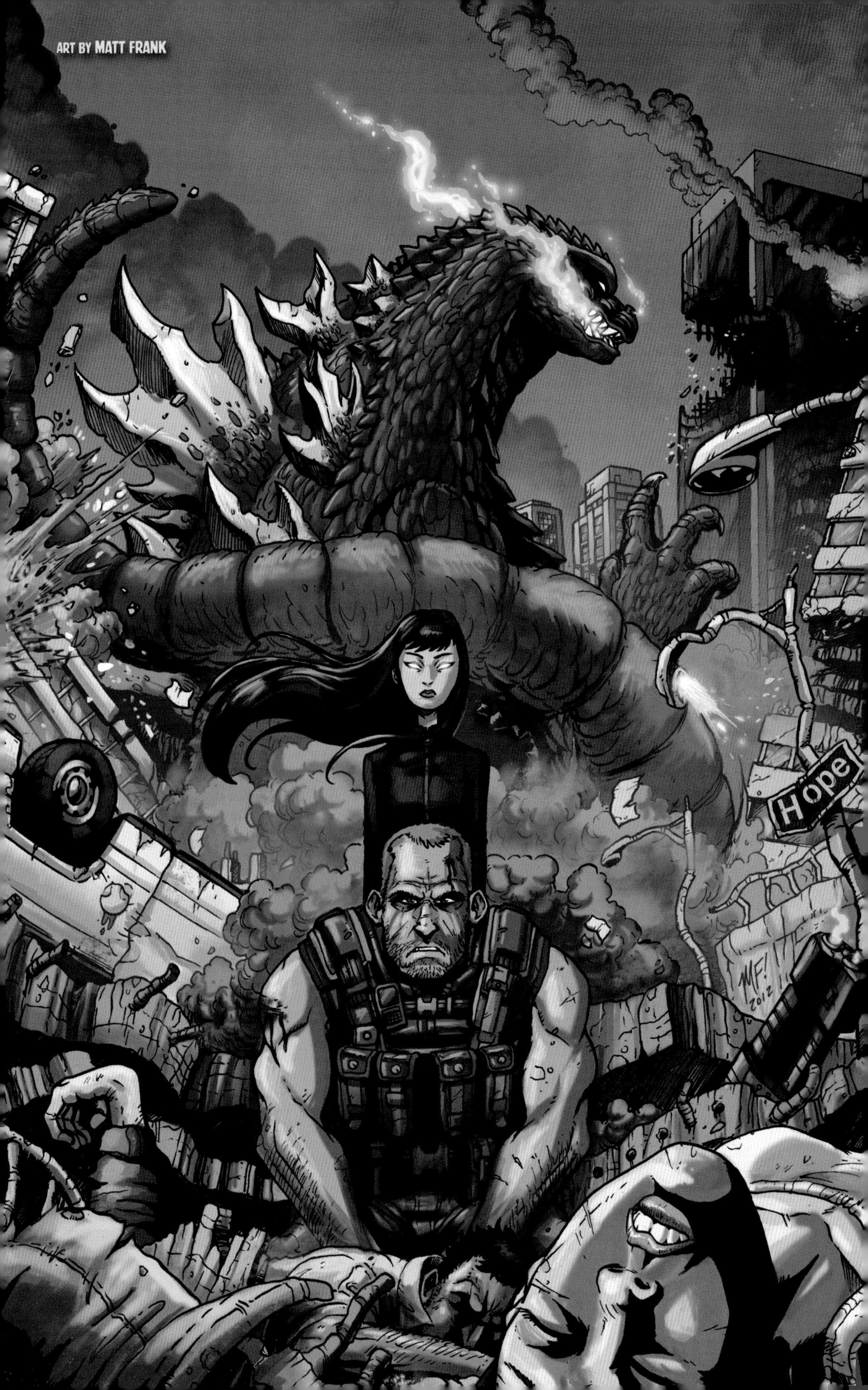
Hope

ART BY DAVE WACHTER

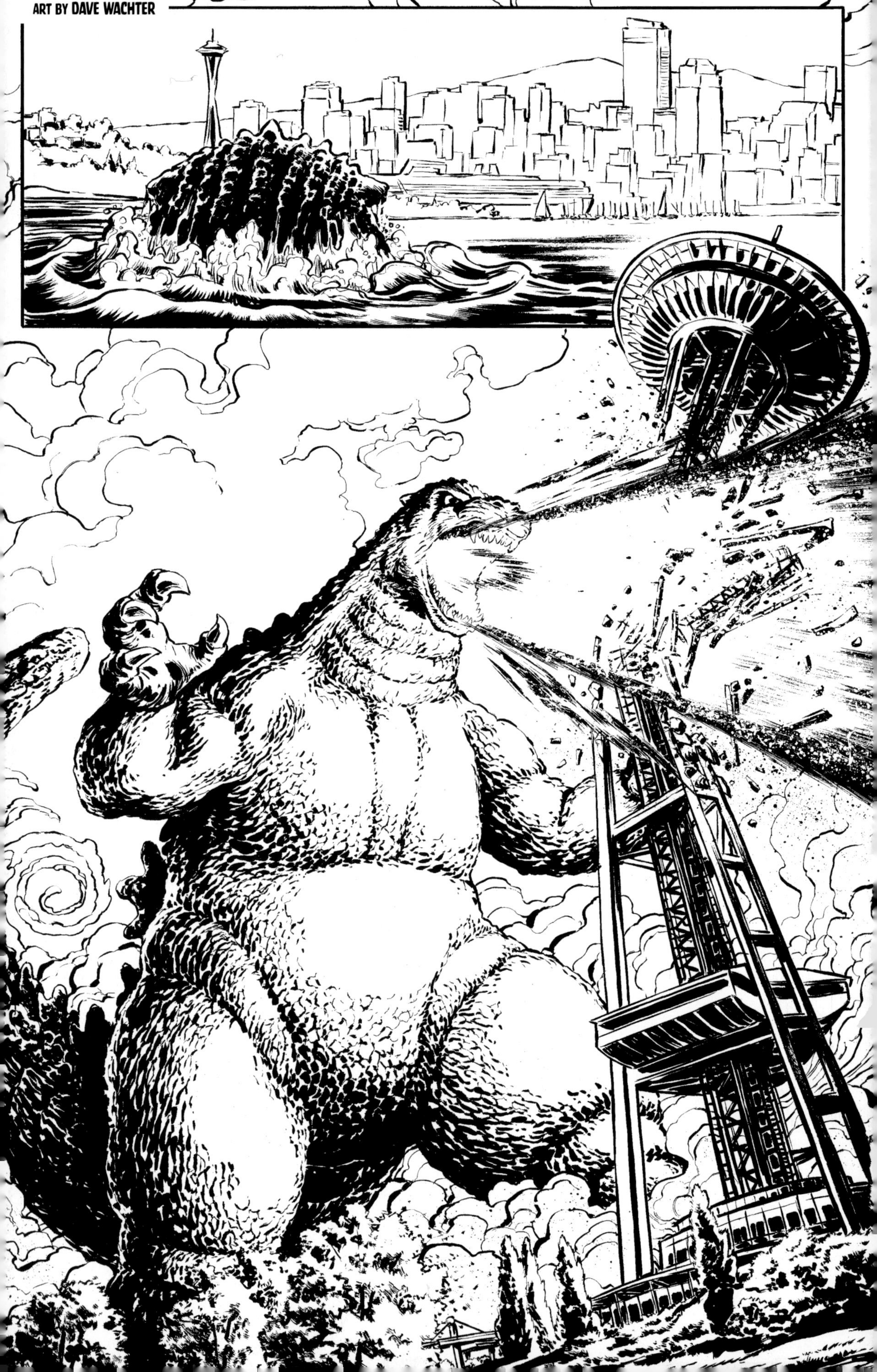

ART BY SIMON GANE

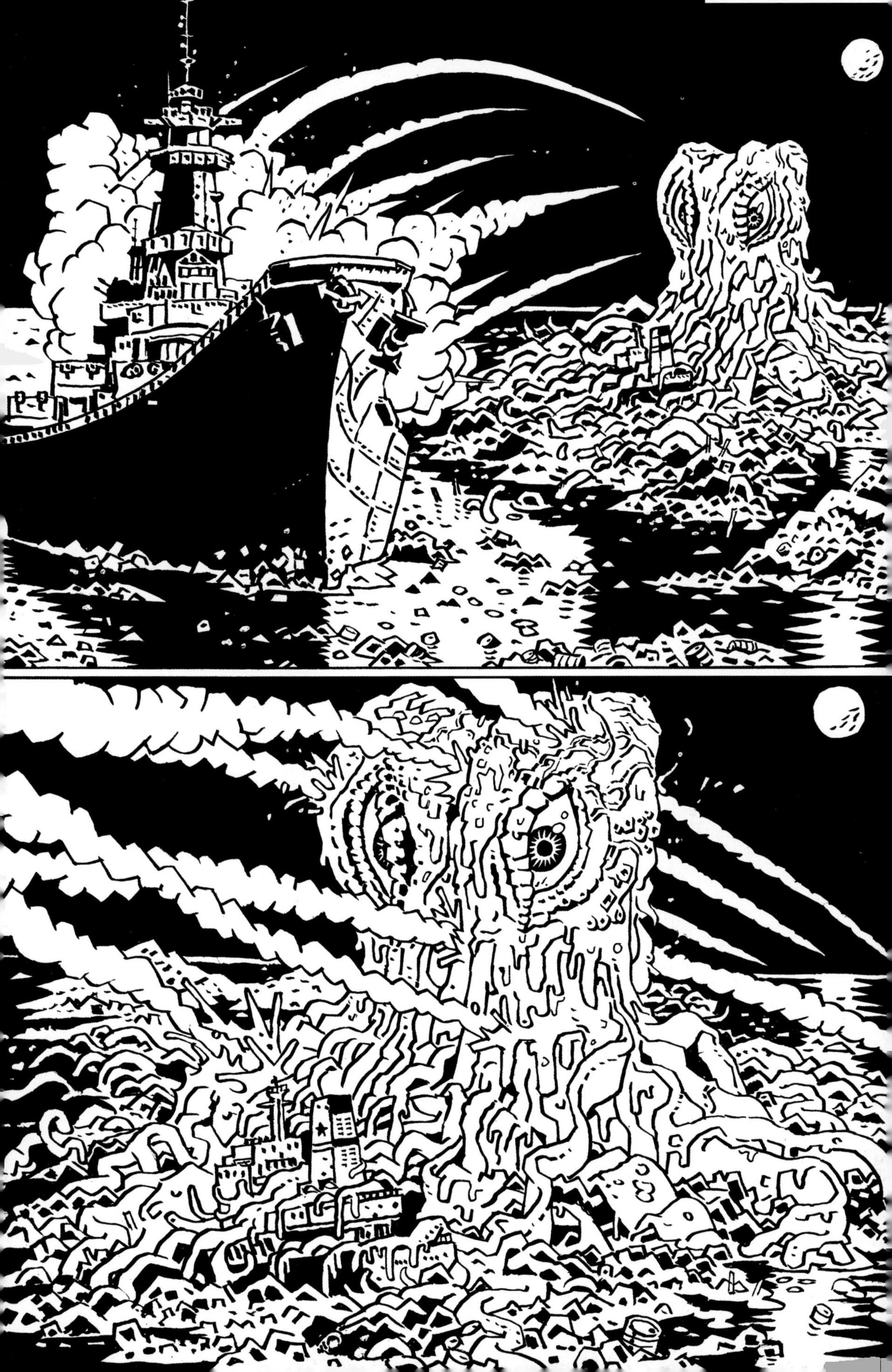

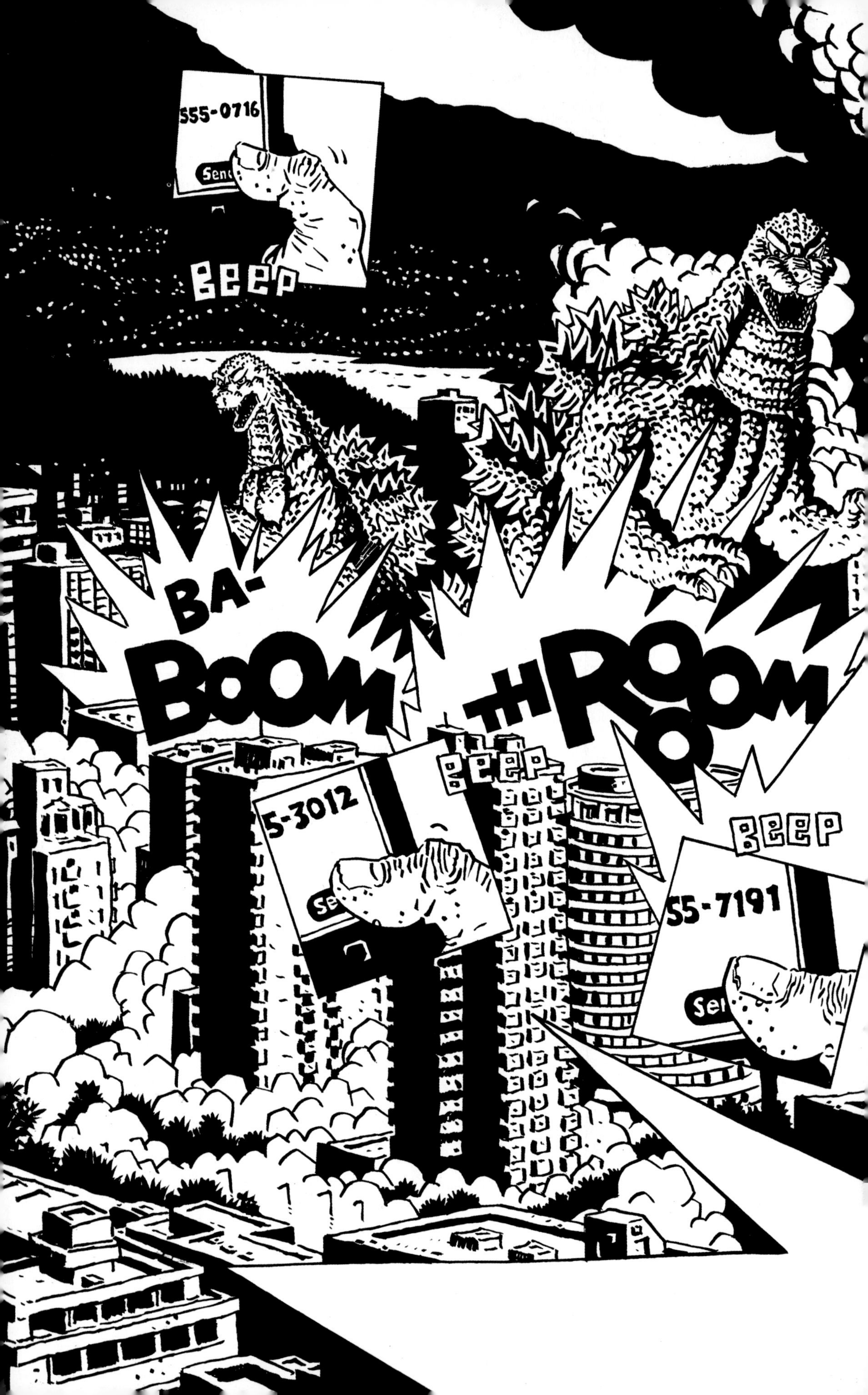

555-0716
BEEP
BA-
BOOM
THROOOM
BEEP
5-3012
BEEP
55-7191

ART BY SIMON GANE

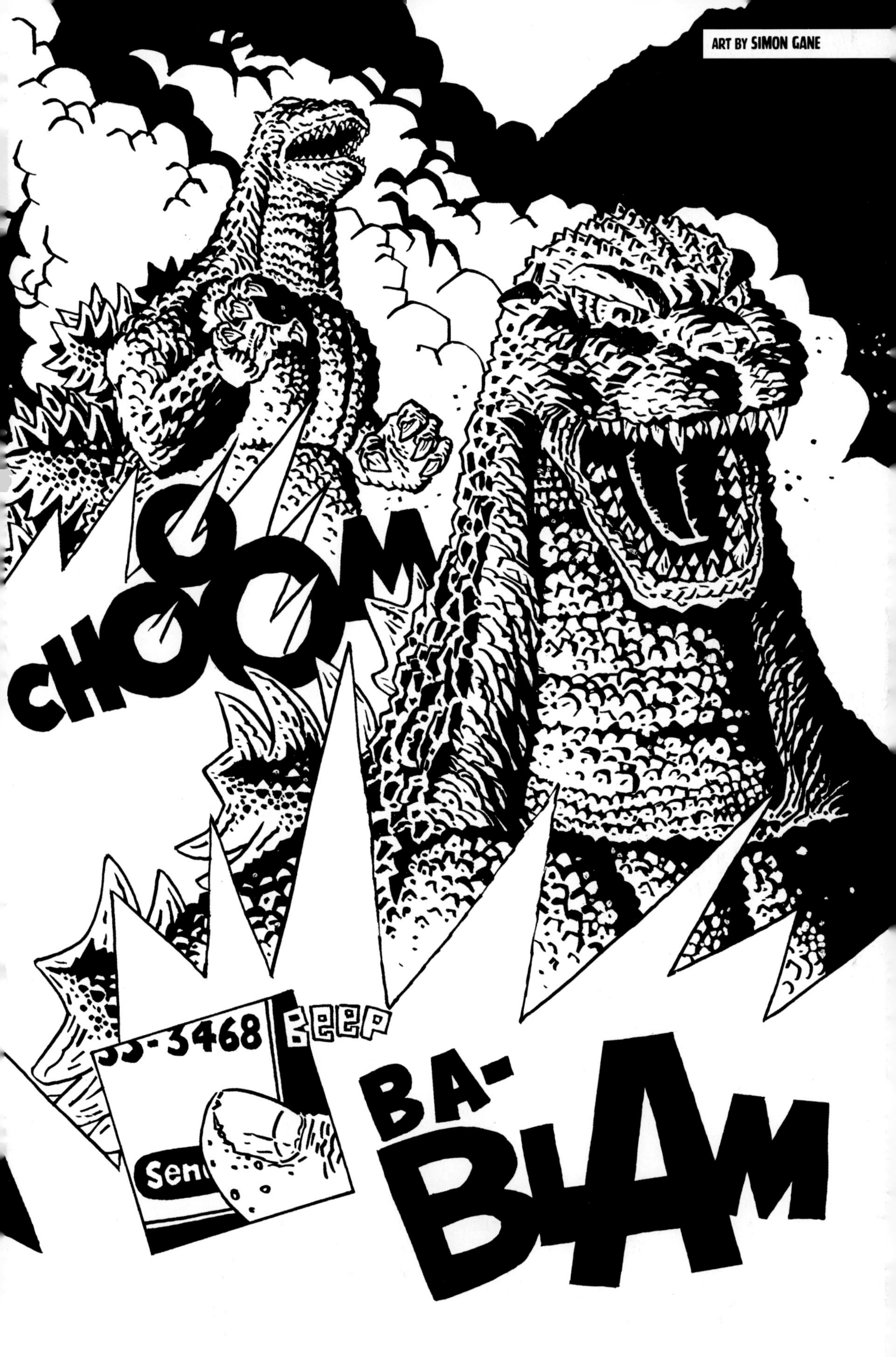
CHOOOM
BEEP
BA-BLAM

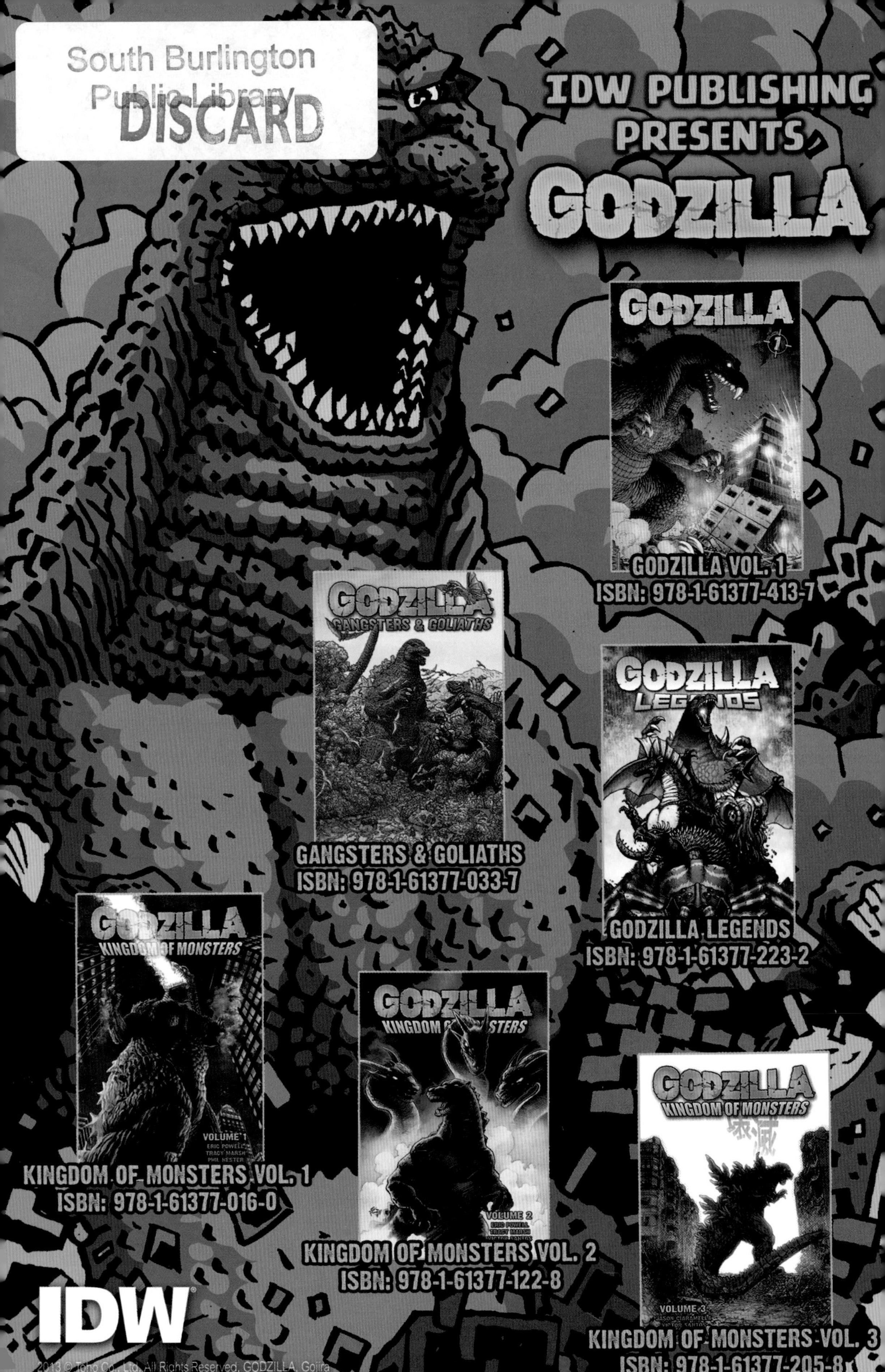
IDW PUBLISHING
PRESENTS
GODZILLA
GODZILLA VOL. 1
ISBN: 978-1-61377-413-7
GANGSTERS & GOLIATHS
ISBN: 978-1-61377-033-7
GODZILLA LEGENDS
ISBN: 978-1-61377-223-2
KINGDOM OF MONSTERS VOL. 1
ISBN: 978-1-61377-016-0
KINGDOM OF MONSTERS VOL. 2
ISBN: 978-1-61377-122-8
KINGDOM OF MONSTERS VOL. 3
ISBN: 978-1-61377-205-8
IDW